Running a Bar

FOR

DUMMIES®

by Ray Foley and Heather Dismore

WILEY

John Wiley & Sons, Inc.

Running a Bar For Dummies®

Published by
John Wiley & Sons, Inc.
111 River St.
Hoboken, NJ 07030-5774
www.wiley.com

For general information on our other products and services, please contact our Customer Care Department within the U.S. at 877-762-2974, outside the U.S. at 317-572-3993, or fax 317-572-4002.

For technical support, please visit www.wiley.com/techsupport.

Wiley publishes in a variety of print and electronic formats and by print-on-demand. Some material included with standard print versions of this book may not be included in e-books or in print-on-demand. If this book refers to media such as a CD or DVD that is not included in the version you purchased, you may download this material at http://booksupport.wiley.com. For more information about Wiley products, visit www.wiley.com.

Library of Congress Control Number: 2006939605

ISBN 978-0-470-04919-8 (pbk); ISBN 978-0-470-14853-2 (ebk); ISBN 978-0-470-46774-9 (ebk); ISBN 978-1-118-05081-1 (ebk)

Manufactured in the United States of America

10 9 8

1B/RU/QS/QX/IN

WILEY

About the Authors

Ray Foley, a former Marine with more than 30 years of bartending and restaurant experience, is the founder and publisher of *BARTENDER* magazine. *BARTENDER* is the only magazine in the world specifically geared toward bartenders and is one of the very few primarily designed for servers of alcohol. *BARTENDER* magazine is enjoying its 27th year, currently has a circulation of more than 150,000, and is steadily growing.

After serving in the United States Marine Corps and attending Seton Hall University, Ray entered the restaurant business as a bartender, which eventually led to his becoming assistant general manager of The Manor in West Orange, New Jersey, with more than 350 employees. At The Manor, he instituted a video-in-house training program — one of the first in the country. Ray is very proud to say that many of his students are now serving in such capacities as owners, managers, and vice presidents of national restaurants, general managers of major hotel chains, as well as bartenders and waiters at some of the nation's finest dining establishments. In 1983, Ray left The Manor to devote his full efforts to *BARTENDER* magazine.

Ray is the author of *The Ultimate Cocktail Book; The Ultimate Little Shooter Book; The Ultimate Little Martini Book; The Ultimate Little Blender Book; Advice from Anonymous; Spirits of Ireland; Jokes, Quotes and Bartoons;* and, of course, *Bartending For Dummies,* now in its third edition. He has also published numerous articles in many magazines, including *Playboy* and *Men's Health,* and has appeared on TV and radio shows, including *The David Susskind Show,* ABC-TV News, CBS News, NBC News, *Good Morning America, The Joe Franklin Show, Larry King Live,* Patricia McCann, WOR-TV, and *Live with Regis and Kathy Lee*. Ray also serves as a consultant to some of the USA's foremost distillers and importers. He is also responsible for naming and inventing new drinks for the liquor industry, including the Fuzzy Navel.

Ray is the founder of the Bartender Hall of Fame, which honors the best bartenders throughout the United States, not only for their abilities as mixologists but for involvement in their communities. Ray is also the founder of The Bartenders' Foundation Inc. This non-profit foundation raises scholarship money for bartenders and their families. Scholarships awarded to bartenders are used to either further their own education or go toward the education of their children.

Ray resides in New Jersey with his wife and partner of 25 years, Jackie, and their son, Ryan. He is also the father of three other wonderful and bright children: Raymond Pindar, William, and Amy.

Ray is foremost and always will be a Bartender.

For more information, please contact Jackie Foley at *BARTENDER* magazine, P.O. Box 158, Liberty Corner, NJ 07938; phone 908-766-6006; fax 908-766-6607; e-mail barmag@aol.com, Web site www.bartender.com.

A veteran of both the restaurant and publishing industries, **Heather Dismore**'s published works include such titles as *Running a Restaurant For Dummies, Jewelry Making & Beading For Dummies* (both published by Wiley), and most recently, *Start Your Restaurant Career,* published by Entrepreneur Press. She has contributed to many books on a variety of subjects, including *Diabetes Cookbook For Dummies,* 2nd Edition, *John Paul II For Dummies,* and *Einstein For Dummies.*

A graduate of DePauw University, she succumbed to the restaurant business while applying to law school. She orchestrated the openings of 15 new restaurants and developed the training, procedural, and purchasing systems that were used as the gold standard in numerous concepts throughout her tenure. She rapidly rose through the ranks at such regional and national chains as The Italian Fisherman, Don Pablo's Mexican Kitchen, and Romano's Macaroni Grill.

She's an active food writer and trend spotter in the food and beverage industry and a regular contributor to FoodChannel.com. She can be contacted at heather@heatherdismore.com. She lives in Missouri with her husband and daughters, who are her first loves, inspiration, and never-ending source of new material.

Dedication

Ray's Dedication:

This book is dedicated to all who serve the public with long hours, tired bodies, and great patience (and still know how to have fun): bartenders, bar employees, owners, and maybe to a couple of great customers!

And, of course, to Jaclyn Marie, whom I love the best, and Ryan Peter, who loves me the best. Both have made my cup overflow.

Heather's Dedication:

I dedicate this book to my college friends with whom I first explored the magic of bars and discovered the mystery contained therein: Tracy, Jeanne, Biddle, Chrissie, Steph, Claire, Staci, Natasha, Lisa, Diz, Vince, Rock, Russ, and all my other DePauw pals.

Authors' Acknowledgments

Ray's Acknowledgments:

First and foremost, I want to thank Heather Dismore for her outstanding writing ability and patience with me. You're the best! Tracy Boggier, Natalie Harris, and Vicki Adang for all their help and assistance; my best friend, Loretta Natiello; Scott Young for all his input and experience; John Cowan, CPA, with more than 30 years' experience at the Nutley Pub and as my bartending partner; Marvin Solomon and his 50 years' experience; Dr. Lawrence Nastro, Rita Mazzarisi, Martin Margolis, attorney-at-law, James Zazzali, George Delgado, Dave Conway, Rene Bardel at Tu Tu Tango, Hymie Lipshitz, and, of course, the best teacher, mentor, general manager, U.S. Marine, and friend, William Boggier.

Heather's Acknowledgments:

A big thank you to our project editor, Natalie Harris, and our copy editor, Vicki Adang, for working their magic with our meager manuscript. To Tracy Boggier, for your confidence in us, your encouragement, and for keeping us on track, whether we liked it or not. To Bill Tobin, for reviewing the facts and figures. As always, thanks to Diane Steele, Joyce Pepple, and Kristin Cocks, for supporting this book from the beginning.

Thank you, Ray Foley. You are a delightful man and an exceptional bartender. I hope to have the opportunity to sit across the bar from you someday soon. Thanks to Pat Duran, a terrific restaurateur and one of the best bar managers in the business.

Thanks to my family who puts up with crazy schedules, my kitchen-table "office," late nights, and sometimes grumpy mornings. I adore you!

Publisher's Acknowledgments

We're proud of this book; please send us your comments through our Dummies online registration form located at www.dummies.com/register/.

Some of the people who helped bring this book to market include the following:

Acquisitions, Editorial, and Media Development

Project Editor: Natalie Faye Harris

Acquisitions Editor: Tracy Boggier

Copy Editor: Vicki Adang

Technical Editor: Bill Tobin

Editorial Manager: Christine Beck

Media Development Manager:
Laura VanWinkle

Editorial Assistants: Erin Calligan, Joe Niesen,
David Lutton, Leeann Harney

Cover Photos: © Michael Neelon / Alamy

Cartoons: Rich Tennant
(www.the5thwave.com)

Composition Services

Project Coordinator: Kristie Rees

Layout and Graphics: Stephanie D. Jumper,
Laura Pence, Alicia B. South, Erin Zeltner

Anniversary Logo Design: Richard Pacifico

Proofreaders: Cynthia Fields, Aptara

Indexer: Aptara

Publishing and Editorial for Consumer Dummies

Kathleen Nebenhaus, Vice President and Executive Publisher

David Palmer, Associate Publisher

Kristin Ferguson-Wagstaffe, Product Development Director

Publishing for Technology Dummies

Andy Cummings, Vice President and Publisher

Composition Services

Debbie Stailey, Director of Composition Services

Contents at a Glance

Table of Contents

Introduction

• •

*T*he bar business is exciting. Every night's a party. We're thrilled you're looking to get involved, and you've definitely come to the right place to get started. From the neighborhood bar to the local wine bar, opportunities in the industry have never been greater. This book is your guide to getting started in the right direction.

A lot of books have been written on being a bartender (heck, coauthor Ray wrote *Bartending For Dummies!*), but to run a bar, you have to be more than just a great bartender. To be the owner, you have to see beyond the glamour of standing behind the bar flipping bottles, pouring draft beers, and chatting up customers. You have to feel the anxiety, and the blood, sweat, and tears that accompany it. As you read this book, we think you will come to understand, if you don't already, that the bar business really is a *business*. You crunch numbers, make sales projections, watch labor costs, and so on, just like in every other business. And ultimately, your success is judged like any other business, on your profitability.

Whether you're a salty bartender or a cocktail waitress looking at your long-term goals, reading this book is a terrific step in launching your own business in the bar industry. Read on for tips on how this book is organized.

About This Book

You don't have to pass an exam or earn a degree to prove you can run your bar. Instead, you have to work at it, gain experience, and have more than a little common sense. We wrote this book to help you to determine what skills you need to get into the business, and we help you figure out where you need to fill in the blanks. After you read the pages between these gorgeous yellow-and-black covers, you'll have a good idea whether this is the racket for you — and you'll have the knowledge to get started on the right foot.

You can find plenty of books that tell you how to open a bar, but you won't find many about how to *keep* it open. This book does both. Why? Because even after opening day arrives, you can never stop improving your service, evaluating your product, scoping out the competition, or researching opportunities in the marketplace. Change is the only constant in this business. To succeed, you must anticipate and act on new trends, new pressures, and whatever else the market throws your way. The spoils go to those who see opportunities before they happen.

Conventions Used in This Book

To help you navigate through this book, we use the following conventions:

- ✔ *Italic* is used for emphasis and to highlight new words or terms that are defined.
- ✔ **Boldfaced** text is used to indicate keywords in bulleted lists or the action part of numbered steps.
- ✔ `Monofont` is used for Web addresses.
- ✔ Sidebars, which look like text enclosed in a shaded gray box, consist of information that's interesting to know but not necessarily critical to your understanding of the chapter or section topic.

Foolish Assumptions

Bar owners have to make assumptions about the patrons sitting on the other side of the bar, and authors have to do the same thing — we have to make assumptions about our readers. With that in mind, we've come up with the following list of assumptions about why you've picked up this book:

- ✔ You're thinking about opening your own bar, and you want practical, how-to advice to accomplish your goals.
- ✔ You're a bartender or other bar employee who wants to take your experience to the next level and manage a bar.
- ✔ You've never worked in a bar but you've had success in other professional endeavors and have skills that you may be able to apply to this business.
- ✔ You buy every book that sports a yellow-and-black cover.
- ✔ You currently own or operate a bar, and you're seeking advice, tips, and suggestions to keep things running smoothly and successfully.

Here's another assumption that we'll address right now, just in case you're carrying this common misconception: Don't think that you should open a bar because you want a cool place to hang out. It's tough to sit down in your bar and actually relax. Typically, you can't turn your management mind-set off just because your friends or family come in. You're too busy watching cocktails being made, looking at paper scraps on the floor, or looking at plates of food going by, doing a sort of on-the-fly quality check. If you take time to actually sit down during a shift, you lose your control or awareness of what's going on. Even if you come in on the one day a month you're off, you'll still probably be distracted by what's going on around you.

How This Book Is Organized

This book is organized into five parts, shaken not stirred, and then topped with soda and garnished with a lime twist. Here's what's in this operation cocktail.

Part 1: Cheers! Getting Started in the Bar Industry

In this part, we give you a crash course in the business, including tips for getting started, understanding your options, creating your concept, and picking your name. We include a detailed timeline from idea to grand opening to get you up and running. We also help you decide whether you have what it takes to make it in the business. Look here for information on getting financing and following the letter of the law.

Part II: Gearing Up to Open the Doors

In this part, we focus on developing your idea and making it a reality. We take you through the critical steps, such as writing a business plan. We help you find just the right location for your bar or make the most of the one you already have. We also help you figure out what you need to stock your bar, from equipment to appliances, bourbon to Budweiser, and everything in between.

Part III: Employees, Customers, and Products: Managing the "Right Stuff"

Here, we help you find the best employees for your bar. We give you tips on how to train them right so you can please the most important person in your bar: your patron. We also give you great hands-on ideas for giving the best possible customer service to keep your bar stools full every night of the week.

Part IV: Managing Your Inventory, Revenue, and Future

This part shows you how to manage what you've created. We help you wrangle every cent out of every dollar without being a cheapskate. We show you how to buy premium products the right way to effectively manage your inventory and cash flow. We give you details on which numbers to watch in the bar business and why. We give you tips on how to bring in new customers for the first time while still keeping your regulars regular. We help you build goodwill in the community and reap the rewards in your business.

Part V: The Part of Tens

In this standard *For Dummies* section, we give you tips for keeping your employees and patrons safe in your place. We help you avoid common problems that plague many a bar owner. We dispel a few myths about the business. And finally, we give you our favorite bar jokes to share with your patrons, your barber, or anyone else who will listen.

Part VI: Appendixes

Not as flashy as the other parts, but equally as important, the appendixes are terrific resources you can go back to again and again. Look here for a listing of alcohol control boards by state. As an added bonus, we threw in a whole bunch of Web sites that are monumentally handy to the above-average bar owner, which you will likely soon be.

Icons Used in This Book

Icons are the cute little pictures that appear in the margins of this book. Here's the guide so you can tell what they are and what they're for:

The Tip icon calls your attention to ideas that can make your job easier and help you sidestep problems. The tips often give you handy ideas on ways to improve your business today.

The Remember icon points out where we reinforce the concepts we discuss. If you're in a time crunch and can't read the entire chapter, you can go straight to this icon and still come away with some very useful information.

The Warning icon alerts you to potential pitfalls and gives you a heads-up on mistakes to avoid. Pay attention when this icon rears its head because it's there to show you something important.

The Technical Stuff icon alerts you to interesting, but not critical, background information about the subject being discussed. You don't have to read the information to understand the ideas and concepts, but you may find it interesting nonetheless.

Where to Go from Here

Because this is a *For Dummies* book, you don't have to read it in order, word for word, front to back, cover to cover. If you prefer, you can check out the corresponding part, chapter, or section and read up on the issue that most interests you, rather than plow through the entire book. You can find out what you want to know without first having read the information that precedes it. In other words, this book gives you get-in-and-get-out convenience. You can start wherever you want and read whatever you want. You can jump around and finish reading when you feel like it. So grab your bar towel and get going. Interested in tips for improving your drink menu today? Turn to Chapter 9. Do you need a test to quiz your soon-to-be hotshot bartender? Take a look at Chapter 10. Looking to get started on a new business plan? Flip over to Chapter 5. Need help choosing a name for your new place? You gotta see Chapter 6!

Part I

Cheers! Getting Started in the Bar Industry

The 5th Wave   By Rich Tennant

In this part . . .

We get you ready to get going in the bar business. First, we outline the basics for you, so you have an overview of just what kinds of issues and experiences you may encounter in your bar or pub. Then we take you through the ins and outs of what the business is like on a day-to-day basis. We also help you explore the process for minding all your legal "Ps & Qs." And we help you refine your ideas for what you want your bar to be by looking at several hot concepts in the bar business.

Chapter 1

Bar Business Basics

● ●

In This Chapter
▶ Understanding the basics of the business
▶ Deciding whether you have the necessary skills

● ●

*T*hink of all the great times people have in bars. They meet for girls' night out, bachelor parties, reunions, birthdays, or just because it's Thursday. They come to celebrate, relax, or have fun. It's a fact: People like bars. So it's not a leap for people to think "Hey, I enjoy hanging out in bars, so I may as well get paid to do what I enjoy — hanging out in bars."

Viewed from the bar stool (on the public side of the bar), it's easy to miss all the hard work that goes on to make hanging out in bars fun for everyone else. When you have to manage every detail — such as hiring the music, choosing the lighting, designing the menu, and picking up trash in the parking lot — the bar business quickly becomes more work than fun, so don't be fooled.

In this chapter, we take you on a quick tour of the business. We explore your reasons for getting into the business and help you check your expectations for your new venture. We introduce you to what you need to know to understand and maximize the true financial performance of your new venture. And finally, we inspire you to keep reaching out to your patrons. Look at the other chapters in this book for more detailed information about these topics and other important points to know about getting your bar going and keeping it running.

Deciding Whether the Bar Business Is Right for You

The bar business world is more than a party every night of the week. It's actually a business. Those owners who look at it as a business ultimately have a much greater chance of succeeding. You can't just give drinks to friends or offer drink specials too deep to turn a profit. You can't order too many bottles of whiskey only to (not) see two of them walk out the door. You have a tremendous opportunity to make a great career out of a fun business if you're willing to put in the effort and use some common sense.

Why do you want to be in the bar business?

The bar business is tough for some people to relate to because you're selling an experience rather than something that's physically packaged that you can hold. Instead, your product is packaged in many layers, from the music you play, to your furniture and lighting choices, to the beers you have on draft. All these things make up your packaging, affect the costs of doing business, and affect your patron's decision to hang out at your place or move on down the street.

Think about these questions when you're contemplating your decision to take the plunge and run your own place:

- ✔ **Do you really like people?** An odd question on the surface perhaps, but running a bar doesn't afford you a lot of quiet, contemplative alone-time. Make sure you can stand the onslaught of conversation and complaints.

- ✔ **How do you handle your own liquor?** For some people, running a bar is like giving a kid the keys to a candy store. The liquor is always available, and they don't seem to know when to say "when."

- ✔ **Are you a night owl?** Think about your own internal clock. When does it turn on and shut off? If you like to be up until 2 or 3 o'clock in the morning, this could be the industry for you.

- ✔ **Are you ready to baby-sit adults?** As the owner or manager of the bar, you have many employees, suppliers, and customers who need your attention. Sometimes you're the one who has to cover a missed shift on the fly. Occasionally, you've got to handle a late shipment of liquor that arrives inconveniently at 6 o'clock on a Friday night. Most likely, you'll need to attend to a patron who needs a cab. Whatever the scenario, tag — you're it.

Make sure you spend some time reading Chapter 2 to get a feel for what the business is really like before you invest serious time and money in developing your ideas.

What do you expect to get out of your place?

Now's the time for you to sit down and create your plan for what your bar should be. Early on, create the pie-in-the-sky version of your ideal place, including a menu (both drink and food), and even draw up mock floor plans. Figure out where you want your stage and TVs to go, how many bars or wells you might have, what your theme is going to be, and so on.

Make sure you figure out what you, as a person, want to get out of the occupation of running a bar. Think about these questions:

- ✔ **How much time do I want to dedicate to work?** Running a bar takes a lot of time, just like managing any other business. The key difference though is that the time tends to be during nontraditional work times. So when the rest of the world is out having a good time, you're providing the good time.

- ✔ **How much time do I need to spend with my family?** If you like to spend nights and weekends at home, this may not be the business for you. But if you're open to finding other times to enjoy each other, you can make it work.

- ✔ **How do I like to spend my free time?** If you enjoy talking with people, listening to music, and playing an occasional game of pool during your free time, you'll probably enjoy this work. But remember to draw a clear line between your business and personal lives.

- ✔ **Do I like having any free time?** When you own your own business, you don't have lots of free time in the beginning. If you hire the right staff members (see Chapter 10 for help) and train them right, you can work your way into delegating some of your jobs.

Eventually, you must take certain steps to plan your business to make it a success before you can open the doors and enjoy it. In fact, we recommend you start planning as soon as you can so you can decide whether your plan is a viable one.

Create a timeline for getting your business up and running (Chapter 13). Decide exactly what kind of bar you want to run (Chapter 4). Choose a name that suits it (Chapter 6). Develop a detailed business plan and use it to find and secure financing (Chapters 5 and 3, respectively). Find the best location for your new bar and get the right licenses and permits as soon as you can (Chapters 6 and 3, respectively).

Starting Fresh or Taking Over an Existing Bar?

The decision to open a bar is a big one. Sometimes people are just sort of considering the idea, and then — out of the blue — they fall in love with an existing location, immediately imagining themselves behind the bar, spit shining glasses. Other people build their dream bar in their mind's eye from the ground up. They have very specific ideas about every physical detail of their place. And naturally, they want to physically build it from the ground up, as well. Depending on your schedule and budget, you can make either scenario a success if you keep certain things in mind, which we explore in this section.

Location, location, location

The bar business is a bit of a different animal. Location definitely matters as it does in any business. But what defines a great location is in the mind of the beholder.

Some people choose to buy or build a bar in an already booming area (and choose to pay higher rent) to get a leg up on getting people in the door. Others think it's better to speculate a bit and get in on the ground floor of an up-and-coming neighborhood, in the hopes that the area will be the next "hot" thing. They save on rent, but usually spend more promoting their business, and have to wait a while to see a return on their investment. The choice is yours.

To help you figure out which way to go, and other specifics about finding the right location for your bar, check out Chapter 6.

Many small neighborhood bars are not in what people would consider ideal locations, but the people who patronize them love them and wouldn't think of going anywhere else. In most cases, these places have been around a long time. If you're taking over a location like this, it's important to figure out what's working already. People have sought this place out for a reason, so you need to figure out what that reason is and don't mess it up. Don't just come in and change everything; instead, meld your ideas with the existing business to make it work for you.

Don't alienate your built-in clientele unless you have to, and then make sure you can replace them with another clientele, through marketing, advertising, and other means.

Getting in with the right people

We're not talking about the Celebrity A-List crowd here. Instead, we mean the barrage of people who can help you alter your space to fit your needs. Most people starting a new business want to change a few things at their new location. Maybe you need to add a wall to create a quiet area away from the stage. Maybe you need to upgrade the bathrooms to comply with the Americans With Disabilities Act regulations. Or maybe you need to install a more comprehensive air-filtration system to keep cigarette smoke away from your customers.

A contractor can save you lots of time and trouble. Don't hesitate to ask questions of a couple of different ones and check their references. Chapter 4 has tips on finding and hiring a contractor.

Here's a quick list of a few hired helpers to keep on speed dial, depending on your concept:

- ✔ **A good equipment-repair technician:** Very important, especially if you've purchased used equipment that always needs to be in working order.

- ✔ **A plumber who works nights and weekends:** Toilets back up even on busy Saturday nights.

- ✔ **A handyman:** Someone who has restaurant experience is a huge plus. You never know when you'll need someone to solder a table leg, replace a window, or fix a crack in your sidewalk on the fly.

- ✔ **An electrician:** He can help you set up dimmers, hide wires and components in places you didn't know were available, and rig up lighting for your stage.

Sometimes you get lucky, and someone on your existing staff has some of these skills. Make use of them. The staffer feels good because you recognize his or her talent, and you can save the cost of a service call.

Staying on Top of the Latest Bar Trends

To be successful in this or, really, in any business, you need to take care of your business today, tomorrow, and years from now. One of the best ways to do this is by staying up on trends in the bar *and* restaurant businesses.

By watching food and beverage trends across all food service outlets, you can

- ✔ Find great additions to your food and drink menu. Watch what mixologists in larger markets are doing for inspiration to create a new cocktail, for example.

- ✔ Consider new categories of food service. If you serve traditional pub grub, maybe you want to try serving some small plates, or *tapas,* that still match your core menu ideas. For more on tapas or other kinds of food menu items, take a gander at Chapter 9.

- ✔ Meld your core concept with what's hot in the industry. You can keep your concept fresh while still keeping your core identity. Look for different fruits that seem popular with patrons (currently guava and pomegranate top the list) and incorporate them into your signature cocktail, for example.

- ✔ Get ideas from promotions and marketing ideas that work in other markets, and be the first to bring them to your town.

Ultimately, you're competing directly with all the other bars in your area. You're also competing indirectly with local restaurant bars and even carryout liquor stores nearby. So keeping an eye on what's going on closer to home is essential. You don't want to copy them and adopt a me-too approach to innovation, but you want to know what they're up to. Check out Chapter 16 for details on how to keep up with and stay a step ahead of your local competition.

Your liquor sales reps can be a great source of information for you in many respects. They also call on restaurants, so they can help keep you in the know about all the goings on around town.

Figuring Out Your Financial and Legal Obligations

Owning a bar is an expensive and potentially risky proposition. As with any new business, you budget your costs, forecast your sales, and hope the sales exceed the expenses. But, to be successful, you have to do more than just hope. You need to do your homework and get your detailed plan together first.

Setting yourself up to succeed

You've probably heard "Failing to plan is planning to fail," and it's as true in this business as it is in any other. Successful businesses don't just happen; people make them happen. Sure, some people do get lucky, but most can only capitalize on that luck if they're watching their business and actively managing it.

Here are some tools that can help you keep an eye on your business, evaluate your successes and failures, and reap the greatest financial rewards:

- **A business plan:** Hands down, a *business plan* is the best tool for figuring out how much money you need to get started, and why, when, and how you're going to turn a profit. Check out Chapter 5 for the steps to create your own. (It's not that painful, we promise.)

- **Income statements:** An *income statement* summarizes your expenses and sales and gives you the bottom-line profit for the month (or the quarter, year, and so on). Take a look at the sample in Chapter 5 to see what this looks like. For more details on using it in your business on an ongoing basis, turn to Chapter 15.

✔ **Cash flow reports:** A *cash flow report* tells you when money is coming in and going out of your bar. It shows you exactly when, where, and how you're spending (and collecting) all that cold, hard cash. Take a look at Chapter 15 for help on creating your own version of this exceedingly helpful tool.

✔ **Inventory counts:** Counting your inventory on a regular basis is crucial to your success. You buy ingredients (like liquor, juice, or even French fries), turn them into products (like cocktails and food items), and then sell them to your patrons. Physically counting your inventory and comparing it to what you should have (based on your invoices and sales numbers) tells you how much of your product is actually making it to the tables and bar top in your bar. It helps you see how much you're wasting, or sadly, how much people are stealing from you. Check out Chapter 14 for tips on managing your inventory to maximize your profits.

Hiring other people to help you steer the ship

Hire an accountant early in the process of setting up your business. She can help you get your numbers together for your business plan, which is a must-do if you're trying to get financing for your venture. Chapters 3 and 5 can give you the details. After you're up and running, you will analyze your monthly financial reports and look for ways to improve the numbers. A good accountant, preferably one with restaurant or bar experience, can help. Take a look at Chapters 14 and 15 to know which numbers to watch and why.

An attorney can help smooth the start-up process by getting all your legal paperwork in order quickly. He can help you review contracts with suppliers, establish partnership agreements, file your permits, or maybe incorporate your business. Depending on how you set up your business, you may need to draft a partnership agreement or two. Watch for details in Chapter 3.

Insurance is a financial necessity for any business owner. You need protection in case a water pipe bursts, a fire breaks out, vandals break in, or worst-case scenario, someone sues you. Make sure you get a good insurance agent from the beginning. Chapter 4 can help you get the right one for you.

Bringing In the Crowds and Keeping Them Coming Back

Getting people in the door is important, and frankly, it's not terribly difficult. The hard part is making sure they have a great time, so great, in fact, that they want to tell their friends and come back night after night, week after week.

Here are some beginning steps to get you thinking about your long-term plans for bringing in the crowds:

- **Figure out what's truly special and unique about your bar.** Write it all down, even if you never show it to anyone else. Take a look at Chapter 4 for help.

- **Decide who your customers are.** Are you interested in drawing a college crowd or after-work yuppies? Do you want sports fans or music lovers?

- **Figure out what kinds of things attract them.** Maybe it's free stuff (like key chains and magnets with your bar's name on them), or maybe it's live music or all football, all day. Check out Chapter 6 for more entertainment options.

- **Look at ways to communicate that your bar matches your customers' wants.** Connect with your customers where they are. Maybe it's in the college newspaper or on a banner in the subway or on the back of a ticket stub from the local baseball team. The possibilities are endless, but you have to get creative to get noticed. See Chapter 16 for more ideas.

Chapter 2

Understanding What It Takes to Own and Operate a Bar

A bar is a place to celebrate, relax, and have fun with friends . . . for the patrons. You, on the other hand, work in this place. While it's definitely fun, it has a serious side. You have to be responsible for everything and everyone in the joint. You have to make sure everything's going smoothly, patrons are happy, and the laws related to running your business are followed to the letter.

In this chapter, we help you get a handle on the reality (not the scripted, "reality TV" version) of what it's like to run a bar. We help you get a sense of the time commitments, the financial obligations, and the sacrifices you make as a bar owner. We also help you sort out your own motivations and expectations to make sure you're going into the business with your eyes wide open.

Social Skills 101: Do You Really Like People (And Their Problems)?

To succeed in the bar business, you have to be accepting of lots of personalities, schedules, and priorities that aren't yours. Whether you're dealing with customers, employees, or a sales rep trying to place the latest in a long line of apple vodkas in your bar, you have to develop a thick skin if you don't have one already.

Patrons are convinced you added too many beers to their tab. Another group knows they were next in line for a pub table. Someone else thinks you're watering down the drinks. All headaches that you have to handle with a smile, or risk losing your clientele.

Employees often have jobs in addition to the one at your bar. Or they may be just working for you temporarily, between "real jobs," or between school years. Although bar employees know they need to be *at* work to get paid, they tend to be very socially active. So you'll have to balance schedule requests, last-minute call-offs from employees who had too much fun the night before, and workers who completely drop off the face of the earth. The bottom line is that, many times, this job isn't an employee's first (or second or third) priority, and you'll need to find a way to deal with it.

You are in the people business. You have to compete for clients and employees. Accommodate them, but don't let either group walk all over you.

Considering your motivation

Why do you want to be in this business? It's not a rhetorical question, or at least it shouldn't be. You should know the answer, even if you don't share it with us. Seriously consider the question and write down the answer.

There are lots of great reasons to want to run a bar. Here are a few of our favorites:

- ✔ You love a fast-paced, dynamic work environment.
- ✔ You love taking on a challenge.
- ✔ You're passionate for mixology.
- ✔ You love tending bar and want to make an investment in your financial future.
- ✔ You have a passion for spirits, beers, and liquor.
- ✔ You're continuing the family tradition.

And the following list contains a few reasons that should send up a red flag in your mind:

- ✔ You think it will be fun.
- ✔ You want a place to hang out.

✔ You're tired of having a "real" job.

✔ You spend most of your time in bars, so you may as well get paid for it.

✔ You want to kick back and take it easy.

If one or more of these reasons sounds familiar, don't be completely discouraged. Just make sure that motivations such as these aren't your only, or even your primary, reasons for wanting to get into the business. And do some further investigation before making the financial, personal, and professional commitment to the business. (See the "Checking your expectations" section for some hints.)

Mastering the key traits of a successful bar owner

Every bar owner injects her own personality into her place. In fact, many people start their own bar because they want it to be different from other places nearby. But most successful bar owners have certain qualities in common. We cover some of these points in more detail later in the chapter, but for now, this list gives you the inside story:

✔ **Business savvy:** Despite people partying it up in your bar, it's not a constant party for you, the bar owner; it's a business. In fact, if more people looked at bars (and restaurants for that matter) as a business, they'd probably have more success. Skills that you've learned, developed, and honed in the "real world" can apply to the bar business, like buying skillfully, managing tactfully, and negotiating shrewdly.

Set up your controls and systems for purchasing, cleaning, scheduling, training (and all the other -ing words you need to run your business) before you open your doors. Consider the long-term consequences of your decisions before it's too late to make the right choice. Learn from your mistakes and build on your success, just like you would in any business.

✔ **High energy:** Owning a bar means lots of long hours on your feet. Employees take their cue for how to deal with the physical stressors of working in a bar from you, their fearless leader. Show them (rather than tell them) how to keep their energy up and keep the personality "on" at all times during their shift. Your bar can't have a positive vibe if you don't.

As a manager or owner, one of your jobs is to promote a positive attitude and energy in the restaurant. You can have positive interactions with customers all day long and make a difference. But if you extend those positive vibes to include exchanges between you and your staff, your staff can in turn extend the good vibes to your customers. That's your goal, because the positive energy can quickly transfer to your clientele as well. If you like to have fun, but you're serious about doing the job right, it shows. And it translates into success.

✔ **Ability to hold your own liquor, or just say no to it:** For some people, managing a bar is like getting the keys to the grown-up candy store, and the temptation is too much to resist. As a barkeep, you often drink as part of your job. Whether you're tasting a new line of flavored rums, checking a freshly tapped keg, sampling a "bad" bottle of wine, or joining your regular customer with a glass of wine or a beer close to closing time, in the course of your daily job you may have occasion to drink. No matter what the circumstances, you still have to count the money at the end of the night. Or you have to be ready to go first thing in the morning.

✔ **Trust:** You need to be able to trust and depend on other people if you want to run a bar. You can't be there all the time that you're open, and if you are, you're going to grow old quickly in an industry that already wears down the best of us. Surround yourself with people who you trust and who you think are smarter than you. Easier said than done, but the successful people in the industry are successful at doing just that.

✔ **Flexibility:** Achieving success and maintaining success are two very different things. As a bar owner, you should be constantly looking at ways to increase your business and keep your clientele interested in your bar, your atmosphere, and your beverages. You have to be in the know about what the other bars are doing and be willing to change your own game plan as necessary.

Look to your liquor reps to help educate you, your staff, and your customers about new products on the market. Try out different entertainment options on different nights of the week to appeal to different groups of people. Run food specials to see what kinds of stuff intrigue your patrons. See Chapter 16 for more ideas about marketing your bar.

Checking your expectations

Running a bar, either yours or someone else's, is a huge commitment. It requires long hours, constant vigilance, and the ability to control potentially chaotic situations — on a daily basis.

Take out a pen and some paper. Divide the paper into two columns. In the first, list all of your expectations for the future of your bar and your career. List everything you can think of, big and small, specific and general, that maps in some way to your career in your bar. Consider what you picture your family life like, goals for the bar, general sales figures, and profit numbers, everything you can think of. This is your chance to put your dreams on paper. Then, in the second column, write down what you expect out of yourself to make this happen. Take into account your contribution in terms of time and money, any sacrifices you'll have to make, and anything else that you can think of.

Figure out how realistic your expectations are. Talk to your business partners to see whether their ideas mesh with yours. Show this list to your significant other, and make sure you're both on the same page about goals and sacrifices the family may make for the business to succeed and vice versa. There's no right or wrong answer. It's all a matter of articulating your ideas, sharing them with the appropriate people, and following through on your commitments.

To get an even better understanding of what your days and nights will be like: Your day will be solving problems. Training and retaining employees. Reading all the newspapers from your area to keep up with the sports and world events because that's what you will talk about all day. You must keep your patience intact. Patience is your greatest asset. You will be dealing with people all day, and they change every day. Ray's old friend used to say, "People are all the same, just different faces and stories." You must love people to stay in this business. You will have fun and learn a lot every day if you keep your ship on course.

Staying on the Positive Side of the Success–Failure Rate

Several different reputable organizations (including top-rated restaurant and hospitality schools at Cornell and Michigan State universities) recently conducted case studies to test the "common knowledge" that "90 percent of restaurants fail in the first year." The data (which takes into account eating and drinking places, including bars) indicates that the first-year failure rate is somewhere between 25 and 30 percent. After ten years, around 70 percent have failed. So, success is far from guaranteed, but it's certainly not impossible.

Failure and attrition is natural in this business, as it is in any industry. New businesses fail and others take their place. That's the beauty and the harsh reality of the world.

Why do so many fail?

Ultimately, most bars fail because they aren't run properly. Sure, we can think of many examples of bars that didn't make it because they had a landlord dispute or some other unforeseen circumstance they couldn't overcome, but most fail because of poor management.

The most common reasons for failure are

- ✔ Irreconcilable differences among the owners. Set up your partnership agreements the right way using Chapter 3 as your guide.

- ✔ Initial underfunding of the bar. Check out Chapter 3 to avoid this problem.

- ✔ Overstocking inventory. Take a peek at Chapters 8 and 14 to head this problem off.

- ✔ Ignoring or mismanaging cash flow (and ebbs). Chapter 15 gives you tools to manage yours.

- ✔ Failing to pay appropriate taxes on time. Read Chapter 3 for tax information, and get an accountant you trust.

- ✔ Skimming, stealing, or other illegal activity. Chapter 14 is required reading to help you keep what's yours.

- ✔ Death by a thousand cuts. Some owners choose to cut corners in food quality, quantity, cleaning regimens, innovation, and so on over time. Over the course of, say, a year, the bar morphs into a mere shadow of its former self. Along the way, it alienates its clientele, who spread the bad news, leaving the bar without repeat business and with disappointed patrons.

Lucky you, you bought this book, so you're more likely to make it into the success category already.

Figuring out why others succeed

Most successful bar owners succeed through sheer force of will, with a dash of common sense, and business savvy to match. They manage their bars as businesses, with procedures and systems. They watch the bottom line and actively train their employees to provide excellent service. They purchase their materials properly and price their menus accordingly. They keep their bars clean and their patrons happy. In short, they have stayed objective and balanced their business goals with their mission to help people have fun.

Understanding the Financial Ramifications

We definitely don't want to discourage you from getting into this exciting and rewarding industry. But for you to succeed, you need to have realistic expectations of the financial commitment and ramifications of running your own bar.

Definitely check out Chapter 3 for more details on getting funding for your business.

Preparing yourself for personal guarantees

Financing is tough for new bar owners. Leasing some equipment is possible (take a look at Chapter 7 for our tips on what to lease). Assuming someone like a bank agrees to give you money, you will probably have to personally guarantee to secure the loan.

A *personal guarantee* is a pledge that you personally (rather than your bar or the corporation that operates your bar) are responsible for the loan, even if the bar defaults on the loan. So, the bank may be loaning the money to the bar, but it expects to get its money from you if the bar goes out of business. (And the bank *will* want its money. Read the next section for more about what could happen if your bar goes belly up.)

This isn't *always* the case, however. In fact, with competition between vendors today, you can get away without signing any personal guarantees at all. The vendors may give you shorter terms on repayment, but the guarantee should be a bargaining point rather than a given.

Because banks consider a bar to be a risky financial investment, many banks will not loan you money. Those banks that will loan you money may require you to guarantee the loan. Again, this isn't *always* the case. It's a bargaining point for a percent interest you pay the bank. Banks often need to be "educated" on the true risk of a bar and their failure rates. Eating and drinking establishments have been cornerstones of the U.S. economy for decades, and there are as many success stories as there are failures. Show the bank the successes and how you plan to be one, too!

Accepting the worst-case scenario

We hope that you have more business than you know what to do with. We hope you have a fat bank account with more operating capital than you need. We wish nothing but success for you in your bar. But, because this book is all about the real deal of the business, we discuss the downside of what may happen if the world doesn't beat a path to your door. Or if you hit a dry season. Or if your suppliers cut you off . . .

You will be put on *COD* (cash on delivery) as your first warning. Suppliers will only give you goods if you pay in cash; getting inventory on credit will be a thing of the past.

Always have two or three suppliers as backups. You may only have hit a bad season for the area. If you're overextended with one supplier, you can keep your doors open by purchasing your goods from one of your backups until you set things right with your primary supplier. This solution isn't a long-term one, though; straighten out the course as soon as you can.

Here are a few warning signs of hard times to come:

- ✔ Nights that should be busy (like Fridays and Saturdays for most areas) are really slow.
- ✔ Your help is quitting. It can happen like rats fleeing a sinking ship.
- ✔ The neighborhood is changing. If you see businesses boarding up, vandalism and crime are sure to follow.
- ✔ You're three months behind in your bills, and you're on COD with everyone.
- ✔ You feel it in your gut that it's time to sell.

It's a great idea to sell while you're still open; you get more money when your business is up and running than when your doors are shut. Talk it out with your family and close friends. It's better to have loved and lost than never to have loved at all. Take a break and try again!

As soon as you see the warning signs, begin taking steps to turn things around. One logical place to start cutting expenses is labor dollars. (Take a look at Chapter 15 for more details.) So, if you send people home early to reduce payroll, you have to start working more to make up for their hours. And remember to watch all your costs from the start. Be careful of any extra benefits you offer because you may have to take them back if business slows down. Taking benefits away tells your employees that something is wrong, and they will jump ship. (If they don't jump ship, they'll be mighty unhappy — and that's bad for business, too.)

Word travels fast in the bar business, so watch what you say. Do not let anyone know when things get tough; it will make matters worse. It will be hard to hire new employees and hard to attract new customers. Your bar is a business, and you need to run it like one. Plan wisely from the day you set your plan in motion.

Personal bankruptcy is a very real possibility if your business fails. Make sure you work with your accountant to protect as many of your assets as possible. You may be able to keep your family's home.

Looking at the upside

If you work hard and plan carefully, your bar will be a superb success, and you will have great fun and a good life. You will be financially stable, and everyone will know your name. You will be asked for advice and also be invited to a lot of parties. Your popularity will increase 30 times what it is now.

You will have tons of friends (maybe because of the free drinks you buy). Our advice is to make sure you take time off from the beginning, even closing one day a week (we suggest Monday). Take time to be with your family. You will have more invitations to events than you can possibly attend. Our advice: *Go!* Take your better half, your best friend, your mom. We give you more pointers about spending time with friends and family later in the chapter, but for now, remember that all work and no play makes for a terrible life. Enjoy!

Balancing Your Bar Life with Your Personal Life

If you've ever worked in a bar (and we really hope you have if you're now considering running your own place), you know that those who run the bar are there well before and after the hours of operation. If the bar is open from 11 a.m. to 2 a.m. for example, someone is probably there between 8 a.m. and 3 a.m. at a minimum, 19 hours a day. That's the best-case scenario. If a pipe bursts, a cooler breaks down, or a toilet backs up, the day gets significantly longer, instantly. So naturally, as the owner of the bar, you're the one who has to deal with all these unforeseen events no matter what time of the day or night. And remember, that's on top of running the everyday, normal stuff of the bar.

All the while, your family's and friends' lives go on. Birthdays happen. Holidays occur. School plays go on whether or not the bar is open. You have to balance the demands of a crazy work schedule with your personal life if you want to be part of both. In this section, we help you get the best of both worlds.

If you're an owner or manager, you will work 70 to 80 hours a week, maybe more when you're getting your bar up and running. Many small-business owners work just as much. The biggest challenge is typically not *how much* you work, but *when* you work.

Combining your professional and social lives

The bar business is fun. Let's face it — that's why most of us are drawn to it in the first place. When you hire your employees, you probably will hire people you are drawn to. You won't hire people who repel you, anyway. If they're quality bar employees, they likely are drawn toward the lively atmosphere offered by the bar and may even enjoy a drink now and then. Because you already have personalities and interests in common, you will on occasion have a drink with the people you work with and those who work for you. It's inevitable.

You have just blended your professional life with your social life. To successfully navigate this potential minefield, you have to drink in moderation and keep your wits about you at all times.

Two common pitfalls await bar owners who hang out and party with people who work with or for them: overindulgence in alcohol and inappropriate personal relationships.

Overindulging in alcohol can lead to embarrassing behavior, like inappropriate sexual advances, drunken tirades, passing out, slurring your words, and so on. As the manager or owner of the bar, you need to maintain your credibility with your staff at all times. An occasional slip in your demeanor while under the influence may be forgiven, but a pattern of overindulging will lead to morale problems, blurring the line between manager and employee.

If you don't know when to say "when," you should probably find another career.

Having personal relationships with your employees can lead to very close relationships — too close, in fact, if the relationships become romantic or sexual. It's not unheard of for people to meet while working in a bar, then marry, and lead happy lives together. But if the relationship doesn't end well (and most don't), it becomes a strain on everyone in the bar, not just the two people in the relationship.

Be very careful in getting too close or too friendly with your employees. If you are known for dating employees, you may be opening yourself up to accusations of sexual harassment. We recommend you date and fraternize with people other than your employees.

It's also inevitable that at some point your friends will come into your place, and you'll sit down and have a drink with them toward the end of the night. But remember, only sit down at the end of the night; everyone will ask you to sit down and have a drink. A simple answer is: "Not right now, maybe later, but thank you." You can sit down for a moment, but you cannot drink with everyone because you must stay sober and keep your wits about you. Remember, you have money to count, employees to manage, patrons to supervise. It's much tougher to cut someone off when they see you drinking yourself.

For safety reasons, consider requiring the closing manager to refrain from drinking. In the bar business, you have significant amounts of cash to count and account for. Math can be tough after a few beers, *and* impaired people are easier to rob than sober ones.

Celebrating holidays, birthdays, and other special times with family and friends

The toughest thing about maintaining your relationships in this business is balancing your work schedule with all the special events that take place in your life. When people are celebrating, they often look to you to entertain them, host them, and generally make sure they're having a good time. So, if you're helping your patrons celebrate, how's your own family celebrating?

Finding ways to celebrate special occasions isn't impossible in the bar business. Here are a few ways that we've found help us immensely:

- ✔ **Communicate with your family and friends.** Understand their expectations and share yours with them.
- ✔ **Keep a master calendar posted for everyone to see.** Write down everything you can so everyone knows who is where, when, and why.

> ✔ **When you're with your family, be *with* your family.** Be fully present, mind, body, and soul. If you're distracted thinking about your business, you may as well just go to the bar.
>
> ✔ **Schedule your own family celebrations before or after the traditional date to work around your work schedule.** If your partner's birthday falls on Super Bowl Sunday (and your bar is slamming busy, so you can't be gone), take her out for a special dinner ahead of time to celebrate her special day.

Okay, we aren't completely delusional. Of course, these things are much easier said than done. But with commitment and consistency, you can make your personal life a priority and have a successful business.

The winter holidays, especially between Thanksgiving Day and New Year's Day, are incredibly hectic in the bar business. Everyone is celebrating, often many nights a week, so you are working. It's not entirely unusual, especially as the owner or manager of the bar, to have just a single day off, or maybe two, during this time. During peak times, it's tough to take time away from what could be an extremely profitable sales period to attend special events in your own family's life.

Getting support from your family

The support of your family is important in any business. But in the bar business, it's essential. Ultimately, you're choosing a profession that takes you away from your family many hours a week, often at special times in their lives, like holidays. You also change your definition of *normal* when it comes to spending time with your family and friends. Instead of being off on Saturdays like normal people, for example, you may regularly be off on Mondays. If you have a family or are considering starting one, make sure your partner understands the ramification that your career choice may have on your family life.

The right approach can make all the difference. You can shift family days around and create your own "regular" schedule. Also, you have the benefit of not having to be at a regular job early in the day. If you have kids, you can spend mornings before day care or school with them and help them start their day because you won't be there to tuck them in for the night.

Like all parents who work outside their homes, you have to make choices about how much time you spend with your kids. You can make family life work, no matter what industry you're in, if it's a priority for you.

Think about nontraditional times you can spend with your kids, no matter what age they are. Here are a few ideas to get you started:

- ✔ If you're working night shifts, consider stopping by school to have lunch with your children because you may not be home for dinner.
- ✔ Take a dinner break, if possible, a couple nights a week and run home to see your family.
- ✔ Spend extra time in the morning with the kids before you take them to day care.
- ✔ Volunteer to coach or be a scout leader on your day off to schedule regular time with your kids.

Above all, be proactive in coming up with solutions to the inevitable schedule conflicts that come up. Don't just expect your partner to solve all the family problems and conflicts. Showing concern and taking responsibility goes a long way in alleviating the stress that being involved in the bar business eventually brings.

Take time off when you can. Your family will appreciate it. And your business will ultimately benefit from a more rested, objective owner.

What if you really need a vacation?

Everyone needs some time away now and then, no matter what business they're in. The best way you can make sure that happens is to put efficient systems in place and train your employees to run things effectively. Giving employees all the information and training they need gives them the confidence to run your business the way you want it to be run.

You also need to find people you trust whom you can lean on for help. Generally, employees want experience and responsibility, so if you give them duties to help make the place run better and so you can go on vacation, you'll end up helping each other out.

Tell your manager where you will be and call once and give the manager a phone number where you can be reached. Tell your manager, "If there is any problem you cannot solve, please call me." In most cases, you will not be bothered once.

You won't be able to solve any serious problem over the phone. Take a vacation, you need it. And if you get a lot of calls . . . you need a new manager.

Take a look at the chapters in Part IV for all the details on how to run your bar the right way. We give you tons o' tips for setting up inventory, purchasing procedures, and cash handling to get your bar into top shape and keep it there.

Chapter 3

Minding the Money and the Law

In This Chapter

▶ Figuring how much money you need

▶ Considering places to get financing

▶ Looking at paperwork and legal requirements

*B*ars and taverns are as welcome as asbestos plants in some towns. If bars aren't run properly, especially when monitoring their customers' alcohol consumption, crime can ensue. Intoxicated patrons can get into fights in the parking lot, get into trouble walking home, or injure themselves or someone else in a car accident. Conversely, your patrons could become victims of muggers looking for an easy target. Because of the potential for problems, most municipalities require extensive paperwork to make sure that people who are licensed to serve liquor do so responsibly. As a result, navigating your way through the paperwork to set up your new business is a challenge, even when everything goes well.

In this chapter, we help you determine how much money you actually need to get up and running, and where to get it. We explain what professionals you may need to help you dot your i's and cross your t's. We also help you navigate the head-spinning world of legalese associated with starting your own business, getting a liquor license, and opening your doors. And we introduce you to your local health inspector.

Figuring Out Your Start-up Costs

Starting a bar is not cheap. Whether you're taking over an existing bar or building your own from scratch, you need money before you can make money. Many expenses happen only once as you start your venture. You have to purchase items like bar stools, soda guns, and bar wells before you can open your doors and collect that first dollar. Your costs for getting a bar started vary based on the location you choose, the modifications you make, your construction costs, the glassware you pick out, the size of your location, and so on. As much as we'd like to give you an idea of how much you actually need to get started, your actual costs vary wildly based on what kind of bar you want to run and where you want to run it.

Chapter 5 contains detailed information on setting up your business plan, but for now we're just going to give you an idea of what kind of costs to expect. Table 3-1 can help you get started. Make lists of all the items you need and how much you expect them to cost, and then consolidate your list on the worksheet. So under furniture and décor, include the cost of your bar stools, tables, chairs, outdoor seating, any furniture in the break room or your office, and so on.

Table 3-1	One-Time Start-up Costs Worksheet	
	Range of Costs	*Final Projection*
Deposits with utilities, landlord, and so on		
Construction, remodeling, and design costs		
Furniture and décor		
Signage		
Fixtures and equipment		
Licenses and permits		
Professional, legal, and consultant's fees		
Initial advertising and PR		
Starting inventory of goods and supplies		
Salaries until doors open		
Operating reserve		
Other		
Total One-Time Start-up Costs:		

Don't forget: You don't stop needing money the day you open your doors. When you're planning for the amount of money you need to get started, plan to include at least three months' worth of operating expenses. This cushion, called an *operating reserve,* helps you stay open until your business level picks up.

Failing to have an adequate operating reserve is the failure of many bars and restaurants early in their life span. Don't become a casualty because you fail to have enough in reserve.

Financing Your New Business

Every deal and sale is different. If you're buying an existing bar, most bar owners will want money upfront, usually from 20 to 50 percent down. That means cash! You will have to borrow the rest. Maybe the owner will finance the remaining balance by taking back a small second mortgage or loan with a good interest rate. Ask!

This section is not on following the money; it's on finding the money. For more info on finding financing, check out *Small Business For Dummies,* 2nd Edition, by Eric Tyson and Jim Schell (Wiley).

Finding money takes time, a good reputation, and a *great* business plan (see Chapter 5). These factors can make the difference between getting the money and not.

Contacting a bank

Few, if any, banks lend people money to open a bar. They lend money on real estate, but very few will lend money for a liquor license. Talk to a loan officer at your local bank or where you keep your savings or checking accounts. It won't hurt, and he may give you a few leads.

When you apply for a loan, you'll be asked to fill out an application and provide details about your financial background. Here's the information — some of which you'll have to supply — that your bank will use to decide whether to lend you money:

- ✔ **Proof of your ability to repay the loan:** Show them in detail how you plan to make money, including a timeline with projected sales and expenses. Use your business plan to get this point across. For details on creating your own business plan, check out Chapter 5.

✔ **Your personal credit history:** The bank runs your personal credit report and assigns you a credit rating. If you want to know what the bank is going to find when it looks at your credit history, you can request a free copy of your credit report by going to www.annualcreditreport.com or calling 1-877-322-8228.

✔ **Equity:** *Equity* is the value of a piece of property or a business after you subtract the mortgage or other loans owed on it. It usually takes the form of your investment in the company. It's sort of like a down payment on a house.

✔ **Collateral:** Any asset that you can use as security, such as your house, your car, and certain kinds of investments, such as certificates of deposit, may count as *collateral,* something the bank will collect if you default on your loan.

✔ **Experience:** Make sure that your business plan includes details of your work and management experience in the business.

Beg, borrow, or sweat: Finding partners

When all else fails, you may have to give part of your dream away by taking on a partner (or two). A *partner* is an investor in your company who owns part of the company and assists in running it.

You have to decide whether it's worth it to you to share your dream to make it come true. Having a partner is like getting married. You must love (or at least like), trust, and respect each other, and be willing to compromise. If you can get away without having a partner, go for it!

If you can't stand the thought of sharing power and want to run your bar your way but still need financial backing, you can always find a couple of *silent partners* (investors who only supply money and have little say in the operations). When you pay investors back, they go away!

Potential business-partner candidates

If you decide you need to take on a partner, here are some places to start looking:

✔ **Consider looking to your family.** Maybe Mom, Dad, Grandma, Granddad, sisters, brothers, or your rich Uncle Walter (don't we all have one?) will be willing to back your business.

Adding the stress of borrowed money to already complicated relationships can be a recipe for disaster. Make sure you're ready for the consequences of getting involved in business with your family. You don't want to lose their support during what's sure to be a tense time in your life.

✔ **Look to friends with knowledge and interest in the industry.** If you've worked with them before, you may already know their philosophies and work ethic. If they match your own, you could do well together.

✔ **Consider a former employer.** If you have a great working relationship with a bar owner you worked for, he may be interested in helping you get started with your own place.

Too many partners lead to too many bosses and, inevitably, to failure! Five partners often means they bring five spouses, and now you have ten opinions and suggestions. It could get tough.

Establishing terms you can live with

Most people make investments to gain a return on their investment: They expect your business to make money. You must set up a written agreement for when and how your investors will recoup their investment with you.

There's no right or wrong way to pay back every investor. Most people have specific things they'll want. Both sides have to compromise to reach an agreement you can both live with. And the sooner you pay them back, the sooner you get to keep all the financial rewards and lose the headache of answering to partners.

Here are some things to consider when you're figuring out how you want to structure your arrangements:

✔ **What rights do partners have?** You should figure out who's responsible for what tasks or areas of the restaurant, who makes which decisions, and who reports to whom.

✔ **Who owns how much?** Make sure you identify who owns how much, no matter what the contribution, including money, time, or both. Spell out the details of your arrangement clearly so that no one has any confusion.

✔ **Who gets a salary?** Spell out who gets a salary and when it starts. Often, as you're building a business, the owners take a small salary (or sometimes no salary) until the business has the money to spare. Make sure that you resolve all financial issues clearly and to the satisfaction of all parties involved.

✔ **How long will it take to repay any loans?** Create a written plan to return loans to investors. Be sure to include details about any interest they're entitled to.

✔ **Which partners are silent?** Everyone has an opinion, and you must clarify how your decisions will ultimately get made. Your first line of defense is to discuss, persuade, and then compromise. But the occasion will arise that requires one person's opinion to win the day. Write down who has final say in these situations before you start your business.

✔ **What happens if someone wants to get out or someone dies?** Make sure that you have an exit procedure outlined in your agreement. Usually, one partner can buy the other out, either in a *lump-sum payment* (all the cash handed over at once) or over time.

Do not give the place away when looking for partners. Create relationships you can live with.

Make sure your lawyer reads every sentence in all agreements, and make sure you know what you're signing. Don't let your dream become a nightmare by agreeing to terms and conditions you can't live with.

Familiarizing Yourself with Liquor and Zoning Laws, and Other Legalities

Check with your local town or city hall about all the laws and requirements *before* you buy a bar. If you find out something that causes you to change your mind about operating a bar, you don't have to go forward with your plans. The police, building inspector, health inspector, and every other inspector in town will tell you the hours and days you can be open and what you can and cannot have in your place. Some towns won't let you open unless you serve food. You won't be able to operate near a school or church (you have to be so many feet from both). Most areas have very specific requirements and regulations; you may even run into a *blue law,* which prohibits certain businesses from opening on Sundays. They still exist in some states!

Make sure to ask the following questions:

✔ What kind of liquor license do I need? What's the fee? How often do I renew it?

✔ What are the restrictions on my hours of operation?

✔ Can I serve food? Do I have to serve food?

✔ Can I open on Sundays? What time?

✔ Do I need a license for music? What's the fee?

✔ Do I need a license for food? What's the fee?

✔ Where do I display the license?

✔ What are the grounds for revocation?

> ✔ How many licenses are issued in the town?
>
> ✔ What areas of town are off limits for my business?
>
> ✔ What are the smoking laws I must abide by?

Obtaining a liquor license

Every bar that serves liquor must have a license to do so. Different agencies regulate the process in different states. Check out Appendix A to find the agency in your state. Make sure you start the process of getting your license early in the timeline of starting up your bar. Depending on the system in your area, getting this license could take a year or more.

The cost of a liquor license varies greatly. The application fee and taxes involved may be only a few hundred dollars. But because many communities limit the number of liquor licenses, you may need to buy one from an existing bar (like the one you're taking over perhaps) or even a license broker, which can wind up costing thousands of dollars. When buying and transferring a liquor license, make sure you have a lawyer who has gone through the process (see the "Bringing In the Big Three: Accountants, Insurance Agents, and Attorneys" section later in this chapter), and ask questions until you understand everything.

Sometimes a town will issue a new license when the population increases. Go to the town government to find out whether you can acquire a license this way and, if so, find out the bidding process. These licenses are usually awarded on a blind bidding scale, sold to the highest bidder. Again, consult with an attorney to walk you through the process.

Most licenses are valid for a year and require an initial license fee. If you maintain good standing with your local agency, you can probably get an automatic renewal for a smaller annual renewal fee. If, however, someone has filed complaints against you for overserving patrons alcoholic beverages, serving minors, or violating other terms of the license, your license may be revoked.

Considering the classes of licenses

Your local governing agency offers liquor licenses in different *classes*. What kind of establishment you have determines what kind of license you need and how much you pay for it. The class of license you need depends completely on what you serve, where you serve it, how you serve it, and whom you serve it to. If you need help deciding what kind of bar you want to run, take a look at Chapter 4.

Here's a list of the broad, common classes of licenses used in many areas. They may be called something different in your area.

- **Tavern:** Some states require taverns to offer a food menu, but others don't. If you serve food but half of your sales are alcohol, your state government may require you to apply for a tavern license. In some states, no such separate license exists.

- **Beer and wine:** This license allows you to serve only beer and wine. Licensees cannot sell liquor or distilled spirits. In some areas, smaller restaurants (40 to 100 seats) can get only this type of license.

- **Restaurant:** This license usually requires that only a certain percentage of your sales come from alcohol. States have varying percentages, but most requirements fall somewhere around 40 percent. Some states have a minimum number of seats required for your establishment to qualify for this license. A restaurant license usually allows you to serve beer, wine, and liquor. Some people call it an *all-liquor license* for that reason.

- **Club:** Private clubs, such as country clubs, golf clubs, and so on, are eligible for a separate license allowing them to serve alcohol to their members. Some states only allow beer and wine in clubs, but others allow for all liquor.

In certain counties, local governments mandate that alcohol may not be sold within its borders. These counties are known as *dry counties.* Most dry counties include an exemption for private clubs, so some creative owners get club licenses and then create a not-terribly-exclusive policy, selling membership cards to their patrons ($1 for a lifetime membership, for example), so they can then sell them cocktails.

- **Brewpub:** Many places brew their own beer, and in some states, you need a separate license to serve it to the public. Check your local agency for details.

Some states issue an *alternating premises,* or AP, liquor license for places like wineries and breweries that allows these establishments to brew and ferment alcohol at certain times and serve patrons at other times.

- **Eating place:** This license is usually reserved for carryout places, such as delis, that may serve food but offer a small amount of carryout beer. Usually, you can only sell beer with this license, and you are restricted in the amount you can sell to each customer (one six-pack per customer, for example).

- **Retail:** A retail license applies to grocery stores, drugstores, liquor stores, or any other retail establishments that sell bottles of liquor.

Some states offer a few other classes that we don't cover in detail here, such as hotel and restaurant, bed and breakfast, arts (for places like theaters that sell alcohol during intermission), and wholesale (for companies that sell liquor to bars and restaurants).

Applying for a new liquor license

Make sure you allow plenty of time to go through this process. The timeline and process vary depending on where you're bar is located, so check with your local office. And remember, allow yourself plenty of time to get this done. Without a liquor license, you can't serve liquor. And if you can't serve liquor, you can't run a bar.

Here are the general steps to follow when you're getting your liquor license:

1. **Figure out which government agency issues licenses in your area.**

   Turn to Appendix A for a state-by-state listing. If for some reason this information isn't correct for your area, conduct an Internet search, check with other bars, or get out the local phone book.

2. **Research the classes of licenses in your area.**

   Request a list from your local agency. Many agencies post descriptions on their Web sites.

   At some point, you will need to talk to a real live person about this. Many agency Web sites are woefully out of date, so don't rely on them for the ultimate answer.

3. **Figure out which class works for your business.**

   Based on what you find out, look at your business, your projected food-to-beverage sales, and the like to determine which license you'll likely need. (Your business plan you draw up in Chapter 5 can help you estimate your sales.) Work with your attorney to make sure that you understand the details.

   You don't get a choice of which class of license you need, per se. Rather, you put together all the information with the appropriate application forms, and the agency hands down a decision. It's not exactly like when you take your vehicle title in and they tell you which class of license plates (tractor-trailer, truck, car, and so on) you need. It's more of a process than that. Nuances and seemingly minor details can sometimes make the difference in how much you pay for your license.

4. **Contact the local agency to find out the availability of licenses, costs, the application process, and a timeline for getting the whole process completed.**

   Your attorney may be able to handle this step for you, but make sure it gets done.

5. **Update your business plan with the information on the cost and timeline.**

   Make sure that you've budgeted both the time and money to get your license before you open your bar. This step is essential, whether you're using your own money or have partners, because if you don't get it done, you can't sell liquor without a license. Revise your plan anytime you run into a new schedule or budget factor.

6. **Apply for the new license or for the transfer of the soon-to-be purchased license.**

   Again, this process varies from state to state, so make sure you complete Step 4 thoroughly so you know what to do.

In addition to your attorney, you might consider using a consulting company that specializes in obtaining liquor licenses. These companies can help you streamline your applications. They file your paperwork and the like — for a fee, of course.

Before you agree to work with any third party to secure a license, check with the state agency that issues licenses and your own attorney. You may be able to avoid additional fees and charges just by making a couple of phone calls. Your local agency may have a list of recommended brokers who handle the buying or selling of existing licenses.

Understanding why you must know your liquor laws upfront

Most areas have very specific liquor laws. The government specifies when, where, in what container, in what quantity, and sometimes even at what price a bar, restaurant, or club can serve alcohol to its customers. These laws can affect how you run your business, like the equipment you must use, the extent of your food menu, and your hours of operations. If you don't follow the law, you risk paying fines, getting sued, facing criminal charges, or losing your bar.

Here are some specifics that may apply to your business. Be sure to check with your governing agency (a list is included in Appendix A) for details.

- ✔ **No discounts:** You may not be allowed to discount liquor in your area. Offers like happy-hour drink specials or 2-for-1 deals are common in some areas and unheard of in others.

- ✔ **No location that may corrupt others:** You may not be able to locate your bar within a certain distance of other buildings, such as churches and schools.

✔ **No doubles:** Some areas set the amount of alcohol in individual cocktails and require that bars use metered pouring systems to dispense the alcohol. These systems may include giving individual-serving size bottles (think airline bottles) to patrons or using automated dispensers.

✔ **No tabs:** In some communities, patrons aren't allowed to run tabs.

✔ **One at a time:** Some states don't allow more than one drink in front of a patron at a time. Others limit only liquor and allow as many draft beers in front of a patron as you can fit on the table.

✔ **Food is required:** You may not be able to serve liquor to a patron if she hasn't also ordered food. Some states require only that the drinker has access to a menu.

✔ **No alcoholic doggy bags:** Some states allow patrons to take their unfinished bottles of wine home. Others prohibit it.

✔ **Limited or no sales on Sunday:** Liquor sales may be limited on Sunday. These laws, lumped together, are called *blue laws*. Some states don't allow the sale of alcohol on Sundays, others allow it in restaurants, and others have no restrictions.

Other legal requirements

Depending on your local laws, you may be required to get these official permits:

✔ **Employer tax ID:** This permit identifies you when you're paying employee taxes and other required fees. It's like your bar's Social Security number. Every business in the country must have a tax ID number.

✔ **Business license:** In some communities, every business owner has to have these permits, whether you run a bar or a dry cleaner.

Depending on your business and your concept, you may also have to get separate permits to operate specific parts of your business. Here are a couple examples:

✔ **Elevator:** You need to get annual inspections done if you have an elevator in your establishment.

✔ **Outdoor seating permit:** Some areas require you to have a separate permit for a patio or outdoor seating.

✔ **Retail tobacco license:** You'll need one of these if you sell cigars or cigarettes.

Getting to Know the Health Inspector

When you're in the town or city hall, take a walk over to your new best friend: the health inspector! Health inspectors drop in on businesses that serve food and beverages to the public and look for cleanliness and proper food-handling procedures, among other things. Ask to see the all the regulations related to owning and running your establishment before you open your doors.

Even if you don't serve food, you still have health codes to follow, so you will get a visit from the health inspector.

Here are some specific questions to ask:

- ✔ Which employees (if any) need a food handlers' permit? How much are the fees?

- ✔ What classes (if any) are employees required to attend? What's the cost to the owner or employee?

- ✔ How many sinks are required behind the bar? In the kitchen?

- ✔ What health code–related signs must be posted? Where must they be posted? The obvious one is "All employees must wash hands before returning to work," but there may be others.

- ✔ Are there any uniform requirements (like hats, gloves, or footwear) for employees?

Your local health inspector will drop by — unannounced, of course — several times a year to make sure the public is protected from food-borne illness and disease spread from employees in bars. If you don't pass inspection, you'll get a report detailing your violations and usually have 24 hours to correct all the problems or face a shutdown. The best way to keep your inspections violation free is to create and maintain excellent standards in your bar. Be prepared any time of the day. Keep the place clean and keep cleaning.

Establishing a regular cleaning schedule

Create daily, weekly, and monthly cleaning schedules to make sure all areas in your bar are cleaned thoroughly on a regular basis. Besides the obvious reason (most people prefer to be in clean and sanitary conditions), the law requires you to keep your bar clean to inhibit the growth of bacteria and pathogens that can be a serious public health risk.

Here are some things that need to be done several times each shift, as needed:

- ✔ Change water in the glass-washing sinks behind the bar.
- ✔ Change sanitizer water.
- ✔ Empty trash.
- ✔ Break down boxes.
- ✔ Clear dirty dishes from tables and the bar top.
- ✔ Wipe down the bar top, tables, and seats after each use.
- ✔ Wash hands.

You can have workers do these cleaning tasks on a shift-by-shift basis:

- ✔ Sweep the walk-in and dish area.
- ✔ Empty and sanitize all ice wells.
- ✔ Mop the entire kitchen.
- ✔ Clean the fryer and filter the fryer oil.
- ✔ Send range grates to the dish machine.
- ✔ Clean and sanitize all surfaces, such as reach-in coolers, prep tables, counters on the line, and so on.
- ✔ Sweep and mop the main bar and any other floor areas.
- ✔ Empty the steam table. Clean, sanitize, and refill the steam table with fresh water.
- ✔ Clean employee bathroom and locker room.
- ✔ Wipe down all table-top items, like salt and pepper shakers and table tents.
- ✔ Clean public restrooms.

Sunday and Monday make great days to do some more-intense cleaning jobs, like these:

- ✔ Empty reach-in coolers and thoroughly clean and sanitize them. Toss any items past their prime.
- ✔ Empty walk-ins and thoroughly clean and sanitize them. Reorganize and replace things as needed.
- ✔ Pull any movable kitchen equipment away from walls. Clean the walls and floor behind them. Grease can build up here over time and catch on fire. Bugs like to find little bits of stuff that fall back here.

Monthly cleaning jobs are reserved for more time-consuming projects. Here are just a few examples:

- ✔ Empty out all salt and pepper containers and run them through the dish area. Let them drain overnight and dry thoroughly before refilling them or you'll have some clumping condiments on your hands.

- ✔ Remove all glassware from shelves and thoroughly clean the shelves before restacking glassware.

- ✔ Hire an exterminator to preventively treat for pests. On "bug night," staff members will need to cover any food items that normally stay out (like crackers, salt and pepper shakers, and so on) to protect them from harmful pesticides.

Failing to do these things on a regular basis will lead to problems with food safety in your restaurant and will eventually show up in lower inspection scores.

Avoiding cross-contamination

Cross-contamination (when bacteria or other organisms present in one food accidentally spread to another) is one of the leading causes of food-borne illness. It can occur at many different points along the food-supply chain, but you have to make sure it doesn't happen in your bar.

Here are a few tips to make sure your place isn't a haven for bacteria and other organisms:

- ✔ Provide plenty of work space for staff working on a variety of foods at the same time. You don't want raw chicken on the same prep table as the salad greens.

- ✔ Clean and sanitize knives and other utensils and equipment before and after use. It may seem like double duty, but bacteria, dust, and other stuff can end up on equipment in between uses.

- ✔ Provide sanitizer buckets with properly concentrated sanitizer solutions and clean towels. Check with your cleaning-product supplier for details on how to use your particular products.

A thorough health inspector will walk around the kitchen as employees are working and confirm that these (and other) regulations are being followed. For example, the inspector will check the strength of the sanitizer solution to make sure it's the right concentration to kill germs.

What about the new smoking laws?

Every day a government (state or local) somewhere passes a no-smoking law for bars and restaurants. Every day! Ask a good lawyer what the law is in your area and what changes are being considered. If you're in a cold area with harsh winters, these laws *will* hurt your business. Be prepared to open a cigar bar or connect a cigar bar to your place.

What has happened in places that have passed a no-smoking law for bars and restaurants? In New Jersey, where Ray runs a bar, the only place people can smoke, other than in their homes, is on a casino floor when they're gambling or outside the casino. For every other public building, people have to smoke outside. An awful lot of bar and restaurant owners added patios with overhangs, heaters, and plastic walls.

Keeping critters out

Bits of food, crumbs, spills, food waste, and other organic material attract unwanted pests. Make sure that when you store any food products you thoroughly cover them. This step helps keep rodents and bugs out of your supplies and out of your bar.

Don't allow wet boxes in the kitchen or storeroom. Keep cardboard boxes outside, if at all possible. Most insects are brought in by deliveries.

Your health inspector will be paying attention to your storage areas so make sure you are, too.

Bringing In the Big Three: Accountants, Insurance Agents, and Attorneys

Get the best professionals you can afford. If you don't know how to find good representation, ask around. Everyone will recommend someone. Make sure the people you hire have previous experience in the bar business. Someone once said, "If you want to play baseball, ask Mickey Mantle, not your dentist." The same goes for operating your bar. Seek the right advice from those who know and have the experience.

Contact the National Restaurant Association (NRA) at www.restaurant.org to see whether it can recommend accountants, attorneys, and insurance agents in your area.

Hiring an accountant

Put an accountant at the top of your list of people to hire to help you with your new business. Before you even open your doors, an accountant can help you create your business plan (see Chapter 5, too). He can explain big words like *depreciation, amortization,* and *capitalization.* He can work with your attorney to show you tax advantages to setting up your business one way versus another.

After you're up and running, your accountant can help prepare the monthly books and reports, prepare taxes, and conduct internal audits and reviews. Work with your accountant to determine what you need to do and what she needs to do to make sure all your paperwork is in order.

Working with an attorney

Working together, your attorney and accountant can help you decide how to set up your business. How you set up your business determines how your bar is taxed, how you earn an income from your business, what your obligations are if your bar should fail, and many other expensive decisions.

Here are the most common options for setting up your business:

- ✔ **Sole proprietorship:** You (and your spouse) are the only owner. You keep all the profits and the debt.

- ✔ **Partnership:** You have one or many partners. You all split the profits (possibly at different percentages based on different rates of investment) and share the debt.

- ✔ **Limited partnership:** Limited partners share in the profits but none of the debt. You pay them back on their investment, but if your business folds, they're not responsible.

- ✔ **Corporation:** A corporation is a legal entity that you can create to own your business. You may be the only shareholder in your corporation, so you still own the whole thing, but you enjoy the legal protection in case your business goes bust.

- ✔ **Limited liability company (LLC):** You gain some protections, similar to those afforded by a corporation, but you have a different tax consequence.

Because we are not lawyers and we do not want to get in a lawsuit, the only legal advice we can give you is to have a lawyer review a contract before you enter into any agreement. It's smart business and could save you a lot of trouble and money in the future.

Protecting yourself with insurance

The law requires you to obtain certain kinds of insurance. The amount of coverage you carry and the *deductible* (which is the amount you're required to pay before your insurance kicks in) you choose affect the amount of your *premiums* (or the amount you pay for your insurance).

Talk with your insurance agent to find the best, most appropriate coverage for your business.

Here is a list of common business insurance coverage:

- ✔ **Property:** Property insurance protects your property in the event of damage. Many policies only cover specific damages. You may want to consider additional coverage that you add to your policy, called a *rider,* like earthquake, flood, wind, and hail insurance, if those natural disasters are likely in your area.

- ✔ **General liability:** Liability insurance protects you in the event that someone sues you for something. Maybe they chipped a tooth on a beer bottle, cut their finger on a broken glass, or fell off a bar stool.

  Check your lease for any required minimums for liability insurance. Your agent should give you recommendations for how much liability insurance you should carry, based on the assets of your business.

- ✔ **Liquor liability:** When you get your liquor license, check with your local agency to see what amount of liquor liability insurance you need.

- ✔ **Workers' compensation:** Usually called workers' comp, this insurance takes care of medical bills for your employees who get injured on the job.

- ✔ **Unemployment insurance:** If you fire an employee or have to lay some of your workers off for business reasons, this insurance pays your out-of-work, ex-employees until they find another job.

The federal government requires workers' comp and unemployment insurance. Protect what you have with the right insurance. See your agent for the best coverage for you.

Taking Over an Existing Bar: Some Things to Watch For

Taking over an existing bar is the quickest way to get up and running. The previous owner can leave customers, stock, and staff in place and hand you the keys. You have a built-in clientele and staff that know the bar, maybe better than you do. You may pay more for an existing bar because assuming you buy a successful bar, it's already making money. You won't wait as long to make a profit, depending, of course, on how much of it you've had to finance.

Here's a list of additional financial things to keep in mind if you're taking over an existing bar:

- **Taxes:** Make sure that all taxes incurred by the previous owner have been paid. If there's anything outstanding, make sure you agree on a plan for taking care of those costs and put it in writing.

- **Stock:** If you are buying the stock (glassware, bottles of alcohol, appliances, furniture, and so on) in the place, make sure a detailed list is included in the contract. Then, the night before you close the deal, or maybe a few hours before you sign on the dotted line, make sure that everything that you and the seller agreed to is still in the bar.

  At this walk-through, if the bar isn't in the condition you've agreed upon or if the stock is missing, do not close the deal. Wait for the lawyers to work out the details. At a minimum, you should be compensated for any items that are missing or the cost involved in returning the bar to the condition you agreed upon.

- **Taking over an existing liquor license:** The fewer licenses in your area, the more the liquor license will cost. Like any commodity, the laws of supply and demand apply. So before you look for a spot to buy or lease, see whether there is a liquor license for sale or available.

Looking Closely at Contractor Paperwork

A *contractor* is a professional who can oversee construction projects in your bar. When you need to hire a contractor to shore up your bar and make it operational, make sure you get everything — and we mean *everything* — in writing. Be sure the start date, deadlines for each part of the job, and a final completion date are included in the contract.

If your bar isn't finished on time, you'll lose business and money. Make sure to include daily penalties if the work isn't finished on schedule. Put everything in writing, and lean heavily on your attorney.

As with any professional, you can find great and not-so-great contractors. Talk to your banker, local government inspectors, and building inspectors for recommendations. Ask a lot of questions of the contractors when it's time to narrow down your choices.

To find a contractor, check with anyone and everyone you know who's built anything. Contractors who build homes also build bars. In some areas, you may find companies that just build restaurants. They are more expensive, but they take care of everything. Depending on your situation, the expertise may be worth the additional money. And always, always check references. Take a look at *Building Your Own Home For Dummies* by Kevin Daum, Janice Brewster, and Peter Economy (Wiley) for more tips on hiring a contractor.

Before you can begin construction or remodeling of your new space, you need to get the appropriate building permits. Check with your contractor and your attorney to make sure that you have the appropriate paperwork in hand before starting construction.

Getting your Certificate of Occupancy

After you finish construction or modification of your space, your local building department must issue a *Certificate of Occupancy* (or your CO) before you can open your doors. After you file your application for the certificate, an inspector from the building department visits your facility and thoroughly inspects the interior and exterior of your location.

Some building departments allow you to file for permits and schedule your inspections online. Check your local office's Web site for information.

The Certificate of Occupancy shows the following:

- ✔ You've followed all building codes. You haven't forgotten to ground all your wires or reconnect your plumbing, for example.

- ✔ Your facility conforms to the current safety requirements. These requirements include making sure that you don't have any asbestos or lead paint around, your fire exits work properly, and so on.

- ✔ Any modifications that you've made to your space are sufficient and appropriate for your new use of the space. Typically, you must submit copies of your plans with your application for the inspector to review.

- ✔ Your building is safe to occupy.

Your CO is valid indefinitely unless or until you make changes or modifications to the structure of your bar. Contact your building department if you plan to add a room, reconfigure your space, or knock down a wall.

Fire codes and capacity

Before you open your bar, you must also get a permit from the fire department. The fire marshal inspects your facility during and after construction to ensure that you have appropriate emergency exits, determine maximum capacity, and check all fire-suppression systems.

Your fire inspector verifies that all your fire extinguishers are in working order, too. So make sure that you have them located in handy places with their current inspection tags attached.

Chapter 4

Deciding What Type of Bar to Have

In This Chapter

▶ Researching your local area

▶ Considering all your options

▶ Putting it together

*T*he best kind of bar to open is . . . Gotcha! We can't fill in this blank for you because ultimately it's a different answer for everyone. It would be like choosing your underwear for you or deciding what kind of deodorant you should wear. Only we're not your mom. We are, though, the authors of this book, and we can help you discover the best bar for *you* to open.

In this chapter, we lead you through developing your plans for what you truly want your bar to be. We look at different aspects of your soon-to-be business, including who your customers are and what your market expects from your place. We also take you through some of the most popular bar formats in the country, identifying specifics along the way.

Determining Your Bar's Potential Market

It may seem like a no-brainer to pattern your bar after the other ten that are on the same street, but it's not a given. What if you could do much better by opening the only falafel-and-margarita bar in town? Okay, maybe that won't work, but what will? We don't recommend just doing what everyone else does. We want you to do your homework and figure out what works for your market, your patrons, and your budget (all before you open it).

Conducting your own market research

Conducting market research is vitally important to getting your bar up and running. *Market research* involves keeping your eye on other bars in your area to figure out what they're doing and why. You need to get a clear picture of what your competition and your clientele will look like. Check out *Small Business Marketing For Dummies,* 2nd Edition, by Barbara Findlay Schenck (Wiley) for help.

Keeping up with your customers and the market doesn't stop when you open the doors. You need to incorporate this process into your regular business practices to stay on top of what's going on in your world. Chapter 16 can help you with this process.

Begin your research by focusing on four areas:

- ✔ **Location:** Determine how important a convenient location is to your soon-to-be patrons. Maybe you're close to your customers' homes or workplaces, or maybe they drive past your place on their commute. Check out Chapter 6 for more information about the importance of the right location.

- ✔ **Menu:** How many drinks or dishes are enough? Will customers be more likely to come in if you have a full menu, or are they just looking for a nightcap? Flip to Chapter 9 for some suggestions.

- ✔ **Price and value:** The *price* is the amount of money that someone pays for an item, like a drink. The *value* is how they perceive what they get (usually in terms of quality and quantity) compared to what they pay. Consider both when you price your menu. Check out Chapter 9 for tips.

- ✔ **Entertainment choices:** Do your patrons like live music, games, pool, darts, or dance tunes? Would they rather be able to have a relaxed conversation or slam into each other on the dance floor? What's available around town that's similar to what you're considering offering? Take a look at Chapter 6 for help choosing your entertainment.

After you understand the basics of the marketplace, you can ask very specific questions that pertain to your specific concept.

You don't have to completely rework your concept to simply fit the mold. But it's better to be armed with information about obstacles early in the game so you can tweak your ideas or add more money to address problems as necessary.

What type of clientele do you want?

Decide who you want your customers to be, and make sure they're likely to frequent your concept. Figure out what demographic group(s) you're likely to attract. The term *demographics* describes characteristics or traits shared by a group. A demographic group includes people within a specific age range or income level, or who share other distinguishing traits like gender or marital status.

Over time, build a profile of your desired patrons and tweak your concept, as appropriate, to appeal to this group. Figure out where they eat and drink. Discover what motivates their decision to choose one place over another. Find out what kind of entertainment choices they opt for. And lucky for you, you can find companies who can help you put this information together. Companies like Claritas (www.claritas.com) can put together specific profiles of consumers in your area. They can give you information about the people within one mile of your bar, two miles, five miles, and so on, to help you make sure your bar is within easy access to people who match your profile.

Unless you own a motorcycle and ride one, don't open a bikers' bar! You should have the same interests, hobbies, and passions as your clientele. You won't be happy faking it just to capitalize on a short-lived trend, and your clients will smell a fake.

Using competitive analysis

Many businesses adopt some form of a *competitive analysis* process, a process that compares them to their competition. Sometimes they look at specific parts of their business, say comparing their respective happy-hour offerings. Or maybe they compare their overall concepts. Whatever the case, you need to develop a tool to help you see what's going on objectively. Table 4-1 is an example of how to set up your own competitive analysis. Use the criteria we've chosen, or adapt it to your own concept to do an objective study of the competition. Study each of your competitors and create an easy-to-read spreadsheet so you can quickly compare them.

Table 4-1	A Sample Competitive Analysis	
Criteria	*Ray's Rec Room*	*The Library, a Campus Bar*
Hours of operation	11 a.m. to 2 a.m.; closed Sunday	noon to 4 a.m.; closed Sunday
Beers on tap	8	2 (light and regular)

(continued)

Table 4-1 *(continued)*

Criteria	Ray's Rec Room	The Library, a Campus Bar
Beers in bottle	6	2 (light and regular)
Food menu	Pub grub, with great wings and burgers	Cheese fries, burritos, and garlic cheeseburgers
Cocktail menu	6 signature cocktails, specializing in martinis	none
Wine list	8 total by the glass, 4 red, 4 white	none
Location	Close to downtown, across from the stadium	Across from the student union
Targeted demographic	Affluent, regulars	Students
Entertainment	Flair bartenders	Garage bands on weekends, jukebox, pool, "Pacman"
Happy hour	None	6–9 p.m. Thursdays, $1 32-oz. pitchers
Promotions		Free cover with student ID
Special Draw		Close to campus

Scratch that niche: Identifying an opportunity

After you get all your information together about the bars in your area, you need to focus your plan (including your business plan and marketing plan) on capitalizing on your strengths and exploiting the competition's weaknesses. Chapter 5 tells you how to put your business plan together.

Here are some ideas to get you started on identifying your *niche* (what you offer that your competitors don't):

✔ **Look for anything missing that you may be able to provide.** In the example in Table 4-1, both bars are closed on Sunday. Maybe you decide this town needs a sports bar where people can watch their favorite teams play on Sunday.

✔ **Think about things that are missing for some groups of customers but present for others.** For example, a 30-something who wants to play pool on a Friday night has no options based on the info in Table 4-1. (I guess she could go check out the pool tables at the college bar, but it might be a little weird.) So you could consider creating a bar with pool tables, darts, and shuffleboard designed for that particular demographic group.

✔ **Pay attention to the breadth of the offerings.** Although both bars in our example serve beer, neither bar has a huge variety. Maybe that could be your thing.

✔ **Consider just how you're going to be different or better.** Carefully consider your market differentiation. If you think you're going to open a bar just like the place down the street and the customers will come to you because of your bright smile, you may want to rethink your concept. What makes you special?

Most people who buy a bar are trying to fill a niche in the area. Why isn't there a pool table around here or a good sports bar or a place to get a good hamburger and a beer? That's the question you try to answer now.

Exploring Your Options: What Kind of Bar Do You Want?

Maybe you knew before you bought this book that you wanted to open a local watering hole where the neighbors would be your regulars, and your market analysis supports that idea. On the other hand, maybe you just can't decide what sort of bar to open. You may even have your heart set on one bar, only to realize that your area is ripe for a totally different type of bar. In this section, we outline some of the most common types of bars. But don't let our ideas limit you. Some of the most unusual bars are the most successful ones.

After you pick what kind of bar and develop your concept, you need to create a complete plan to go with it. Create your décor, menu, staff uniforms, and logo to work together. Check out Chapter 6 for choosing and buying decor.

And of course there are wine bars, martini bars, car bars (NASCAR), cowboy bars, and candy bars (Snickers, yum!).

We definitely recommend taking field trips to existing bars to help you make your decision. So, grab your wallet (with money and ID) and get out there and visit some bars (a tough assignment, we know!).

Sports bar

Sports bars are popular today. They're usually decorated with extensive sports memorabilia, like hockey sticks, jerseys, action shots of athletes, uniform pieces, and so on.

Typically, their draw is a better selection of televised sports than customers can get at home. Fans who live halfway across the country from their favorite teams can go to a bar to watch the games, even if the local affiliates don't show them. The bars boast many TVs, often showing separate games and events on each. Patrons generally sit near the TV showing the event that interests them most.

Menu options typically include traditional American fare like burgers, sandwiches, chicken wings, and chili. Some may offer pizza and salads as well. Beer and mixed drinks are popular here. Higher-end bars may also choose to include ribs or steaks on the menu. They may also have a line of signature cocktails.

Local drinking establishment

These bars are known primarily for good drinks and good conversation. This is the place "where everyone knows your name." The clientele is fairly regular, and low key. Beer and mixed drinks are the "usual" orders here, but a bottle of wine may make an appearance on your menu. Food is typically much lower on the list of priorities and may only consist of peanuts or pickled eggs served from a huge jar behind the bar. The only entertainment is likely a jukebox, but you could expand the entertainment choices to include a video game, darts, or a pool table. Look for a basic selection of beers and mixed drinks here.

If you choose to run this kind of a bar, you can focus on a certain theme, like an Irish pub, a beer bar, or a whiskey bar, and carry the theme through in your name, décor, and menu.

Upscale lounge

Upscale lounge is just a fancy phrase that simply means high-class, expensive bar. Décor is typically what sets this bar apart from the rest. Typically, ultra-modern, sleek designs and über-trendy fixtures set the tone. The flooring is almost always something special; part of it may be illuminated from underneath or have flowing water under glass tiles. Bar stools, tables, and chairs may have a retro feel but still be very trendy. Wall décor may include original works of art, artsy photos, and mood lighting. Patrons are often young, trendy, and beautiful. People are often there to see and be seen with the "right" people. Entertainment is often limited to music, often with a trendy DJ to spin it.

The drink menus typically contain only premium and super-premium spirits in their house-created cocktails. (See Chapter 9 for more about the different categories of liquors.) Drink descriptions detail specific ingredients (like Kaffir lime leaves and unrefined sugar), include various processes (like muddled, shaken, blended), and usually name the liquors by brand.

The staff in this type of bar is known for impeccable service, so if you think you may go this route, you'll need to hire experienced, quality employees and be ready to pay for their expertise. You may need to hire a great flair bartender to flip bottles to delight your patrons.

Martini bar or lounge

Martini bars tend to be trendy, yet nostalgic. They celebrate the tradition of the cocktail by elevating one of the most beloved, the martini, to renewed heights. They usually have a list of house martinis and may have a list of the house's take on traditional cocktails like Sidecars, Stingers, and Rusty Nails. See Chapter 12 if you need recipes for these (and other) cocktails.

Many martini bars are furnished with usable antique couches and chairs, set up in conversational groupings rather than a dining room–type floor plan. The décor tends to have a vintage feel, often inspired by time periods, like the 1940s, 1950s, or even the 1960s. The clientele is often a mix of trendy people, yuppies, and anyone else who's interested in the atmosphere.

Often, smooth music accompanies the smooth drinks. Music choices for a martini bar might include

- ✔ Jazz melodies.
- ✔ Swing, Big Band, '40s-era tunes.
- ✔ Lounge music like Dean Martin, Wayne Newton, or Frank Sinatra.
- ✔ New takes on any of the above styles of music. Newer artists are putting out retro-inspired music they call "space-age pop," "atomica," "bachelor pad music," or "cocktail jazz." Much of it has an organ-meets-orchestra-meets-elevator-music feel to it, preferably with maracas. Take a listen to www.luxuriamusic.com to hear examples of this music.

These ideas are not absolute rules. It's your place, so play what you want. A real live, retro lounge act may be a fun way to round out your theme and satisfy patrons who want live music.

Wine bar

Oddly enough, as the name would suggest, a wine bar specializes in wine. In most cases, a wine bar's inventory includes a wide variety of wine, varying vintages, many, many vineyards, and likely many different price points. Some wine bars have 80–150 wines available by the glass, then another 100 (or more) by the bottle. Many wine bars only serve wine, no beer or liquor available.

Wine, in volume, can be very expensive. To stock a reasonable level of inventory, be prepared to spend thousands of dollars. And you need to have (or hire someone with) the expertise to talk about wine in general and the wines on your list, specifically. The expert who can talk for hours about the nuances of wine is called a *sommelier*. People want to know why one wine is better or more expensive than another. They want help deciphering the difference between a Beaujolais and a Burgundy. Even your bartenders and servers will need extensive training, extending at least to your wine list. You need to be prepared to put in the time.

Because of the incredible variety and range of wines available worldwide today, more people from all walks of life are interested wine. The best way to learn about wine is to taste it, so if you're going to open a wine bar, expect a varied clientele. But, because wine is not cheap, your clientele will have a decent amount of disposable income. The wine is the entertainment, so other than some soothing music, you can skip the other entertainment options.

Wine bars often serve food. Most often, the menu is designed to complement the food. The sommelier and chef work together to develop food and wine pairings, and sometimes create flights of wine to match a meal. A *flight* is made up of small servings (usually around 2 or 3 ounces each) of several different wines, sold together.

To take a peek at some wine bars, check out these Web sites:

- ✔ EOS Wine Bar in San Francisco: `www.eossf.com/wine.html`
- ✔ Morrell Wine Bar and Café in New York: `www.morrellwinebar.com`
- ✔ Les Zygomates Wine Bar and Bistro in Boston: `www.winebar.com`

Bar and grill

What's another way to spell "bar and grill?" R-E-S-T-A-U-R-A-N-T. Okay, basically a bar and grill is a restaurant without high chairs. And usually, the lounge or bar area is not separate from the dining area. So in some states (like Indiana), kids can't go in to a bar and grill (or a restaurant for that matter) if there's no barrier between the bar and the dining area.

Brewpubs: A two-fer-one business

A *brewpub* is more than a bar; it's a bar and brewery, all in one. You control your production, manufacturing, warehousing, inventory, and everything else. You can decide what styles of beer to serve, whether you want a wheat beer, a pilsner, or a stout. You can name the beers whatever you want. You can even start a sideline business of selling your beer to other places in town. Sounds good, right? Well, it can be good, but it requires a whole other level of expertise to start your own brewpub. (So basically you need this book plus a master brewer to get going.)

If you're looking to start a brewpub, spend some time perfecting your beers in the brewery before you decide to open the pub. You can roll out the pub after you've built a loyal following for your beer. Otherwise, you have a really tough nut to crack, essentially opening two businesses at the same time.

A bar and grill typically has a more expansive menu than just a bar. If you open this type of bar, you'll have, presumably, a grill to make burgers and sandwiches. You may have a fryer as well for things like, um, fries and wings. Heck, maybe you'll even toss a couple of salads on the menu for good health and good measure.

You can choose a theme for a bar and grill and carry it through the menu and décor. You will sell quite a bit of beer but will likely have success with select mixed drinks as well.

Entertainment can run the gamut from video games, to pool and darts, to live music, or even karaoke. Many bar and grills have TVs for the sports enthusiast or the stay-at-home moms who need their soap opera fix with their lunchtime glass of wine. Your entertainment options are open with this kind of bar.

If you're interested in running a bar that's pretty much a restaurant, check out *Running a Restaurant For Dummies* (Wiley) for more information.

Several casual restaurants (like Applebee's) have quietly dropped the words "Bar & Grill" from their name, opting for the more family-friendly "restaurant" instead.

Live entertainment venue

Some bars are absolutely known for their entertainment. (We immediately think of the now-defunct legendary CBGB in the Bowery in New York, the bar that launched hundreds of careers like the Ramones and Blondie in the '70s and '80s.) People drink at these places, to be sure, but they're not typically looking for specialty cocktails; the music is the draw.

Here are a few ideas if you're looking to open a bar focused on live entertainment:

- ✔ **Original bands trying to break into the business:** These bands are popular among the college-age set.

- ✔ **Cover bands:** These bands sing familiar songs in their own particular style. They often have a broad appeal because although the band may not be well known, everyone likes to sing along to "Brown Eyed Girl" and "Mustang Sally."

- ✔ **Local favorites:** These bands often do a mixture of cover tunes and their own originals that locals love.

- ✔ **Country & Western:** You *can* have *both* kinds of music: country *and* western. Depending on your geographic location, this may be a huge hit for you, either because that's what people like or because it's a novelty.

For more information on booking and signing live entertainment, check out Chapter 6.

Remembering to Choose One Theme and Be Good at It

Can you be everything to everybody? No, you can't. But you can choose something and be the absolute best at it. (Now we *do* sound like your mom.) Although there's no absolute formula for how to succeed, one tenet rings true in this business: *Hot food, cold beer.* We like to add great service, but it doesn't seem as catchy that way.

Yes, you can have a cowboy bar with a martini menu and a beer bar with the best hamburgers. You can break the theme of your place, but only for one or two items. (Ray always wanted to own a pizza place and give out fortune cookies with the meal.)

The most important thing is to have a great drink menu. You run a *bar,* after all. When you are doing a theme, carry it through both your drink and dining menus. Jazz bars should name a couple of cocktails after songs or instruments, like the Brass Trumpet, for example. A cowboy bar should have a cocktail named the Bull Rider. A sports bar should have a Foul Ball cocktail. Have fun with your theme. You can even ask your customers to suggest creative names.

Part II

Gearing Up
to Open the Doors

The 5th Wave
By Rich Tennant

"Our customer survey indicates 30% of our customers think our service is inconsistent, 40% would like a change in the menu, and 50% think it would be real cute if we all wore matching colored vests."

In this part . . .

This part is your guide to getting all the specifics of your new bar in place. We help you put your business plan together, an essential step for anyone starting a new business of any kind. We give you advice on choosing the right name and finding the perfect location to launch the bar of your dreams. We introduce you to the key products in the industry and help you decide which ones are a good match for your bar. We help you create your menus, stock your bar, and buy the right equipment to match your plans. We even get you started with developing entertainment options (from pool tables and jukeboxes to booking live acts) to make your new watering hole the talk of the town.

Chapter 5

Putting Your Business Plan Together

- -

In This Chapter

▶ Understanding what a business plan is

▶ Creating your business plan

▶ Presenting your financials on paper

- -

*R*unning a bar is not an endeavor to be entered into lightly. Although the business is a fun one, you have to approach it as a business to be financially successful. To keep your bar running in the black, you must create a business plan, follow it closely, and make adjustments as needed. Over the years, your business plan can become a living, breathing document that helps you manage your bar successfully.

A business plan can be a great tool in setting yourself up to succeed in this business. It's your map to get from Point A (starting out) to Point B (retiring to the Caribbean, or whatever your personal goal may be). The more detailed your map is, the less likely you are to get lost along the way. Before you take the big trip, planning out your route can help you avoid lost time (in the business world, time equals money) and make the journey much less hectic.

In this chapter, we cover the basics of the bar business plan and show you why you need one. We also give you tips for putting it all together.

What's a Business Plan and Why Should You Create One?

A *business plan* is a written document that includes information about your business, your goals, your strategies, and your financial expectations. Essentially, it's your road map or blueprint for creating a successful business, and it helps you figure out how (and when) your bar will make money.

This document persuades investors to invest in you and landlords to rent to you. Sometimes, it will be the document that helps you form your team. If you have partners, the document also helps you plot the course. Of course, you can adjust the sails as the winds change, but the business plan keeps your focus on that specific point on the horizon.

Here are the basic pieces of most bar business plans, which we cover in detail in the following sections:

- ✔ **Cover page and table of contents:** The cover page sets a professional tone for your business plan. The table of contents helps readers see at a glance what information is in your plan and where they can find it.

- ✔ **Definition of your business concept:** In this section, you tell your readers what they can expect when they visit your bar. You can include general information about the atmosphere, the types of food and drinks you'll serve, and the customers who will frequent your bar.

- ✔ **Sample drink and food menu:** Here is where you can be more specific about the food — from appetizers to full meals — and drinks — from a wide variety of wines to every mixed drink imaginable — you'll serve.

- ✔ **Market analysis and clientele demographics:** This section of your business plan explains how your bar will be different from other watering holes and describes your intended clients.

- ✔ **Financial data:** This is likely to be the most read section of your report. You use this section to show investors how you'll spend your money to have a successful start-up and then how you'll keep your bar running in the black.

- ✔ **Management team:** This part of your business plan explains who is responsible for running the bar (that would be you, maybe your bar manager, and a head bartender, if it's a selling point). It helps readers understand your qualifications for operating a successful bar.

A business plan helps you ensure that you do all the background research you need to for optimal success, helps you corral your creative thoughts and define exactly what you want your new business to be, and helps you head off obstacles before they become big problems.

For more help writing (and using) your business plan, take a look at *Small Business For Dummies,* 2nd Edition, by Eric Tyson and Jim Schell; *Small Business Kit For Dummies* by Richard D. Harroch; and *Small Business Marketing For Dummies,* 2nd Edition, by Barbara Findlay Schenck, all published by Wiley.

Considering the Benefits of Having a Business Plan

Many bar owners skip creating a business plan; they think it's not worth their time because they can't accurately predict the future, or they may not know where to begin. Or they're intimidated by creating such an official-sounding document, if they even know what a business plan is. Most owners who skip this step fail to see that their bar is, first and foremost, a business. And with a failure rate of 30 percent in the first year, those who plan have a greater chance to succeed. In fact, creating a business plan may be one of the most important steps you take in creating a bar that's built to succeed. If you already know you want to create a business plan, skip on ahead to "Looking at the Parts of Your Plan," later in this chapter.

We firmly believe that your time is well spent creating a solid foundation for the business you're building.

A business plan is a road map to your bar's success. Without a map, you won't know where you are on your road to success or when you can expect to reach that destination. Failing to plan can result in detours (lost time) that cost you money in the long run. Many successful businesses regularly update their business plans, every year or two (or more often if you prefer), to make sure that they're on track.

You can use a business plan to regularly assess how well your bar is

- ✔ **Meeting your financial goals:** Are you getting enough sales on Friday nights to justify staying open on slow post-football Sundays in February, for example?

- ✔ **Keeping current with changes in the market:** Should you consider adding a mud-wrestling pit on Wednesday nights to compete with the new one at Slammin' Sally's across the road?

- ✔ **Addressing your customers' needs:** If your new goal is to have a competitive dart league on Thursdays, how's it affecting the regulars?

Even if you are 100 percent opposed to creating a business plan, create some sort of financial forecasting tool that helps you see your cash flow. It's too easy to see all the money coming in without a plan for how it must go out in order for you to stay in business. We recommend that you use the financial tools in Chapter 14 to run your business successfully, but if you find something that works better for you, use it.

Looking at the Parts of Your Plan

Because writing a business plan is a big job, even for those with extensive experience in the industry, we break it down for you, piece by piece, in this section. We split off the financials into their very own section because they're the toughest part of this nut to crack. Make sure you don't miss them in "Putting Your Financial Forecasts on Paper," later in this chapter.

The cover page and table of contents

The cover page identifies your plan and distinguishes it from plans for other bars, restaurants, or companies that your potential investors may be looking at. Include the name of your bar, the address (assuming your have one), any *taglines* (a catchy phrase, such as *"The* place for all your sports needs") you plan to use, your name and contact information, and your logo, if you have one. These details add a touch of professionalism that shows you're serious about your business.

The table of contents provides readers with an outline for perusing your plan and includes page numbers so they can flip right to the section that interests them at the moment.

Your business concept

The first official page of your business plan should describe your business concept. (We usually don't count the cover page and table of contents as *real* pages. They're really just there to help your potential investors navigate their way through your plan.) Your *business concept* describes your business in five or six sentences. Think about it as a paragraph or two that envisions what you want your bar to be when it grows up.

Pretend you're talking to your ideal bar customers. You have 30 seconds to persuade them that your bar is the place for them to spend their time (and money). Figure out what you want them to know. Take a look at the two examples in this section to see what a finished description looks like.

Here are some questions that you need to ask yourself to get started writing your own business concept.

✔ What kind of bar are you going to run? (See Chapter 4 for more details.)

✔ How is it different from other bars? (See Chapter 4.)

✔ What's the atmosphere and décor like? (See Chapter 6.)

✔ What (if any) specialty drinks (or liquors, beers, and so on) will you serve? (See Chapter 9.)

✔ What entertainment (if any) will you have? (See Chapter 6.)

✔ What kind of food (if any) will you serve? (See Chapter 9.)

✔ What's your clientele like? Who are they? (See Chapter 4.)

✔ What distinctive features can your patrons expect at your place? (See Chapter 4.)

All the answers may not make it into the final description, but it helps you to know all the information anyway.

Ultimately, you can use your business concept to create a succinct mission statement for employees, a tagline to go on your drink menus, catchphrases for T-shirts and bumper stickers, or as the introduction to the financial report after you've franchised your new bar internationally. (Dream big, right?)

Example of a business concept for an Irish pub

The Irish Wolfhound is the premier pub and social gathering place in Manhattan, Kansas, offering high-quality food, drinks, and entertainment in an upscale, casual environment with ample seating. We offer a broad menu of midpriced appetizers and authentic entrees served in generous portions. In addition, we stock a full-service, gleaming mahogany bar, featuring a wide selection of major domestic, imported, and specialty beers, including authentic Irish beers, such as Guinness Stout. Our friendly Irish bartender, with a brogue to match, serves patrons, and he may even take an occasional break to throw a round of darts with you. Decorated with intricately hand-carved wooden panels straight from the Book of Kells, *The Irish Wolfhound* is full of character, warmth, and comfort.

Example of a business concept for a tequila bar

Añejo (named for the Spanish word for *aged* that describes premium tequila) is proud to serve the most extensive collection of tequila on the planet. With more than 120 varieties available, we have something for everyone. For the true connoisseur, the bar offers rested (aged 2–11 months) and aged (one year or more) tequilas. We offer an extensive menu of margaritas, featuring Sauza tequilas, in a variety of flavors, including blueberry, banana, mango, peach, piña colada, prickly pear, raspberry, strawberry, and lime. To complement the tequilas' flavors, we've created a tapas menu, including crab ceviche with avocado, and corn-and-black-bean salsa with blue corn chips. With a festive atmosphere, *Añejo* is a great place to relax after work or get your night started.

A sample drink and food menu

Include a copy of your menus in your business plan. Take the time to actually make the menus look like finished, professional menus, rather than just lists of drinks or products. The menus help make your place more real in the minds of your investors and give them a specific picture of what your bar will be like and why it's special. For details on developing, formatting, and figuring a cost for your menu, check out Chapter 9.

Market analysis and clientele demographics

Here, you show the world in detail how your business is different from the rest. List concrete examples of other bars in your area (or somewhere else, if appropriate) that are similar to yours and point out your differences. Consider their menus, prices, locations, entertainment offerings, hours of operation, clientele, staffing, atmosphere, and anything else that seems relevant to your business. This sounds like a lot of work, but you should have done a lot of this analysis when you decided what type of bar to open (see Chapter 4).

Discuss who your patrons will be. Include answers to questions such as: What is the age range and income level of the people you're trying to attract? How much time and money are they likely to spend in your establishment? Will they be sports fans or theater-goers? Confirm that you have sufficient numbers of potential customers to draw from in your market to make your business a success. Also explain why your concept and marketing plan will appeal to them. For more on developing your marketing plan and keep guests coming in the door, check out Chapter 16.

Your management team

This section of your business plan provides information about (surprise!) your management team. Your management team may consist of partners with a financial stake, operational managers, or even key employees. Whoever matters to your audience should make an appearance here. Summarize (in four to five sentences) the experience, expertise, and strengths of your team in this section. Include industry-related experience, accolades, and accomplishments. Place this section up front in your plan if your team is a strong selling point; otherwise, it's usually better placed at the end of the document.

Include information about key personnel here (even if they're not managers) if it might positively impact the reader. For example, if your head bartender won the Flair Bartending Associations Pro tour the last six years running, you probably want to include that information.

Putting Your Financial Forecasts on Paper

At some point, your business plan ultimately comes down to numbers. The financials section explains how much money your venture will cost, how you're going to spend the cash, and how you're going to build upon it. This section also offers your investors some kind of return on their investment. Every potential investor will look at this section of your business plan, even if they look at nothing else. In many ways, it's the most important piece of the puzzle, and it's usually the most daunting piece. But lucky you! You have this book to help you out.

When you *forecast* your financials, you predict how much money you'll take in or spend in a given period of time. In the same way a meteorologist makes predictions about the weather with some degree of accuracy, you can make predictions about your bar. Will your forecasts be 100 percent correct in every instance? Definitely not. But these forecasts are better than just making guesses. Take a look at the following sections for details about how to predict different numbers that are important to your business.

Include three sets of numbers for each forecast in your business plan:

- ✔ A low-end number that projects your worst-case scenario. Yes, Murphy and his Law make their way into bars now and again.

- ✔ A best-case scenario number that shows all the potential you can imagine if everything goes your way. You'll be retiring in no time!

- ✔ The midrange number that takes into account when some things go your way and other things don't. In real life, this is usually the most likely situation, even if you run your bar perfectly.

Use a calendar to actually count the number of days in your real operating months. In the scenario in Figure 5-1 (in the "Forecasting your sales" section later in this chapter), January, March, and May each had 27 operating days, while February had 24. Both the income and expenses were higher for those days.

Here are a few basic elements you should make sure to include in the financial section of your business plan:

- ✔ **Forecasted sales:** This spreadsheet shows anyone reading your plan how you predict your sales will grow over a period of time. (Very handy when trying to persuade investors to give you greenbacks.)

- ✔ **Forecasted expenses:** This prediction highlights how you expect to spend your money. It shows start-up expenses as well as daily expenses.

- ✔ **Forecasted cash flow:** This document shows how you plan for money to come in *and* go out of your business.

- ✔ **Income statement:** Sometimes called a profit and loss (or P&L) statement, this standard accounting tool helps you check the health of your business. It shows you how you're making and losing money (or how you plan to, if you're just getting started).

- ✔ **Balance sheet:** This spreadsheet is a summary, comparing your business's *assets* (cash, receivables, inventory, or anything valuable the business owns) and your business's *liabilities* (money you owe). It's basically a snapshot used to assess the health of your business at a specific point in time.

We cover these elements in more detail in the following sections.

Forecasting your sales

Your *forecasted sales* are the sales you expect to take in over a given time. We recommend you start your exercise in forecasting here. If you don't know how much money you're making, you can't figure out what you can spend!

In Figure 5-1, we show you a forecast for a tavern in the Midwest. It has 14 bar stools and six 4-top tables, for a total seating of 38 people at any one time. Of course, in bars, people do stand and drink during peak times, so we've taken that into account as well. It serves pub grub like burgers and sandwiches, draft and bottled beers, and just about any cocktail you can order. It has a very limited wine list, basically one of each color. And finally, the tavern isn't open on Sundays. (The owners, of course, may change that plan during football season, but they'll see how it goes.)

Cover Counts and Check Average							
FOOD	**Monday**	**Tuesday**	**Wed.**	**Thurs.**	**Fri.**	**Sat.**	**Averages**
Lunch	25	25	25	30	30	30	27.5
C/A	$7.00	$7.00	$7.00	$10.00	$10.00	$18.00	$9.83
Dinner	20	25	25	25	50	50	32.5
C/A	$15.00	$15.00	$15.00	$15.00	$20.00	$25.00	$17.50
SUBTOTAL FOOD:	**$475.00**	**$550.00**	**$550.00**	**$675.00**	**$1,300.00**	**$1,790.00**	**$890.00**
BEV.	**Monday**	**Tuesday**	**Wed.**	**Thurs.**	**Fri.**	**Sat.**	**Averages**
Lunch	25	25	25	30	30	30	27.5
C/A	$4.00	$4.00	$4.00	$4.00	$6.00	$6.00	$4.67
Dinner	20	25	25	25	50	50	32.5
C/A	$12.00	$12.00	$12.00	$12.00	$20.00	$20.00	$14.67
SUBTOTAL BEV.	**$340.00**	**$400.00**	**$400.00**	**$420.00**	**$1,180.00**	**$1,180.00**	**$653.33**
DAILY TOTALS:	**$815.00**	**$950.00**	**$950.00**	**$1,095.00**	**$2,480.00**	**$2,970.00**	**$1,543.33**
AVERAGE DAILY FOOD SALES:				**$890.00**			
AVERAGE DAILY BEV. SALES:				**$653.33**			
AVERAGE DAILY SALES:				**$1,543.33**			
TOTAL WEEKLY FOOD SALES:				**$5,340.00**			
TOTAL WEEKLY BEV. SALES:				**$3,920.00**			
TOTAL GROSS WEEKLY SALES:				**$9,260.00**			
ANNUALIZED FOOD SALES:				**$277,680.00**			
ANNUALIZED BEVERAGE SALES:				**$203,840.00**			
ANNUALIZED GROSS SALES:				**$481,520.00**			

ANNUALIZED SALES FORECAST:				
	2007	2008	2009	
FOOD SALES	$277,680	$305,448	$335,993	
BEVERAGE SALES	$203,840	$224,224	$246,646	

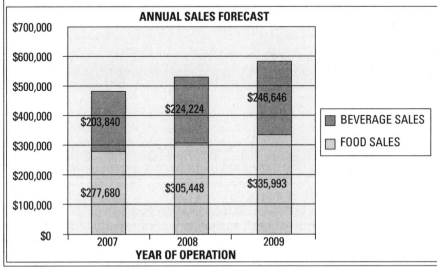

Figure 5-1: Sample sales forecast.

To start forecasting, estimate how many people will be in your joint at different times of the day (often called your number of *covers*), and how much each person will spend (usually referred to as the *check average,* abbreviated C/A in the figure).

Here are the steps we followed to get this forecast:

1. **Predict how many patrons you will have at each meal period.**

   We're looking at 25 lunch patrons during the early weekdays and 30 lunch patrons Thursday, Friday, and Saturday.

2. **Estimate what each patron will spend.**

   Based on our menu, we estimate that each person will spend, on average, $7 on food and $4 on a drink during lunch.

   Notice we said *average.* Some patrons may order iced tea at $1.50 with free refills, while others will order three martinis at $7 each. It's not an exact science, but you gotta start somewhere.

3. **Multiply your covers by your check average to get your total sales for the day.**

   We recommend breaking down food and beverage sales separately (as we did in Figure 5-1), so you can see more specifically where you're taking in money.

4. **Add your total sales for each day together and divide by the number of days to get your weekly average.**

5. **Multiply your weekly average by 52 weeks to get annual sales.**

6. **Estimate your growth percentage year over year.**

   In our example, we're planning on growing our sales by 10 percent each year. So we would multiply our 2007 numbers by 1.1 (or 110 percent) to figure out how that percentage translates into real dollars.

This example is a simple representation of an average week. But many say that in this business there are no average weeks. Make sure you take into account any seasonal events that may affect your business, such as sports seasons, resort-based ebbs and flows, and holidays.

Forecasting your expenses

Forecasting your expenses is similar to creating your home budget, only it's a whole lot more detailed. When you *forecast your expenses,* you anticipate every possible expense that you may incur, but you hope to reduce those expenses and control costs as you actually spend the money. For example, if you estimate your monthly home grocery bill at $100 a week, but you find an excellent sale, you're going to save the money rather than just fork it over to the grocer anyway. It's the same with forecasting your expenses for your bar: Plan for the worst case, then manage the money to the best of your abilities.

To help you think of every possible thing you may need to get your bar up and running, Figure 5-2 is the list of accounting codes the National Restaurant Association (NRA; www.restaurant.org) recommends. If you're starting a bar from scratch, use this list to help you anticipate expenses you may otherwise skip. The NRA also offers research you can use to help predict your expenses or check whether any of your expenses are out of line. Your local restaurant association should also be able to help you estimate some expenses by obtaining data from other members. This information adds credibility when you're asked how you derived your figures.

Pick up a copy of *Accounting For Dummies* by John A. Tracy (Wiley) to get more help on using these and other accounting tools.

When you put together your real financial forecast, include a full year of data and make sure you include every expense you can think of. Check out Figure 5-3 for a sample expense forecast that covers a six-month period. Make sure you remember to include your best, worst, and midrange set of numbers for a complete picture. (Yes, complete the worksheet three times.) In particular, look at the last column in the chart, Total Percentage of Sales. We used the forecasted sales from Figure 5-1 to figure out the sales for each month. Then we multiplied the monthly total by the percentage specified in each row to figure out how much we could spend on each particular line item each month.

The expenses in Figure 5-3 are broken down into two categories:

- ✔ **Controllable expenses:** These are expense you have control over. For example, you choose how much liquor to buy, how you pour it, control it's usage and waste, and so on. These expenses often go up as your sales go up.

- ✔ **Non-controllable expenses:** These expenses, such as the rent, occur regularly. You have to pay these costs no matter how much you buy and sell.

Technically speaking, you should also accrue for depreciation, interest, and other accounting-ish items you may not think about on your own. Get with your accountant for details on how to get this done.

CHART OF ACCOUNTS
P&L ACCOUNTS

Code	Account	Code	Account
3000	**SALES**	4500	**MARKETING**
3010	Food	4510	Selling & Promotion
3020	Liquor	4520	Advertising
3030	Beer	4530	Public Relations
3040	Wine	4540	Research
		4545	Complimentary Food & Beverages
4000	**COST OF SALES**	4550	Discounted Food & Beverages
4001	Food -		
4002	Meat	4600	**UTILITIES**
4003	Seafood	4610	Electrical
4004	Poultry	4620	Gas
4005	Produce	4630	Water
4006	Bakery	4640	Trash Removal
4007	Dairy		
4008	Grocery & Dry Goods	4700	**GENERAL & ADMINISTRATIVE**
4009	Non-alcoholic Beverages	4705	Office Supplies
4020	Liquor	4710	Postage & Delivery
4030	Bar Consumables	4715	Telephone / Communications
4040	Beer	4720	Payroll Processing
4050	Wine	4725	Insurance - General
4060	Paper (QSR)	4730	Dues & Subscriptions
		4735	Travel Expenses
4100	**SALARIES & WAGES**	4740	Credit Card Discounts
4110	Management	4745	Bad Debts
4120	Dining Room	4750	Cash (Over) / Short
4130	Bar	4755	Bank Deposit Services
4140	Kitchen	4760	Bank Charges
4150	Dishroom	4765	Accounting Services
4160	Office	4770	Legal & Professional
		4775	Security / Alarm
4200	**EMPLOYEE BENEFITS**	4780	Training
4210	Payroll Taxes	4785	Miscellaneous
4220	Worker's Compensation Insurance		
4230	Group Insurance	4800	**REPAIRS & MAINTENANCE**
4240	Management Meals	4810	Maintenance Contracts
4250	Employee Meals	4820	R&M - Equipment
4260	Awards & Prizes	4830	R&M - Building
4270	Employee Parties & Sports Activities	4840	Grounds Maintenance
4280	Medical Expenses	4850	Parking Lot
4300	**DIRECT OPERATING EXPENSES**	5000	**OCCUPANCY COSTS**
4305	Auto & Truck Expense	5010	Rent
4310	Uniforms	5020	Equipment Rental
4315	Laundry & Dry Cleaning	5030	Real Estate Taxes
4320	Linen	5040	Personal Property Taxes
4325	Tableware	5050	Insurance-Property & Casualty
4330	Silverware	5060	Other Municipal Taxes
4335	Kitchen Utensils		
4340	Paper Supplies	6000	**DEPRECIATION & AMORTIZATION**
4345	Bar Supplies	6010	Buildings
4350	Restaurant Supplies	6020	Furniture, Fixtures & Equipment
4355	Cleaning Supplies	6030	Amortization of Leasehold Improvements
4360	Contract Cleaning		
4365	Menu & Wine List	7000	**OTHER (INCOME) EXPENSE**
4370	Pest Control	7010	Vending Commissions
4375	Flowers & Decorations	7020	Telephone Commissions
4380	Licenses & Permits	7030	Waste Sales
4385	Banquet & Event Expenses	7040	Interest Expense
4390	Other Operating Expenses	7050	Officers Salaries & Expenses
		7060	Corporate Office Expenses
4400	**MUSIC & ENTERTAINMENT**		
4410	Musicians & Entertainers	8000	**INCOME TAXES**
4420	Cable TV/Wire Services	8010	Federal Income Tax
4430	Royalties to ASCAP, BMI	8020	State Income Tax

Figure 5-2:
Chart of restaurant income and expense accounts.

Figure 5-3:
A sideways
glance at a
sample six-
month
expense
forecast.

	JAN	FEB	MAR	APR	MAY	JUN	TOTAL	Total Percentage Of Sales
CONTROLLABLE EXPENSES								
Cost of Sales								
FOOD	$1,802	$1,602	$1,802	$1,669	$1,802	$1,736	$10,413	25.00%
BEVERAGE	$662	$588	$662	$613	$662	$637	$3,824	15.00%
TOTAL COST OF SALES	$2,464	$2,190	$2,464	$2,282	$2,464	$2,373	$14,236	40.00%
Payroll								
SALARIES	$4,167	$3,704	$4,167	$3,858	$4,167	$4,013	$24,076	10.00%
HOURLY WAGES	$6,251	$5,556	$6,251	$5,788	$6,251	$6,019	$36,116	15.00%
BENEFITS	$3,334	$2,963	$3,334	$3,087	$3,334	$3,210	$19,262	8.00%
CONTRACT LABOR	$0	$0	$0	$0	$0	$0	$0	0.00%
TOTAL PAYROLL	$13,752	$12,223	$13,752	$12,733	$13,752	$13,242	$79,454	33.00%
Other Controllable Expenses								
DIRECT OPERATING EXPENSES	$1,042	$926	$1,042	$965	$1,042	$1,003	$6,020	2.50%
MUSIC & ENTERTAINING	$208	$185	$208	$193	$208	$201	$1,203	0.50%
MARKETING	$2,084	$1,852	$2,084	$1,929	$2,084	$2,006	$12,039	2.50%
ENERGY & UTILITES	$833	$741	$833	$772	$833	$803	$4,815	2.00%
GENERAL & ADMINISTRATIVE	$1,354	$1,204	$1,354	$1,254	$1,354	$1,304	$7,824	3.25%
REPAIRS & MAINTENANCE	$417	$370	$417	$386	$417	$401	$2,408	1.00%
TOTAL Other Controllable Expenses	$5,938	$5,278	$5,938	$5,499	$5,938	$5,718	$34,309	11.75%
Non-Controllable Expenses								
RENT	$2,917	$2,593	$2,917	$2,701	$2,917	$2,809	$16,854	7.00%
REAL ESTATE TAXES	$625	$556	$625	$579	$625	$602	$3,612	1.50%
LEASE EXPENSES	$292	$259	$292	$270	$292	$281	$1,686	0.70%
FF&E RESERVE	$833	$741	$833	$772	$833	$803	$4,815	2.00%
INSURANCE	$833	$741	$833	$772	$833	$803	$4,815	2.00%
TOTAL OTHER EXPENSES	$5,500	$4,890	$5,500	$5,094	$5,500	$5,298	$31,782	13.20%

Forecasting your cash flow

In a nutshell, your *cash flow projection* shows you month by month where the money is coming in and going out. It sort of marries the sales and forecasts reports and shows you when you'll have what money. It helps you manage your money on a timeline. Take a look at Figure 5-4 for an example of a six-month cash flow projection. For more details on keeping your eye on your cash flow, see Chapter 15.

You could actually create a week-by-week (or even day-by-day) report after you're up and going, but for the business plan, you really only need this month-by-month version.

Generating an income statement

Your *income statement* is a tool that estimates your profit by taking your forecasted sales and subtracting your forecasted expenses. In Figure 5-5, we show you a sample using the same numbers we use throughout the chapter.

Some people call this tool a profit and loss statement or P&L. Whatever you call it, it works the same way.

Creating a balance sheet

A balance sheet is a summary of your business's assets and liabilities on a given date. It takes into account all the business's *assets,* including inventory on hand, your *receivables* (or money owed to the business), cash on hand or in any accounts, equipment, vehicles, and so on, and compares them to its *liabilities* (money the business owes to people like investors and creditors). You use the balance sheet to assess the health of your business at a specific point in time. It helps you show investors or anyone else looking at your books that your business is worth as much as it owes. If you haven't yet invested a single dollar in the business and you don't owe anyone money, it will look like the blank form in Figure 5-6.

CASH FLOW PROJECTIONS							
Q1 AND Q2 FY'07							
CASH RECEIPTS	JAN	FEB	MAR	APR	MAY	JUN	TOTAL
FOOD SALES	$24,030	$21,360	$24,030	$22,250	$24,030	$23,140	$138,840
BEVERAGE SALES	$17,640	$15,680	$17,640	$16,333	$17,640	$16,987	$101,920
SALES RECEIVABLES	$0	$0	$0	$0	$0	$0	$0
TOTAL CASH RECEIPTS	$41,670	$37,040	$41,670	$38,583	$41,670	$40,127	$240,760
CASH DISBURSEMENTS							
COST OF SALES, FOOD	$7,209	$6,408	$7,209	$6,675	$7,209	$6,942	$41,652
COST OF SALES, BEVERAGE	$4,410	$3,920	$4,410	$4,083	$4,410	$4,247	$25,480
TOTAL COST OF SALES	$11,619	$10,328	$11,619	$10,758	$11,619	$11,189	$67,132
CONTROLLABLE EXPENSES							
PAYROLL							
SALARIES	$4,167	$3,704	$4,167	$3,858	$4,167	$4,013	$24,076
HOURLY WAGES	$6,251	$5,556	$6,251	$5,788	$6,251	$6,019	$36,116
BENEFITS	$3,334	$2,963	$3,334	$3,087	$3,334	$3,210	$19,262
CONTRACT LABOR	$0	$0	$0	$0	$0	$0	$0
TOTAL PAYROLL	$13,752	$12,223	$13,752	$12,733	$13,752	$13,242	$79,454
OPERATING EXPENSES							
DIRECT OPERATING EXPENSES	$1,042	$926	$1,042	$965	$1,042	$1,003	$6,020
MUSIC & ENTERTAINING	$208	$185	$208	$193	$208	$201	$1,203
MARKETING	$2,084	$1,852	$2,084	$1,929	$2,084	$2,006	$12,039
ENERGY & UTILITES	$833	$741	$833	$772	$833	$803	$4,815
GENERAL & ADMINISTRATIVE	$1,354	$1,204	$1,354	$1,254	$1,354	$1,304	$7,824
REPAIRS & MAINTENANCE	$417	$370	$417	$386	$417	$401	$2,408
TOTAL OPERATING EXPENSES	5,938	$5,278	$5,938	$5,499	$5,938	$5,718	$34,309
OTHER EXPENSES							
RENT	$2,917	$2,593	$2,917	$2,701	$2,917	$2,809	$16,854
REAL ESTATE TAXES	$625	$556	$625	$579	$625	$602	$3,612
LEASE EXPENSES	$292	$259	$292	$270	$292	$281	$1,686
FF&E RESERVE	$833	$741	$833	$772	$833	$803	$4,815
INSURANCE	$833	$741	$833	$772	$833	$803	$4,815
TOTAL OTHER EXPENSES	$5,500	$4,890	$5,500	$5,094	$5,500	$5,298	$31,782
INTEREST	$417	$370	$417	$386	$417	$401	$2,408
OTHER DEDUCTIONS	$0	$0	$0	$0	$0	$0	$0
TOTAL CASH DISBURSEMENTS	$37,226	$33,089	$37,226	$34,470	$37,226	$35,848	$215,085
CASH FLOW FROM OPERATIONS							
CASH RECEIPTS	$41,670	$37,040	$41,670	$38,583	$41,670	$40,127	$240,760
LESS: CASH DISPURSEMENTS	$37,226	$33,089	$37,226	$34,470	$37,226	$35,848	$215,085
NET FROM OPERATIONS	$4,444	$3,951	$4,444	$4,113	$4,444	$4,279	$25,675
CASH ON HAND							
OPENING BALANCE	$0	$3,944	$5,895	$8,339	$10,452	$11,896	
PLUS: NEW LOAN (DEBT)	$0	$0	$0	$0	$0	$0	
PLUS: NEW INVESTMENT	$0	$0	$0	$0	$0	$0	
PLUS: SALE OF FIXED ASSETS	$0	$0	$0	$0	$0	$0	
PLUS: NET FROM OPERATIONS	$4,444	$3,951	$4,444	$4,113	$4,444	$4,279	
TOTAL CASH AVAILABLE	$4,444	$7,895	$10,339	$12,452	$14,896	$16,175	
LESS: DEBT REDUCTION	$500	$1,000	$1,000	$1,000	$1,000	$1,000	
LESS: NEW FIXED ASSETS	$0	$0	$0	$0	$0	$0	
LESS: PROFIT DISTRIBUTIONS	$0	$1,000	$1,000	$1,000	$2,000	$2,000	
TOTAL CASH PAID OUT	$500	$2,000	$2,000	$1,000	$3,000	$3,000	
ENDING CASH POSITION	$3,944	$5,895	$8,339	$10,452	$11,896	$13,175	$13,175

Figure 5-4:
Sample
cash flow
projection
for six
months.

PROJECTED INCOME STATEMENT: Q1 AND Q2 FY'07								
	JAN	FEB	MAR	APR	MAY	JUN	TOTAL	TOTAL
REVENUES								
FOOD SALES	$24,030	$21,360	$24,030	$22,250	$24,030	$23,140	$138,840	57.67%
BEVERAGE SALES	$17,640	$15,680	$17,640	$16,333	$17,640	$16,987	$101,920	42.33%
OTHER INCOME	$0	$0	$0	$0	$0	$0	$0	0.00%
TOTAL REVENUE	**$41,670**	**$37,040**	**$41,670**	**$38,583**	**$41,670**	**$40,127**	**$240,760**	**100.00%**
EXPENSES								
FOOD COST	$7,209	$6,408	$7,209	$6,675	$7,209	$6,942	$41,652	17.30%
BEVERAGE COST	$4,410	$3,920	$4,410	$4,083	$4,410	$4,247	$25,480	10.58%
TOTAL COGS	**$11,619**	**$10,328**	**$11,619**	**$10,758**	**$11,619**	**$11,189**	**$67,132**	**27.88%**
PAYROLL								
SALARIES	$4,167	$3,704	$4,167	$3,858	$4,167	$4,013	$24,076	10.00%
HOURLY WAGES	$6,251	$5,556	$6,251	$5,788	$6,251	$6,019	$36,116	15.00%
BENEFITS	$3,334	$2,963	$3,334	$3,087	$3,334	$3,210	$19,262	8.00%
CONTRACT LABOR	$0	$0	$0	$0	$0	$0	$0	0.00%
TOTAL PAYROLL	**$13,752**	**$12,223**	**$13,752**	**$12,733**	**$13,752**	**$13,242**	**$79,454**	**33.00%**
OPERATING EXPENSES								
DIRECT OPERATING EXPENSES	$1,042	$926	$1,042	$965	$1,042	$1,003	$6,020	2.50%
MUSIC & ENTERTAINING	$208	$185	$208	$193	$208	$201	$1,203	0.50%
MARKETING	$2,084	$1,852	$2,084	$1,929	$2,084	$2,006	$12,039	5.00%
ENERGY & UTILITES	$833	$741	$833	$772	$833	$803	$4,815	2.00%
GENERAL & ADMINISTRATIVE	$1,354	$1,204	$1,354	$1,254	$1,354	$1,304	$7,824	3.25%
REPAIRS & MAINTENANCE	$417	$370	$417	$386	$417	$401	$2,408	1.00%
TOTAL OPERATING EXPENSES	**$5,938**	**$5,278**	**$5,938**	**$5,499**	**$5,938**	**$5,718**	**$34,309**	**14.25%**
GROSS OPERATING PROFIT	**$10,361**	**$9,211**	**$10,361**	**$9,593**	**$10,361**	**$9,978**	**$59,865**	**24.87%**
OTHER EXPENSES								
RENT	$2,917	$2,593	$2,917	$2,701	$2,917	$2,809	$16,854	7.00%
REAL ESTATE TAXES	$625	$556	$625	$579	$625	$602	$3,612	1.50%
LEASE EXPENSES	$292	$259	$292	$270	$292	$281	$1,686	0.70%
FF&E RESERVE	$833	$741	$833	$772	$833	$803	$4,815	2.00%
INSURANCE	$833	$741	$833	$772	$833	$803	$4,815	2.00%
TOTAL OTHER EXPENSES	**$5,500**	**$4,890**	**$5,500**	**$5,094**	**$5,500**	**$5,298**	**$31,782**	**13.20%**
ADJUSTED PROFIT	**$4,861**	**$4,321**	**$4,861**	**$4,499**	**$4,861**	**$4,680**	**$28,083**	**11.67%**
INTEREST	$416.70	$370.40	$416.70	$385.83	$416.70	$401.27	$2,407.60	1.00%
DEPRECIATION	$541.71	$481.52	$541.71	$501.58	$541.71	$521.65	$3,129.88	1.30%
NET PROFIT/LOSS	**$3,903**	**$3,469**	**$3,903**	**$3,612**	**$3,903**	**$3,757**	**$22,545**	**9.37%**

Figure 5-5:
Sample
income
statement.

Assets			
Current Assets:			
Cash		$0	
Accounts Receivable	$0		
Less: Reserve for Bad Debts	0	0	
Merchandise Inventory		0	
Prepaid Expenses		0	
Notes Receivable		0	
Total Current Assets			$0
Fixed Assets:			
Vehicles	0		
Less: Accumulated Depreciation	0	0	
Furniture and Fixtures	0		
Less: Accumulated Depreciation	0	0	
Equipment	0		
Less: Accumulated Depreciation	0	0	
Buildings	0		
Less: Accumulated Depreciation	0	0	
Land	0		
Total Fixed Assets			0
Other Assets:			
Goodwill		0	
Total Other Assets			0
Total Assets			$0
Liabilities and Capital			
Current Liabilities:			
Accounts Payable		$0	
Sales Taxes Payable		0	
Payroll Taxes Payable		0	
Accrued Wages Payable		0	
Unearned Revenues		0	
Short-Term Notes Payable		0	
Short-Term Bank Loan Payable		0	
Total Current Liabilities			$0
Long-Term Liabilities:			
Long-Term Notes Payable		0	
Mortgage Payable		0	
Total Long-Term Liabilities			0
Total Liabilities			0
Capital:			
Owner's Equity		0	
Net Profit		0	
Total Capital			0
Total Liabilities and Capital			$0

Figure 5-6:
Sample
balance
sheet.

Chapter 6

Selecting Your Bar's Site, Décor, and Name

. . . .

In This Chapter

▶ Choosing the best location for your bar

▶ Picking the right name

▶ Decorating your bar

▶ Getting the right equipment to entertain your patrons

▶ Developing your music plan

. . . .

*Y*our bar should have a certain mood, a feel, an atmosphere that draws people in and makes them want to linger and spend their money. You, as the owner, set the tone for the experience your customers have in your place from the first moment you start planning. By choosing the location that fits your idea, your goals, and your patrons, *you* set the stage. When selecting your name, you give your patrons something to talk about that sticks with them and paints a picture before they've even walked in the door. After they're inside, the décor, entertainment, and music options complete the experience.

In this chapter, we walk you through each step of that process, from choosing just the right spot to open your place to giving your baby (oops, we mean your bar) a name. We offer suggestions on the ideal furniture and other design elements to please your patrons visually. And we help you choose how to entertain them so they come back again and again.

Finding Your Bar's Ideal Location

Location, location, location is the cardinal rule in real estate. But what does that have to do with your bar? Ultimately, you have to choose which location fits your business, your patrons, and your goals. And remember, the better the location, the more expensive it is. You get what you pay for, so be creative and you can save money.

Here are a few general ideas to get you thinking about the right place for your bar:

- Consider a spot near offices, near residential neighborhoods, in strip malls, or near a sporting complex. These areas can be great locations because people are already in the area using related services. Your prospective patrons can just stop by on their way to or from these places.

- Corners are desirable because people can see you from two streets instead of one. You'll get more exposure, instead of being buried in the middle of the block. But remember, you typically pay more for corner locations, so balance the added exposure with your budget to find the best answer for your business.

- Check with your city or county zoning boards about your intended use of different locations. Each town has specific laws about where you can open a bar. Most governments won't let you operate a bar within so many feet of a school or church, for example. Take a look at Chapter 3 for details on getting a liquor license.

In this section, we break down the process of looking for just the right location for your bar, with lots of specifics along the way.

Is location truly everything?

At the end of the day, yes, location really is everything when it comes to picking a site for your bar. But what constitutes a prime location is different things to different people. Most people look at the real estate market and potential locations in one of two ways:

- **A sure thing:** Many people start a bar in an already hip, trendy area of town and hope to make some profit. Locations where people are often mingling provide a built-in customer base. But these locations come at a price, usually in the form of high rent.

- **Speculation on neighborhood turnaround:** Some folks choose to be prospectors and hit an area before it becomes a great entertainment neighborhood. If you go this route, you typically pay less rent, but you won't have a built-in customer base, at least for a while. You may need to spend more on marketing and advertising just to get people to your door. Just keep in mind that with the greatest potential for profit comes the greatest possibility of failure. Your real estate agent should be able to help you find up-and-coming locations.

If you choose to establish your bar in an area before it becomes hot, you may not realize your business potential for a couple of years. Make sure that you have enough cash to sustain the wait.

Identifying possible areas

Many different locations can make a great location for your bar. You can consider downtown areas, suburban areas, even abandoned warehouses. With a little research and a lot of vision, you can find just the right place for your place.

Everything starts with the local real estate market. Here are a few ways to find potential locations:

- **Work with a commercial real estate agent or business broker.** Some real estate agents specialize in buying and selling businesses and business property. They may work independently or in a division of a large real estate company. Finding someone who knows the restaurant and bar market is preferable.

- **Drive around neighborhoods you think you might be interested in.** Get out of your car and take a walk around the area. Look for locations that interest you, even if it's not obvious that they're up for sale or lease.

- **Check in with your local chamber of commerce.** It's a good source for resources. You can get insights into key tourist areas, tax benefits and consequences of certain areas, and demographic information about your community.

- **Contact your local restaurant or bar owners' association**. These organizations typically have a small membership, and everyone knows who's coming and going. Check out www.restaurant.org to find a chapter near you.

- **Get info from your local governing bodies.** Town councils, zoning boards, and any other agency or board that doles out licenses is likely to know of new development and rezoning opportunities.

- **Talk with liquor, wine, and beer salespeople.** They are sometimes the first to hear about locations opening up and zoning changes.

How much does size matter?

Most bars seat fewer than 75 people at tables and 20 or fewer at the bar. Bars are warm and friendly places. Keep yours small and tight for employees and customers. You should be able to yell to someone and be heard on the other side of the room. You're running a bar! It should be a place where everyone knows your name, you can relax, have good conversation, watch a great ball game, listen to a great jukebox, eat a great meal, have a great cocktail or beer, play pool or other bar games, and spend some time enjoying your life. *This is a bar!*

If you want a bigger place, check out *Running a Restaurant For Dummies* (Wiley) written by coauthor Heather Dismore, along with Michael Garvey and Andrew Dismore.

Knowing what to avoid

In a perfect world, people will beat a path to your bar's door, no matter where you're located. But in the real world, outside factors affect your business more than you may guess. Your best bet is to pinpoint and avoid things that may keep customers away from your bar.

By asking questions of other shopkeepers in the area you're considering, you can get the scoop on what's being planned and what's currently going on in the neighborhood. You can also get a feel for what kind of clientele you may attract. You may also get an inkling about what kinds of services in the area might turn off your potential patrons.

It's very hard to say what to avoid; some of the formerly worst neighborhoods are now the trendiest.

For starters, avoid locations that feature:

- ✔ **Businesses that your customers may find unsavory.** Consider the impact of close proximity to places such as adult video or bookstores, free clinics, and pawn shops. Your patrons may feel uncomfortable and may stop coming altogether.

- ✔ **Permanent construction zones.** You don't want heavy machinery and trucks going through the area during prime business hours. Patrons may have a tough time navigating their way through the construction mess. If the construction is short term or pervasive throughout your area, you may not be able to avoid it. But if your heart is set on the area, give it your best shot.

Spend the necessary time talking to the people at your city, county, and state transportation departments. They can tell you what their long-term plans (one-, three-, and five-year time frames) are regarding road projects in the areas you're considering. Surviving and/or recovering from an extended road construction project can be difficult or impossible. Many of your potential customers will choose other routes to their destinations and never even find out that you exist. The ones who know about you won't want to deal with the hassle.

On the flip side, you may be able to negotiate a better deal if the site is going through a transitional time. Eventually, the construction is going to clear up, and until it does, you may be able to draw the construction workers in for a brewski after a long day on the job.

- ✔ **Remote or hard-to-find addresses.** If they can't find it, they won't! (Did Yogi say that?) Don't locate your bar in a remote or hard-to-get-to location. Walking through alleys or driving more than 10 or 15 minutes is unlikely to happen. People are less likely these days to venture far from home when drinking.

On the other hand, some patrons look for out-of-the-way places or get-aways. Do an Internet search for "hideaway bar," and you'll find many successful, longstanding establishments. Whether they're hiding from their spouse, boss, or AA sponsor, many people like to drink at remote and hard-to-find places. You just have to decide if that's the kind of place that you want to have.

Contact your local law enforcement agency to get the scoop on crime rates in your potential location. Find out what kinds of crimes occur and how often, and get any information about what the agency expects to happen in the future.

Competition for bar business is stiff. Choose the most attractive location you can afford. Don't just think "If I build it, they will come." Unless of course a whispering cornfield says it to you. Then by all means, build it wherever you want, Mr. Costner.

Considering traffic and parking in the area

Traffic is the movement of vehicles *and* people along a route. Notice we said people as well as vehicles. Consider foot traffic, private vehicles, and public transportation when you evaluate the ease of getting to your place.

Here are some things to look for to ensure you have good traffic flow and ample parking:

- **Consider the sheer number of people.** Granted you can't stand there all day with a counter watching people walk by (you've got work to do, darn it!), but if your business plan requires you to have 200 people a night to break even and you don't have a single person of drinking age near your place, you need to know right away.

- **Figure out where people are going.** Are they commuting, shopping, or eating and drinking in nearby establishments? Formulate ideas about how (and for how long) you can lure them into your new bar. Think about what may keep them in the bar stools and keep them coming back.

- **Look at the pace at which they're moving.** Are people harried, or are they strolling leisurely? Do they look like they may be interested in stopping in for a beer, or are they in too much of a hurry? If people are driving, are the vehicles moving fairly steadily? Are there tie-ups that keep cars from moving? Do people need to wait for a left-turn arrow to turn into your parking lot?

- **Make sure you have parking near your bar.** Your patrons shouldn't have more than a three-block walk to your bar. If parking is free, even better. Make sure those three blocks are a safe walk for your patrons. If you have to hire a valet, it will cost you some cash, so budget for it.

If you're located in an urban area, parking is less of a concern than if you're in a suburban area. More walkers will visit your bar in the city; suburbanites tend to drive.

✔ **Consider whether patrons have easy access to your location.** If they have to drive past your bar, turn left at the next light, and then backtrack to get to you, they may not bother.

Thinking about a location's security

Security is a key concern for any business owner. Bars tend to be cash rich, although credit and debit cards definitely claim their share of sales. When the cash flows (or at least the perception that it flows), bars can be a tempting target for thieves.

You can head off security problems before they start by making sure that your bar includes these safety features:

✔ Working locks and alarms on exterior doors or other secure areas.

✔ Working security system with cameras.

✔ Safe access to and from the garbage area. Your trash may be dumped a few times during the night.

✔ Plenty of food storage in secured areas.

✔ Well-lit exterior and parking lots.

✔ A working safe.

A little bit of time and money on your part will take care of these matters.

No matter where your bar is located, however, you can keep yourself, your managers, your employees, and your patrons safe by heeding this advice:

✔ **Avoid buildings with blind interior and exterior corners.** *Blind corners,* like blind driveways, are corners that can't be seen from the normal flow of traffic. These spots are a perfect place for a thief to ambush someone.

✔ **Stay away from buildings with poorly lit stairwells and hallways.** If you do choose a location that's poorly lit, make sure you immediately make improvements to remedy the situation.

✔ **Consider potential terrorist targets when selecting your location.** This particular point may not be the most important one in making your decision, but if you're considering a location near a courthouse, a power plant, or a federal building, you run the risk that you may have to temporarily close your doors during bomb threats, evacuations, and the like.

These potential terrorist targets may be terrifically busy locations, and you may have absolutely no problems and instead reap the rewards of a built-in population ready to imbibe with you. Just consider the full picture before you sign on the dotted line.

Comparing an apple (martini) to an orange (whip): The final choice

No two locations are alike, so if you find more than one likely area for your bar, it can be tough to pick one over the other. After all, if you choose one (because of the 24-foot mahogany bar), you may be giving up another great space (with the kitchen that's already perfect for you). Although this can be a good problem to have, you still have a tough decision to make.

After you've narrowed your choices down to a few locations, do some good, old-fashioned detective work to get an intimate feel for the area.

✔ **Be a pedestrian:** Walk ten blocks in every direction, and see what's going on. Talk to everyone: shop owners, gas station attendants, people walking down the street, bus drivers, train conductors, ticket sellers. Say hello, ask if they have a minute to talk, and tell them your plans. It may surprise you that people like to talk and give you ideas and opinions.

Be an investigator. Look up and down the street, peek in the alleys, go into every store, and see what business is like. Stop, look, and listen.

✔ **Act like a commuter:** Get on the bus or the train, if one is nearby. Take the ride and look around. Figure out how easy or difficult it is for a commuter to make a stop at your place on the way home. Check out the public transportation stops for advertising opportunities.

If you set up shop in an area with bus or train lines nearby, make sure you keep the local public transportation schedules handy. People will ask you about them.

Ideally, you'll stay in your location a long time; this is a very big move. Get to know everyone and everything.

You can also research the history of your proposed space, building, and neighborhood. Find out what was there before and what has succeeded and failed. Try to figure out why businesses in the area made it or didn't survive. Here are a few ways to get started on your research:

✔ **Ask landlords for information.** At a minimum, they can give you the names of previous tenants or information about the businesses that have come before yours.

✔ **Visit the library.** Resources such as archived court records, old newspapers, and local histories at your library can be helpful if the space you're interested in has been around for a long time. Check with a librarian in areas like Local History, or other similar areas, to help you find relevant information.

✔ **Talk to past owners and lessors.** They may share invaluable information on their problems and solutions for the space, saving you some trial and error down the road.

✔ **Check in with your local building department.** All renovations, additions, and many minor construction projects require permits, which must be granted by the building department. The building department keeps a copy of all plans and permits on file. You can use this information to look at infrastructure improvements or gauge the date of different construction projects to help you make an informed location selection.

✔ **Contact your local restaurant association.** If the space you're considering used to be a bar or restaurant, the group may have the scoop on why it's not now (or why the owner's selling). Go to www.restaurant.org to find a chapter near you.

In the end, you have to be the final decision maker about what you need most out of a location. You have to look at what each location offers and choose the best one for your bar.

Choosing and Establishing Your Bar's Name

It may be true that "a rose by any other name would smell as sweet." Not so for a bar! Great bar names evoke pictures in patrons' minds. Sometimes they choose one bar over another based on the name alone.

People choose names based on important people in their lives, historical or fictional characters, heritage, or simply where the bar is located. Maybe you have a favorite uncle who loved to drink scotch in a big chair by the fireplace, so you name your bar Uncle Matty's Bar. Or maybe you're Irish by heritage and want to evoke that feel in your place, so you name your bar the Donegal Tavern. Whatever your reasons, you can create a name that represents your vision and connects with your patrons.

At the end of the day, the single most important thing about naming your bar is that the name and the atmosphere must be in synch. Your name must match your concept or theme. People should hear the name and have a pretty decent idea of what to expect when they walk into your place. (Besides, if you come up with a great name and logo for your bar, you can print and sell some great T-shirts!)

What's in a bar name?

BARTENDER magazine (www.bartender.com) has a page called BARGOS, where bar owners send their logos and name of the bar. Here are a few of our favorites to get your creative juices flowing.

TC's Speakeasy

Splash

Cocktail Bob's

Rumrunners

DRINKS

Budapest Blondes

Jersey's Bar and Grill (located in Redondo Beach, California)

Manhattan's (in Milford, Massachusetts)

Brown Bag Saloon

Lucky Lady

Dew Drop Inn

Drift Inn

Last Call

Cell Block

Huffy's Mule Barn

Monkey Bars

Grasshoppers

Cats Meow

The Squealing Pig

Dogs Place

Lions Head

The Hairy Lemon

Four Seasons

Bamboo Grill

Thirsty Turtle

Big Heads

Turtle Bay

Runaway Bay

Foxy's

The Back Room

Downstairs

Sidebar

Lotus

and of course, Bob's, Ray's, Bill's John's, Mary's, Jackie's, Heather's, and Hymie's

The name: A few words about your bar

When you name your bar, you have your single greatest opportunity to connect your vision for your place with potential patrons. You need to give them something to remember in a positive way.

Here are a few things to think about when choosing a name for your place.

> ✔ **Consider geographic locations.** This can be based in reality (Mountain View Bar in Denver) or wishful thinking (Beachfront Bar in St. Louis). Try words like *by the sea, lakeside, landings, creeks, ocean view, river, arctic, trackside, station, depot, train stop, living room, bedroom, hotel bars, lobby, terrace, factory, home,* and *house.*

✔ **Think about different themes.** Just about anything's a possibility here: sports bars, billiard bars, biker bars, eateries, jazz; '60s, '70s, and '80s bars; seafood, steak, lobster, and ethnic bars.

✔ **Base it on your specialty.** If you're specializing in wine, you could use words like *cellar, cave, cork, grape, vat,* and *wine* in naming your place. If you're specializing in beer, consider words related to beer and brewing, like *hops, wort, barley, malt, ferment,* styles of beer (*ale, stout,* and so on), *brewhaus,* or *brewpub.*

✔ **Get creative with the specific type of establishment you run.** Words like *bar, place, saloon, joint, lounge, bistro, café, bar and grill, grille, club, pub, tap room, manor, palace, tavern, inn,* and *sports bar* can pair with a first (or last) name to finish it up. Just add your name to the front of one of these, after you decide which one you want to be: Ray's Manor, Ray's Bar, Heather's Saloon, Heather's Bistro, or Heather's Pub.

✔ **Play off the area of town where you're located.** A bar located in the financial district could be called *In the Red.* Near government and political buildings could be a great place to launch a bar called *Hot Air Saloon.*

Now that you're armed with this information, you have to pick a name for *your bar* (we think this name is already taken). This is the fun part; you will get many suggestions from everyone. Take your time, and choose a great name. This is a very important decision. It will be with you for a long time.

Protecting your bar name and trademarks

As you build your business, you build your reputation. Your patrons have an expectation when they step in the door. If you're successful, they associate all the terrific things about your bar with its name and atmosphere. The last thing you want someone to do is to sabotage your hard work by stealing your name and using it to open his own place.

Consider how you want to use your name. Are you hoping to sell merchandise (like beer mugs and T-shirts) that includes your name and logo? And think about where you want to use your name. Maybe you just want to stay local, or maybe you want the option to expand and franchise someday. Depending on your answer, you need to search for your name in a couple of different ways.

Performing a search on your potential name

Go to your favorite search engine (like Google, Yahoo, or Ask.com) on the Internet. Search for bars (or restaurants, delis, and so on) that have the same name or a name similar to the one you're choosing.

Next, consider using a domain name lookup service, such as Whois.com (www.whois.com), to find out whether a particular Web site address that corresponds to your name is taken and, if it is, who owns it. If the Web address you want to use is available, you can register the domain name for as little as $4.95 a year to hold on to it. And this site offer a service to buy a domain name for you, even if it's already registered with someone else. It may cost a bit to get one that's already been taken, assuming the owner is even interested in selling it. (For more on using a Web site to promote your bar, see Chapter 16.)

Trademarking your name

Plan ahead and *trademark* (or register) your name, logo, taglines, and so on. Get the proper paperwork to protect your intellectual property in your state and in the entire country. This prevents other bar owners from slapping your bar's name on their business. The nerve!

A trademark or intellectual property attorney can help you navigate through the confusing landscape, but here are the basic steps you need to follow:

1. **Incorporate your restaurant.**

   This step makes you a legal entity. Look for more information about incorporation in Chapter 3.

2. **File an application with the county or state office that deals with trademarks.**

   This step makes the corporation the sole owner of your trademarks in your *class of goods or services* (delicatessen, restaurant, and carryout restaurant are examples of a few classes of services currently registered) in your state.

   This legal jargon basically means that no other restaurant or food service company in your state can use the same name, logos, and the like. If a skateboard company wants to use the name to market its skateboard, it can probably do so, unless you file separate applications for each and every class of goods or services around.

3. **File an application with the U.S. Patent and Trademark Office (USPTO).**

   This step protects your marks throughout the country. Check out the USPTO Web site at www.uspto.gov to search the database of registered trademarks.

   If you plan to expand your bar, franchise your name, or have several locations, have your attorney file for international trademarks as well.

Don't assume that because your future mark isn't listed that someone hasn't applied for it. The only way to be completely sure is to file your own application and get it approved. Check out *Patents, Copyrights & Trademarks For Dummies* by Henri Charmasson (Wiley) for more information on this process.

Picking Out Your Bar's Décor

Choosing a bar's décor is critical to creating just the right atmosphere for your customers. The décor you choose sends a message to your patrons about your place and who your clientele is. It can even give them clues about what kind of drinks you pour and what entertainment you offer. Plus, it's among the super-fun jobs in opening your own place.

Ultimately, you have to decide what style fits with your bar. Are you looking for sleek modern lines? Do you want retro '50s-inspired bar stools to match your retro jukebox? Maybe you're looking for classic wood chairs and tables to evoke a warm and comforting tone. What you buy sets the tone for your bar. This section can help you get started finding the right décor for your bar.

As much as we'd like to give you some guidelines about how much you should plan to spend on furnishing, lighting, and decorating your bar, it's just impossible. Your budget, the size of your bar, the number of furniture pieces and lighting fixtures you need, and your tastes will determine how much you'll spend.

Finding furniture

There's no shortage of furniture to furnish your bar. So many styles, colors, and heights to choose from, so little time. In most cases, you probably want the furniture to coordinate to some extent. Unless, of course, you're going for an eclectic style.

Figuring out what you need

No two bars are the same. What works for us may not work for you and vice versa. But most bars have a few common elements that you need to consider when setting up your furniture budget.

Here's a good place to start when you're figuring out what pieces you actually need:

- **Bar stools:** What's a bar without bar stools? You can find these guys in a variety of heights, materials, styles, and colors. Literally, the possibilities are endless. Consider whether you want a back on the stool, and if you do, how high you want it. Some modern-style bar stools have a low back that gently cups the patron's backside. Others are high-back bar stools that help keep even the most lounging lizard in his seat. Some come with a hydraulic lift (think barber chair) that lets customers adjust their seat, while others are a fixed height. You can find aluminum, wood, chrome, wrought iron, or stainless steel frames. And if you choose upholstered stools, you can select vinyl, leather, or cloth in many different colors and patterns. Some stools swivel; some don't. Some are mounted to the floor; others can be dragged from one side of the bar to the other. Expect to pay between $100 and $400 apiece for these, depending on the materials and features you want.

Most bar stools come in varying heights. Consider the height of your bar before you buy your stools. Take a look at the sidebar "What's the right bar height?" later in this chapter for help.

✔ **Chairs:** If you're the matchy-matchy kind of decorator, you can pick from all sorts of chairs to match your bar stools. In fact, often when you order bar stools and chairs, you can simply select the same basic chair in varying heights to fit your bar, counter, or tables. The number of chairs you need corresponds directly to the number of tables you choose. Always choose even numbers, either two or four chairs for each table, depending on its size.

✔ **Tables:** Tables come in three basic heights: dining room, counter, and bar height. You can get tables in lots of materials, styles, and colors, just like any other furniture, so the sky (and your budget) is the limit. Some even have a little ledge and hooks under them to hold things like purses and cellphones. And if you choose tall tables, consider looking for some that have footrests for comfort.

Consider your menu when you choose your tables. The size of the tabletop varies (anywhere from 20 to 48 inches in diameter), and your patrons need more space if your plates are big. You can skip the big 60-inch table for a bar. Large parties typically just push small tables together, and a big table ties up too much space.

✔ **Outdoor tables and chairs if you have outdoor seating:** You need durable, lightweight, and easy-to-clean furniture for outdoor seating. Look for wrought iron, resin, or PVC depending on what fits your style and budget.

If you opt for glass-top tables, make sure you buy tempered glass. If the table flips over in the wind, it will break like auto glass into small, relatively harmless pieces, rather than sharp, jagged shards.

Finding places to buy furniture

We suggest always buying your furniture locally. The salespeople at these companies can become your customers. Check your local furniture stores and restaurant supply houses in your immediate area, but here are a couple more recommendations:

AAA Furniture Wholesalers, 10301 Harwin Drive, Houston, TX 77036; phone 1-888-AAA-FURN (1-888-222-3876) or 713-777-5888, fax 713-777-0585; e-mail aaafw@netscape.com, Web site www.aaafurnitureusa.com.

Derry's Ltd., phone 703-980-2666 or 212-831-3293; e-mail sales@derrys.com, Web site www.derrys.com.

E-J Industries, Inc., 1275 S. Campbell, Chicago, IL 60608; phone 312-226-5023, fax 312-226-5976; e-mail `info@sitonbooths.com`, Web site `www.ejindus.com`.

Gasser Chair Company, Inc., 4136 Loganway, Youngstown, OH 44505; phone 330-759-2234, fax 330-759-9844; e-mail `sales@gasserchair.com`, Web site `www.gasserchair.com`.

Harbour House Bar Crafting and Furnishing, 15 Meadow St., Norwalk, CT 06854; phone 800-755-1227 or 203-838-7280, fax 203-838-7290; e-mail `info@harbourhouse.com`, Web site `http://harbourhouse.berlinproductions.com`.

If you can find quality used furniture, snap it up! Used furniture is always a good deal. Many bars go out of business in the first two years (unless they read this book) and get rid of their furniture, which probably hasn't seen too much wear and tear. Some of this furniture can be purchased at very good prices, but buy only what you need. Don't buy something because the price is great unless you have a lot of storage.

Looking at lighting

Lighting options are as varied as the people who buy them. One thing is essential though: You have to be able to adjust the light level in the bar as the sunlight comes and goes. Plus you definitely need to turn the lights up at the end of the night to give everything a thorough cleaning.

Common lighting options include

- **Pendant:** A *pendant* light is a single light fixture that hangs directly from the ceiling. It has a single lamp and shade.

- **Track lighting:** *Track lights* usually come in a system, often with four to six lamps per set. The track is installed on the ceiling, and the lights slide along the track. This setup allows you to position the individual lamps where you need them.

- **Recessed lighting:** *Recessed lighting* is actually fixtures and bulbs installed in holes cut into the ceiling. The bulbs may extend slightly from the ceiling, but most of the fixture is in the ceiling.

- **Sconces:** These fixtures are mounted flush against the wall. They offer great mood lighting. You can find sconces shaped like streetlamps, candles, glowing boxes, you name it.

- **Chandeliers:** The word *chandelier* may conjure images of opulently cut crystals hanging from the ceilings of ballrooms or swanky hotels, and you may run the other direction. But the term *chandelier* really just means a light fixture that hangs from the ceiling with multiple arms or branches of lights. They're made in many styles, colors, and sizes, from incredibly ornate to simple and sleek.

✔ **Flush mount:** These fixtures are installed flush with the ceiling and offer general lighting. (They don't illuminate particular areas; they just generally light a room.) They're most often used in bars (or areas in bars) where the ceiling is low or standard. If you have high ceilings, choose a hanging light of some sort for the majority of your lighting needs.

✔ **Rope:** Rope lights are flexible tubes of light used to accent areas of your bar, rather than provide lighting per se. Use them to line the corners of the ceiling, outline artwork, or even write a message that you don't want your customers to miss.

Always check with your local electrician and electrical houses for lighting recommendations. These people can become your customers and, face it, in your business, you always need an electrician. So hook up with two electricians in your area and always have their phone numbers available.

What's the right bar height?

A standard bar height is 42 inches from the floor to the *top* of the bar. Of course, yours may be higher or lower, so measure it. Then take these steps to figure out what height stools you need.

1. **Measure the distance from the bottom edge of the bar on the side where patrons sit to the floor.**

   Remember, sometimes bars have thick wood trim on the public side of the bar that patrons sit under. We're assuming it's a 2-inch thick counter, so the bottom sits 40 inches from the floor.

2. **Subtract 10 or 11 inches or so for your patrons' legs to fit comfortably. The resulting number is the optimal seat height.**

   We used 10 because it's a nice round number, so we're now 30 inches from the floor. We would look for 30-inch bar stools.

Remember, the seat height is the distance from the ground to the top of the stool's *seat,* not the seat back. Seat backs vary widely, so we're not talking about that here. We're only looking for the most comfortable seat height for your customers when they belly up to your bar.

Here are a few other measurements you might find handy in your search for the perfect furniture.

✔ The average dining-room table runs between 28 to 30 inches high, and your average dining-room chair has a seat height of around 18 inches.

✔ The average bar table is 42 inches high and takes a 30- to 32-inch stool.

✔ The typical counter-height table is 36 inches high. Counter stools to match these typically have a seat height around 24 to 26 inches.

✔ Extra-tall bars can be high as 48 inches. You need stools with seat heights between 34 and 36 inches to sit comfortably. Make sure you follow the steps to measure the height to get a perfect fit.

If math isn't your thing, create a bar-stool model using a regular chair and phone books (or newspapers, magazines, whatever you can pile on the seat). Stack the books to your desired height on the chair. Push it all under your bar to see if it fits. (Be careful if you try to sit on it.) If you're happy with the fit, measure it and you're in business.

For some ideas to get you started thinking about what lighting choices might be good for your bar, check out these online retailers:

Destination Lighting; phone 800-653-6556; Web site www.destinationlighting.com.

Meyda Tiffany, 55 Oriskany Blvd., Yorkville, NY 13495; phone 800-222-4009 or 315-768-3711, fax 800-651-3453 or 315-768-1428; e-mail sales@meyda.com, Web site www.meyda.com.

Never buy used lighting. Used lighting can be dangerous; you never know how the previous owner tinkered with it. And lighting has to meet certain codes, which is why you should always consult a licensed electrician for help with lighting.

Figuring out flooring

Easy-to-clean, durable, and slip-proof are key words to consider when deciding on flooring for your bar. Popular choices include wood, concrete, natural stone (like slate and granite), vinyl, linoleum, brick, laminates, and ceramic tile. Many kitchens opt for a slip-resistant tile that's easy to scrub down at the end of the night.

We recommend that you stay away from marble or tile floors. Both are slippery and increase breakage. And stay away from shag carpeting — it's just ugly!

To get an idea of commercial flooring options check out these online retailers:

✔ **Armstrong Flooring:** www.armstrong.com/commflooringna

✔ **Elite Crete Systems:** www.elitecrete.com

✔ **Exceptional Flooring:** www.exceptionalflooring.com/flooring.html

✔ **Tarkett Commercial:** www.domcotarkettcommercial.com/us

You can also check your local carpenters, flooring houses, carpet showrooms, Home Depot, and Lowe's, but make sure you look at commercial products, not residential.

Legally, you need to use commercial-quality flooring materials that meet the ADA (Americans with Disabilities Act) requirements, rather than residential-grade flooring. You keep your customers safe and get a longer-lasting product.

Working on the walls

Walls can be as simple as white plaster you decorate with pictures of your favorite sports stars or as complicated as hand-painted murals. No material is off limits these days.

Here are just a few common wall treatments you can find in bars today.

- ✔ **Vinyl wall covering:** This is thick, commercial-grade wallpaper. It comes in lots of textures and patterns and is highly durable. You can find covering that looks like natural stone, leather, handmade paper, or individual tiles. You can find wall covering with a fabric look, stripes, wood paneling, or even saw grass.

  Take a look at Wallpaper Wholesaler (www.wallpaperwholesaler. com) and click on "Commercial Wallcovering" to get a feel for the variety available. Command 54 (www.command54.com) offers edgier designs.

- ✔ **Acoustic wall carpet:** It can cut down on noise. Some people choose to cover half the wall (either the top or bottom) so they can decorate the rest.

- ✔ **Paneling:** Whether you use rustic, barely finished boards or gleaming mahogany wainscoting, you can't go wrong with wood. It gives your bar a cozy, warm feeling that makes people want to stay.

- ✔ **Brick:** Exposed brick is a great way to bring in an older, traditional feel to the bar. If you don't have the luxury of a location that already has brick, you can cover your walls (or even a single wall) to make it look like brick.

- ✔ **Faux finishes:** Using paint, you can create the look of aged Venetian plaster, fibers, or a window to an imaginary courtyard.

After you put all that work into choosing your wall treatment, you're probably going to want to cover it up with signs or pictures or trinkets. This, however, doesn't have to cost you any money. Hurray!

Many (if not all) beer and liquor companies have bar signs, clocks, neon signs, and artwork for free. Ask your rep!

You can also ask your customers for items from their companies. (The 21 Club in New York became very famous not only as a fine restaurant and a one-time speakeasy, but for taking the trucks and toys different patrons had given them and hanging them from the ceiling.) You will be surprised by how willing your customers are to give you things for the bar. So ask them already!

Other ideas would be to have a theme, like the most clocks on the wall in North America, signed sports memorabilia, collectible mugs, bobble heads, or movie posters. Start a bottle collection, or have the best of something. Anything to have people say, "Did you see the stuff at Your Place?" which leads to, "Have you had the — at Your Place?"

Fun and Games: TVs, Video Games, Pool Tables, and More

Let us entertain you! Like it or not, you're in the entertainment business, and the more ways you can entertain customers — and let them escape their daily lives — the better. Popular choices for entertainment include television, video games, and more traditional games like pool tables and shuffleboard.

It's not necessary to have all of these choices, but a couple could help. Not everyone likes to talk; some customers like to play. Entertainment keeps patrons in your bar, and the longer they stay, the more they drink. Choose the best diversions to make the most of your bar.

Tuning in with TVs and programming

You have to decide how many televisions your bar needs based on your goals for your bar. If your bar serves as the local watering hole and you just want to keep a news channel on in the background, one smaller model is probably okay (but make sure people can still make out the images from a few yards away). But if you're opening a sports bar and will be showing the weekend's hottest sporting events, you'll need a couple of larger screens.

Many different types of TVs are available, including high-definition, diagonal, flat panel, projection, tube, and combo. The technology changes every year, and the prices keep coming down. Make sure the model you choose can accommodate components such as sound systems, satellite receivers, video games, and interactive bar games (check out the "Video and interactive games" section later in this chapter for more on these).

As you're researching the hundreds of models on the market, talk to an expert at your local appliance store. He can recommend a quality brand that will serve your needs. When it's time to have your TVs installed, make sure your installer is experienced, can hook up all the components, and is available for repairs.

Picking the right spot and installing the TV

You can put a TV just about anywhere these days. In most cases, choose high locations, at standing eye level or higher, so that most patrons can see the TVs. When it's time to choose the location for the TV, mark a spot and then walk around and make sure there aren't too many *blind spots* (areas blocked by poles or supporting beams). If most patrons won't be able to see the screen, choose a different location.

You have a couple of options when it comes to installing televisions:

✔ **Flush mount to the wall:** This option is popular for flat-panel plasma or LCD TVs. An experienced technician can hide all the wires and components for a clean, sophisticated look.

✔ **Mounting brackets:** You can find ceiling and wall mounts, and even corner brackets, to match your location. Look for a unit that swivels so you can reposition the TV as you need to.

✔ **Cabinets:** You may prefer the look of cabinets or shelving to hold your TV. Make sure you measure your TV (both the size and weight) to get furniture that will work for your equipment.

Keep the remote behind the bar, otherwise the only time you'll ever see it is when you first program the TV's settings. Only one person should be in charge of the remote: the bartender or the manager.

Signals from outer space: Satellite systems

Depending on what type of bar you're running, you may want to get a satellite TV system. These systems are great because you can get all kinds of sporting events you can't get with regular cable television. Say you want to watch Finnish curling. Satellite has it. And it also has music channels for whatever fits your mood.

With a satellite system, you need a separate receiver for each TV if you want to show different programs at the same time.

The big names in satellite systems are

✔ **DirecTV For Business** (www.directv.com, click on the "DirecTV for Business" link in the upper right-hand corner): DirecTV's big draw for bars is its NFL Sunday Ticket (which gives you every NFL game no matter where it's played) and Mega March Madness (its exclusive coverage of the NCAA Basketball tournament). The company offers XM satellite music commercial-free for businesses.

✔ **Dish Network** (http://commercial.dishnetwork.com): This company also has lots of sports programming, such as MLS Direct Kick (soccer) and ESPN Full Court (basketball). It offers Sirius satellite music.

Make sure you purchase a license to broadcast the programming in your bar or you could get into legal trouble. Also, read the fine print before you sell tickets to patrons to watch a premium event like a pay-per-view fight to make sure you're complying with all the requirements.

Considering games for your bar

Games are extremely popular pastimes for bar patrons. Most require you to purchase or lease some equipment. When you have games in your bar, you can sponsor tournaments. Just think of all those people penciling in game night at your bar on their weekly calendar. We hear the cash register ringing already!

Traditional live bar games

The first recorded incident of playing pool in an American tavern occurred in 1775. But experts agree that earlier versions appeared in the British colonies, in what's now the United States, in the 1600s. These early games were based on European games, and the first incident of what most Americans play today, commonly known as "Eight Ball," occurred in the early 1900s. Darts made itself a bar mainstay in the early 1900s as well, after the king and queen of England were spotted tossing a few on a tour of a local pub.

Everyone wants to be the best at something, and these games are meant for competition and fun. Many places have contests for the best dart player, pool player, and so forth. Give out prizes and trophies; these help build bigger and better crowds.

Here's a list of popular bar games, along with suggestions for where to look for more information:

- ✔ **Darts:** You can choose several dart options, from the traditional, self-healing boards with live (and sharp) darts to the electronic dart machines with blunt tips that can injure only a few people. Ask your liquor rep about getting a dartboard; many of the scotch companies have quality sets. And check out the National Dart Association (www. ndadarts.com) or Planet Darts (http://planetdarts.com) for information on game play or setting up a league.

- ✔ **Pool:** Pool (also called billiards) is and will always be one of the number-one games in bars. The American Poolplayers Association (www.poolplayers.com) is the final word on rules and organizes tournaments. You can choose a pool table from a local game-supply store or one of these companies:

  - Aramith/Preciball: www.saluc.com

  - Bumper Tube: www.bumpertube.com

- ✔ **Table shuffleboard:** Table shuffleboard is similar to its cruise ship cousin in that players push a weight along a game board hoping to slide it to its target. Another great tournament choice. Check out eShuffleboard.com (www.eshuffleboard.com), which includes links for buying a shuffleboard table, and the Table Shuffleboard Association (www.tableshuffleboard.org) for more information.

✔ **Pinball:** It's a classic game of skill beloved by many. More important to you, pinball machines are a great source of revenue. Check these sites for a quality machine:

- American Vending Sales: `http://americanvending.com`

- Fun Merchandise: `www.funmerchandise.com`

- The Pinball Factory: `www.pinball.com`

- Pinball Sales: `www.pinballsales.com`

- Stern Pinball: `www.sternpinball.com`

Video and interactive games

Whether it's electronic casino games, like blackjack or Texas Hold'em, trivia, play-along sports games, or video games, more patrons are testing their skills and knowledge in bars than ever before. In fact, some bars, like Dave and Buster's or Great American Midway, built their concept around games for adults. And remember, the more they play, the longer they stay.

If you think you want to offer some of the national, interactive games, check out NTN Buzztime. NTN broadcasts live, interactive entertainment through its Buzztime Network to more than 4,000 bars and restaurants across the United States. Players can compete for points, rankings, and prizes. Contact them by calling 888-752-9686, e-mailing `sales@ntn.com`, or visiting their Web site at `www.ntn.com`.

If your patrons would rather play traditional arcade games, you can cater to their needs. Choose free-standing video games with the classics like _Pacman, Galaga, Centipede,_ or _Mario Brothers._ You can also get an Arcade Legends game with 50 classic games in one machine; then you don't have to narrow down your choices. Or go with something more au courant like _Police Trainer, Golden Tee Golf,_ or _Big Buck Hunter._

You can also choose video-game systems (like Xbox 360 or PlayStation 3) to hook to your TVs. You can't set them up to be a pay-to-play system (yet!), but you can provide them as a service to your clients.

If your machines don't take bills, consider getting a change machine. It will save your bartenders and waitstaff some time and headaches.

As with just about any other equipment for your bar, you can lease game equipment and jukeboxes (See "Getting your jukebox," later in this chapter, for more details). If you buy it, you own it forever, keeping all the profits. But you'll pay a high hourly repair rate if the equipment breaks down. Leasing ensures that the leasing company takes care of all repairs and maintenance, while you split the revenue fifty-fifty. Plus, you can switch leased machines out with other games if your customers get bored.

Music, Professor! Jukeboxes, DJs, and Live Tunes

Music is the final piece in setting the tone for your bar. A jukebox is a great choice to allow people to play what they want to hear when they want to hear it. You can also get live music, such as bands, DJs, and karaoke systems, for special occasions. This section gets you started.

It is not absolutely necessary to have music in your bar, but if you choose to have it, do it right. Ask your customers what they want to hear. Ask employees what kind of music is hot in the area. See how their ideas match your ideas for your bar.

Getting your jukebox

A jukebox is a bar standard (not to mention a great revenue stream). Even if you're going to have other music options, you probably need a jukebox. If you've been in a bar lately (and man, we really hope you have), you have probably seen the two basic styles available, a CD jukebox and a digital jukebox. The CD jukebox holds complete CDs of music. The digital variety updates its playlist using the Internet and offers new tunes to your patrons regularly. They are constantly being updated.

When installing your jukebox, make sure that the volume and on/off switches are located behind the bar or in a closet that only certain people can access. Also make sure you have some tokens or slugs that you can use to start some music.

Consider using a great patriotic song to play during *last call* (the magical moment that signals the last opportunity for a patron to order a drink for the evening). The song should get everyone's attention, and then you can turn up the volume to ensure your customers know it's closing time.

Here's how to find a local distributor for these specific brands:

- ✔ NSM Jukeboxes: www.bmigaming.com
- ✔ Rock Ola: www.rock-ola.com
- ✔ Rowe International: www.roweinternational.com/distributor_network.html
- ✔ Wurlitzer: www.deutsche-wurlitzerusa.com

Wurlitzer just launched its CD/iPod jukebox that holds 100 CDs and hooks to an iPod to offer up another 60GB of space (approximately 10,000 songs). The company also has a jukebox that plays old vinyl records. (For those of you who may not know, records are what we played before CDs. Hard to imagine, we know.)

Check out your Yellow Pages for listings under "Vending" and "Amusement." Many of these companies offer all things coin-operated, including jukeboxes and video games.

Finding and signing live performers

In most cases, performers will find you as soon as they hear that a new bar is opening. Talk to other bar owners to see who the biggest draw is.

Naturally, you should audition performers or go hear them sing at someone else's bar. Before you hire, tell them the rules:

- ✔ **Specify how many breaks they should take.** For example, maybe you agree to one 15-minute break every hour. Your call.

- ✔ **Agree to discounts on the price of their drinks and the limit for the discount.** Identify who qualifies for the discount as well. You may want only band members to get the discount, rather than girlfriends, boyfriends, or family members. You may not have to give them a discount at all, or you can take the bar tab out of what you pay the band.

- ✔ **Develop a groupies policy.** You do not want your bar full of groupies who buy one drink and sit there all night. You lose customers and possibly your bartender if it continues.

- ✔ **Determine your free or discounted meals policy.** Identify who you feed and the price they pay.

- ✔ **Approve the set list.** You need to make sure that their song choices appeal to your patrons. (Remember the original Blues Brothers movie, "We play both kinds of music: country *and* western.")

- ✔ **Negotiate the cost to you.** Some bands set a *cover charge* (an admission price that patrons pay to hear the band play) and keep it. Others split the cover charge with bar owners and take a percentage of sales. Others simply get a flat fee for performing for a certain amount of time. Figure out what the plan is before you're slapped with a bill at the end of a long night.

You can even have amateur or open-mike night at your place if you want some live entertainment but don't want to pay a lot. You may or may not have a lot of patrons participate, but remember: You get what you pay for.

Hiring a DJ or karaoke company

A DJ or a karaoke company is basically a live performer, so all the rules for bands in the previous section apply here. Lay down the ground rules ahead of time.

You can hire your very own DJ to play the latest rock, rap, or country hits for your place. Having your own DJ is cheaper in the long run than hiring an outside company to come in and entertain the crowd every weekend. You can also have a guest DJ once a week. The best bet is to have a DJ on one of your slow nights and, of course, Fridays and Saturdays. These resources can help get you started:

- ✔ ProSound: www.pssl.com
- ✔ Rock and Soul: www.rockandsoul.com
- ✔ Top DJ Gear: www.topdjgear.com

If you want to buy your own karaoke equipment, here are some places to look:

- ✔ Ace Karaoke: www.acekaraoke.com
- ✔ Cheap Karaoke: www.cheapkaraoke.com
- ✔ Karaoke Now: www.karaokenow.com

You may save yourself some money, but you have to have someone to run the equipment for you. Even a karaoke night needs an emcee of some sort. You can hire this out at first while you're getting your place going, and then hire a part-time person to act as a DJ or emcee on designated nights.

Chapter 7

Stocking Up on Smallwares and Equipment

In This Chapter
▶ Getting your bar equipment together
▶ Checking out kitchen appliances
▶ Selecting your smallwares
▶ Setting up your table
▶ Looking at equipment financing options

*T*he wide, wide world of bar equipment can be overwhelming. Trying to figure out what you need, where you need to put it, and whom to get it from can be a daunting task.

You're only as good as the tools and employees you have. Hire good people, you get great workers. Buy good equipment with good warranties, you have less trouble (and trouble *will* find you in this business — you won't have to look for it). Take your time and shop around for all your equipment. Buy quality tools and appliances once, and you won't have to fix them or take them back.

This chapter is here to help. We show you what you need (and don't need). We help you figure out how to pay for it. And we give you tips on how to put it all together without breaking your budget.

Picking Out Your Bar Equipment

In this section, we cover everything from glassware and shakers to *smallwares* — those little, necessary things that every bar needs, like serving ware and linens. We help you figure out which items you need (and more importantly, which ones you don't) to get your bar stocked the right way.

Getting your glassware

You could spend a fortune in terms of dollars and storage space to keep a slew of glasses for every occasion. Customers expect cocktails and drinks to be served in specific glasses. Although that's all well and good, we recommend you keep it simple. And how much you'll spend depends on the style of glasses, size, price, number, and so on.

Here are the glasses you really need (check out Figure 7-1 to get a better idea of what each one looks like):

- ✔ **Shot glass:** You serve, um, shots in these. Some people also use them to measure liquor for cocktails.

- ✔ **Wine glass:** Choose an all-purpose wine glass for both red and white wine, rather than one for each type. Most people choose a 5- or 8-ounce size. In a pinch, you can also use wine glasses to serve drinks that you'd normally serve in a rocks, highball, or collins glass. Of course, if you plan to run a wine bar, invest in a variety of glasses to match the variety of wines you serve. Your customers will expect nothing less.

- ✔ **Rocks glass:** Drinks served *on the rocks,* or with ice, like martinis and manhattans, are often served in these glasses. Some people call them old-fashioned glasses, not because they're not hip, but because a cocktail of the same name is served in them. Use the 5- or 6-ounce variety.

- ✔ **Highball and collins glasses:** You can choose one or the other, depending on your preference. Use them to make popular drinks, such as a Bloody Mary or Tom Collins, and cocktails ordered *tall* (or served in a taller glass containing the same amount of alcohol, but with extra mixers). We recommend a 10- to 12-ounce glass.

- ✔ **Martini glass:** The age of the cocktail is back in full swing. You definitely need many martini glasses, specially because 40 percent of cocktails are called martinis. Don't buy really large martini glasses unless martinis are going to be your specialty cocktail. Stick with a 4- or 5-ounce size.

Only serve martinis in martini glasses if you serve them *up,* or without ice. Ice in a martini glass is awkward, so serve martinis on the rocks in a rocks glass, detailed earlier in this list.

✔ **Beer glass:** The most common choices are pint glass (either 16- or 20-ounce), pilsner, mug, or beer glass. Ask your beer distributor for good buys. Fancier choices include the tulip and wheat beer glasses. If you're going to be known for your beers (especially draft beer), consider investing in a few different types to match your styles of beer. Check out Chapter 12 for more information on different styles of beer.

Consider carrying two sizes of beer glasses, say a pint (16-ounce) glass and a 10- or 12-ounce glass or mug. You can offer draft beers at two different price points, offering a better value to the customer who chooses the more expensive pour.

✔ **Coffee glass/mug:** Many bars use your average, everyday coffee mugs for coffee drinks, but some invest in special mugs to differentiate coffee from coffee cocktails. Choose what fits your budget and your bar.

Do not buy any glasses unless you have a rack to wash them in. We repeat: *Do not buy any glasses unless you have a rack to wash them in.* You should be able to buy racks from the same company you buy your glasses from. Without the proper rack, glassware can and will get broken in the dish machine. If yours is a busy bar, don't try to rely on just an in-sink washing unit to do the job. You need to be able to wash racks of glasses at a time in the machine in the kitchen. You can also use the racks to store the glasses.

If you really want to get fancy (and your budget and glass storage space allows), add a few other stems to your glassware entourage, like these:

✔ **Snifter:** This glass is reserved for cognac and brandy.

✔ **Champagne:** Two styles are available (flute and saucer), but the flute is more common these days.

✔ **Margarita:** Many versions of this glass are currently available from very rustic, hand-blown versions, to elegantly simple ones that resemble champagne saucers.

✔ **Cordial:** A cordial glass can be used to serve cordials, layered shots, port, or anything else served in small, but potent quantities.

Touching on basic bar tools

Every professional uses the proper tools to do his or her job well, and a bartender is no exception. For tips on how to use some of these tools to make the best drinks around, check out Chapter 12 and Ray's *Bartending For Dummies,* 3rd Edition (Wiley).

Figure 7-1:
Glassware
options.

If you stumble on used versions of these supplies and they appear to be in good condition, go ahead and buy them. Don't spend your time looking for used ones though, because the small savings you get isn't really worth the time.

✓ **Bar rail and service mats:** A *bar rail mat* is a long, narrow rubber mat that lies on the edge of the bar. Bartenders place in-progress cocktails on them as they pour, mix, and garnish drinks. The mats catch small spills and clean easily as you run them through the dishwasher. *Service mats* are thin, rubberized mats placed on the service bar counter, where bartenders place completed drinks ordered by waitstaff.

If you don't mind doing a little advertising for the liquor companies, you often can get these mats, as well as bar towels, mirrors, beverage napkins, straw holders, garnish caddies, glass rimmers, cork screws, and water pitchers, for free from your liquor rep. Because every company will offer you something, take the items and put the extras in your storeroom.

✓ **Bar spoon:** This is simply a long spoon for stirring cocktails, shown in Figure 7-2. Keep these handy so bartenders aren't tempted to use their fingers.

Figure 7-2: Miscellaneous bar tools: (1) bar spoon, (2) blender, (3) ice tongs, (4) ice scoop, (5) wine bucket, (6) jigger or measuring cup, (7) knife and cutting board, (8) muddler, (9) pitcher, and (10) glass rimmer.

✔ **Bottle openers:** Choose wall-mounted (with a catcher) or handheld openers to open beer bottles quickly. Take a look at Figure 7-3 for a few different options.

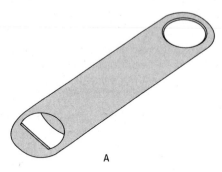

A

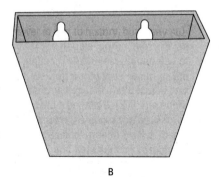

B

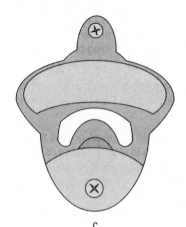

Figure 7-3:
Bottle
openers.

C

A waiter's wine opener, pictured in Figure 7-8, can also be used to open beer bottles, but it's not nearly as fast as either a flat or wall-mounted opener. Choose wisely, grasshopper.

✔ **Garnish caddy:** A *garnish caddy* is a divided tray that holds several different types of garnishes, such as lime wedges, olives, and onions. Take a look at Figure 7-4 to see an example of a garnish caddy.

✔ **Glass rimmer:** This tool helps you add decorative and tasty garnishes to the rim of your cocktail glasses. Take a look at the device in Figure 7-2.

✔ **Ice bucket:** You need at least one large plastic bucket to carry ice from the ice machine in the kitchen out to the bar to restock your wells. Consider using the rolling version if you can because these large buckets (5 gallons or more) get heavy. You can save some strain on your champagne company if you buy a couple of cases of their champagne.

Only use this ice bucket for ice. Label it in big bold letters **ICE ONLY** and store it near the ice machine. After you put trash, food, or anything else in the bucket, it's no longer suitable for ice, even if you clean and sanitize it. Foreign items impart an unpleasant smell and flavor to ice long afterward. The bucket will never be quite clean enough again.

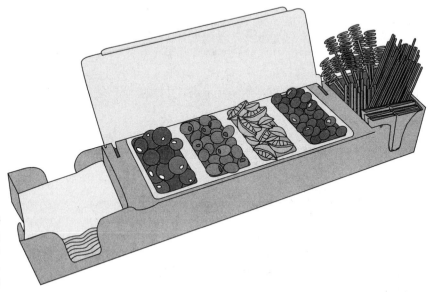

Figure 7-4:
Garnish
caddy.

- **Ice scoop:** We highly recommend metal or plastic scoops. You can run them through the dish machine to sanitize them thoroughly and often. You can see one in Figure 7-2.

  Never, ever use your hands, a glass, or anything other than a proper scoop to scoop ice. It contaminates the ice, making it unusable for serving to customers.

  If you break this rule (shame on you!), you could break a glass in the ice or spread germs to your patrons. After you (or more likely someone who works for you because *you* are reading this warning) commit this grievous sin, you must *burn the ice well* (Melt the ice with hot water, remove any foreign objects, thoroughly sanitize the well, and restock with ice.) before it can be used again.

- **Jigger:** A *jigger* is a metal, double-ended measuring cup. Typically it measures ½ ounce on one end, and 2 ounces on the other. Check it out in Figure 7-2.

- **Knives and cutting board:** We recommend that you keep at least one sharp paring knife and a cutting board behind the bar specifically for cutting garnishes. It's best to have one set for your bar and one set for your kitchen (if you're serving food) so they're handy when you need them. We recommend a hard-plastic cutting board that can be sanitized easily and run through your dish machine.

- **Muddler:** Use this small wooden bat or pestle to *muddle,* or crush, herbs and fruit (like mint and limes for Mojitos) for cocktails. Treat this wooden tool as you would a wooden cutting board or wooden spoon. Hand wash only! Take a look at this tool in Figure 7-2.

- **Pourers:** These plastic pitchers are handy if you don't have juice on your soda guns. Keep backups of OJ, Bloody Mary mix, and cranberry juice handy in these in the reach-in cooler behind the bar. Take a look at pourers in Figure 7-5.

- **Shakers:** These must-have tools let you thoroughly mix cocktails and give them a little foam. Most bartenders use one of two basic styles of shakers:

  Boston shaker: These shakers have a glass piece and a tin piece. The roughly 16-ounce glass fits into the tin, which is shaped like a cone, and you shake the drink. Never *ever* pound the tin against the bar. If the pieces get stuck, run the shaker under hot water and slowly work the parts apart. The Boston shaker also comes in a shorter size with just the metal part, and this usually fits over the glass you serve the drink in. Shake with ice, pull the shaker apart from the glass, and serve the cocktail on the rocks in the glass.

  Standard cocktail shaker: These shakers usually have a tight top and a strainer that is fitted onto the bottom half. They come in many types of designs. Some, but not many, bars use them. If they do, they are usually only for display. There must be at least 1,000 different styles, from planes to birds, and they make great collector items. (Ray has more than 300 different ones.)

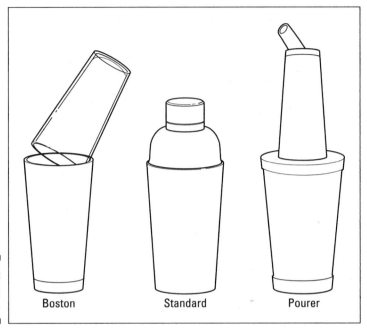

Figure 7-5:
Shakers and
a pourer.

Boston   Standard   Pourer

✔ **Sinks:** You need a few sinks behind the bar — three to set up a dish-washing system (see the "Acquiring Bar Appliances" section, later in this chapter, for details) and a fourth exclusively for hand washing.

✔ **Soda gun system:** Your soda gun connects to your bag-in-the-box (BIB) system. Soda syrup is mixed on demand with soda as the bartender makes the cocktail.

✔ **Speed rails:** Speed rails are metal trays that hold many of the commonly poured liquors. Many bars use speed rails, in addition to their wells, to keep more liquors within reach. Speed rails are usually set up on the opposite side of the bar and in the area where most cocktails are made. They are either attached or hung on the sink portion of the bar, near the ice bins. Speed rails contain items that are usually called for, such as vodka, gin, scotch, bourbon, or whatever is the most called-for item at your place. Your bartender will decide which brands or category to place in the rails.

✔ **Strainers:** Strainers are handy if you serve cocktails *up,* or without ice (some people say "straight up" for added effect, but the words mean the same thing). Check out Figure 7-6 for the ever-popular Hawthorn strainer. Some shakers include their own strainers, but we prefer the Hawthorn because it's the original. Color us sentimental. To use the Hawthorn, just place the strainer over the end of the shaker containing your shaken cocktail with the coil facing into the shaker. Pour the drink into your serving glass, through the strainer, and catch the ice.

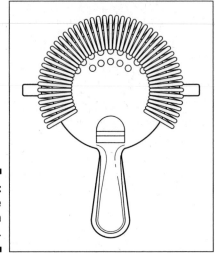

Figure 7-6:
The
Hawthorn
strainer.

✔ **Wells:** A *well* is a dedicated area where (usually) a single bartender works to make drinks. A well should have liquor, ice, garnishes, mixers (often in the form of a soda gun), and easy access to glassware. Check out Figure 7-7 to see how a well could be laid out.

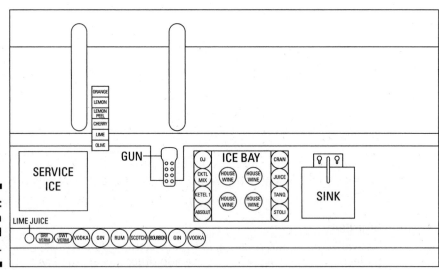

Figure 7-7:
Layout of a
standard
bar well.

✔ **Wine buckets:** You only need wine buckets if you're serving bottles of white wine and champagne that you want to keep chilled at the patron's table. If you're selling wine by the glass only, you can skip this particular tool. Wine buckets come in metal or plastic, and you may be able to secure a couple from your wine salesperson when you order wine or champagne. You can also buy them wherever you get smallwares. If you buy them, get a couple of stands to hold the buckets, rather than put the bucket on the table. Three buckets is probably enough, depending on the size of your wine/champagne business.

✔ **Wine openers:** Wine openers come in many varieties these days. If you serve a lot of wine, consider getting a counter-mounted version. If you only have the occasional *oenophile* (or wine lover), a pocket-sized version like the waiter wine key will do you just fine. Take a look at them both in Figure 7-8.

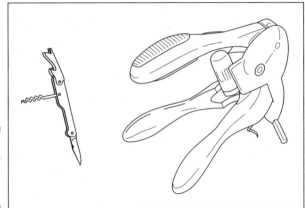

Figure 7-8:
Examples of
wine
openers.

Stocking up on smallwares

Smallwares describes all the small stuff in the bar, such as knives, forks, plates, ramekins, and paper goods. They aren't terribly exciting, but they're necessary.

Flatware

Flatware can be purchased in five-piece settings: dinner fork, salad fork, knife, tablespoon, and teaspoon. You can add other pieces, such as a fish fork, butter knife, and steak knife, if you need them. It's becoming more common to just provide two regular-sized forks, rather than a standard fork and a smaller salad fork. Choose which plan works better for you.

Dishware

The category of dishware typically includes plates, platters (particularly good if you serve multiple items on the same plate), soup bowls, and bread-and-butter plates. Choose a basic commercial pattern for your dishware. Look for sturdy and functional. And make sure you can easily get pieces to match because items will get broken.

Ramekins (they look like small bowls) are handy for serving sides and condiments to your patrons if you serve food in your bar. You can also use them to bring extra garnishes for that patron who needs ten cherries for his Amaretto Sour.

Linens

Linens include things like towels, tablecloths, napkins, and even kitchen uniforms. You can buy or rent your linens. Most restaurants rent them. Bars are split.

- ✔ **If you buy,** make sure the linens are all made from fabrics that are wash and wear or wash and use. Make sure you have a washer and dryer on site to get these ready for the next day. This really will save you money if you can do it yourself.

- ✔ **If you rent,** keep a good inventory and inspect everything. Do not accept tablecloths or napkins that are frayed or have holes in them! If you rent your linens, check them in and check them out. Create a notebook with a list of all the linens you use, how many of each you rent, and the dates in and out. This way, you will know where your linens are and how much is going bye-bye.

Don't let your staff leave with linens you own or rent. In particular, uniform pieces, such as chef coats, seem to disappear if you don't set up a firm policy on placing them in the dirty linen bin or hanging them back up in employees' lockers after use.

Avoid linen abuse. It's not just a cleanliness issue, it's also a cost issue because you have to pay to wash a napkin that's been used. It seems small, but it adds up quickly! Post signs prohibiting linen abuse:

1. Do not wipe floors with linens.

2. Do not shine shoes with napkins.

3. Please do not abuse linens.

Signed by Ray Foley, Linen Police

Miscellaneous supplies

You need just a few more items for your bar that don't fit neatly into any of these categories.

✔ Ashtrays, assuming you can still smoke in bars in your state

✔ Trashcans with extra _liners_ (bar lingo for trash bags)

✔ Pens and pencils

✔ Telephone books and a diary for behind the bar (See Chapter 18 for tips on using a diary effectively.)

✔ Extra pitchers for juice and water

✔ Floor mats to cushion feet, knees, and backs, and to reduce the danger of slipping

✔ Straws and stirrers

✔ Cocktail napkins, sometimes called _bevnaps_

Stocking the table

Most tables have something on them when a customer sits down. Maybe you have a table tent with your beer selection listed, a drink menu, salt and pepper shakers, or other items people will need when enjoying your establishment. Ultimately, the table size and your idea of what's important will determine what you place on the table. If you serve a lot of burgers, consider keeping things like ketchup and mustard on the table, within easy reach. If you don't, you can probably bring it as needed, saving table space.

Just to clear up a bit of jargon confusion, the items discussed here are definitely not smallwares (see the previous section). The actual vessels (salt and pepper shaker) might be, but once they're filled and out in the dining room, they move into the category of table stock. Items like Worcestershire and hot sauce aren't smallwares in any sense.

When stocking your table, remember to leave room for drinks and food. Do not overcrowd your patrons. They want somewhere to put purses, cellphones, planners, laptops, and other necessities.

You'll need to place these items on the table:

✔ Salt and pepper shakers

✔ Flower arrangement or centerpiece (a candle, for example)

✔ Maybe one table tent listing house specials

Place other items in the waiter station, including these oft-used ones:

- Ketchup
- Mustard
- Hot sauce
- Worcestershire sauce
- Peppermills
- Sugar and sweetener (for coffee and tea)
- Creamer

When the kitchen closes, take all of these items off the tables and put them in the waiter station or you will lose them!

Acquiring Bar Appliances

In this section, we cover appliances, which are pretty much bar tools with a plug. Quite a distinction, we know. If you need help figuring out where to get this stuff, take a look at the section "Leasing versus Buying, New versus Used," later in this chapter.

Here's a list of appliances you need for your bar:

- **Blender:** Most bars do have blenders, even though bartenders like to hide them. Because you will get patrons who want frozen daiquiris, margaritas, Piña Coladas, and other frozen cocktails, you need a good-quality commercial blender with some kind of warranty. Check it out in Figure 7-2.

  The most popular bar blender brands are Vita-Mix (www.vitamix.com), Hamilton Beach (www.hamiltonbeach.com), and Waring Blenders (www.waringproducts.com).

- **Coolers:** No, we do not mean that you should put the heavy-duty plastic, tailgating toy box behind your bar. The term *cooler* actually refers to a refrigerator in bar-speak. You can find a variety of sizes to fit in different spots behind your bar and in your kitchen.

  - *Reach-in coolers* are small coolers, roughly the size of a dorm or under-the-desk fridge. Bartenders reach in to get what they need out of them. *Highboy coolers* are reach-in coolers situated about waist level, maybe on top of a counter. *Lowboy coolers* fit under the counter. Bartenders keep backup garnishes, bottled beer, juice, and other perishables they need regularly in these small coolers.

- *Beer coolers* are large, chest coolers below the bar top. The door is located on top of the chest, and it slides open, allowing easy access to quick-selling beers.

- Many bars also have walk-in coolers in or near the kitchen. Commonly known as *walk-ins,* these refrigerated rooms allow staff members to walk into them. You can store large, perishable items such as kegs, cases of beer, or a flat of salad greens in your walk-in. Typically, bartenders move what they need from the walk-ins to the reach-in before their shifts start to keep things handy.

✔ **Ice machine:** Making great drinks requires using great ice. And great ice requires a water purification system and a quality ice maker.

✔ **Smoke eaters:** These commercial clean-air systems are a must in any bar or tavern that has a smoking section or allows smoking at the bar. See `www.smokeeaters.org` on the Web or call 1-877-688-2703 for more information.

✔ **Submersible dishwasher:** This dishwashing unit is standard in a restaurant, but it's typically a backup appliance in a bar. A submersible dishwasher is only for glassware. It usually fills the first of a *three-sink system.* The first sink is for washing (or gently rubbing the glasses around on the rotating brushes). The second sink is for rinsing the soap off the glasses. The last sink contains sanitizer to dip the glasses in to kill off any lingering germs.

Selecting Kitchen Appliances

Your menu really dictates what appliances you need (or more accurately, your appliances determine what foods you can serve). Unless you're intent on making food a top priority at your bar, your menu should really take advantage of basic kitchen equipment. Take a look at Chapter 9 for tips on how to get your menu and your kitchen totally in synch.

Keep handy a list of electricians and mechanics in your area. The longer your equipment is down, the more money you're losing. It's important, very important, to keep everything in working order.

The next section, "Leasing versus Buying, New versus Used," addresses where to find appliances, how to pay for them, and things to watch out for. Here we cover the basics of what kinds of equipment most bars use, but your list may vary:

- **Grills:** These are a staple in any bar that serves food, which is why so many call themselves "Bar and Grill." You can cook many different things, from burgers to steaks, or even eggs and bacon. Choose both a *flattop grill* (like a big skillet) and a *grated grill* (with an open flame) if you have the money and space. You can easily use them both.

  Grills are good candidates for buying used, especially if they're gas.

- **Broilers:** These appliances are fairly versatile and come in many sizes. The large size can be used for things like steaks and chops. A smaller version is handy for quickly melting cheese on soup, nachos, and open-faced sandwiches.

- **Ovens:** You'll need one of these if you plan to serve anything that can't be prepared on the grill or broiler. Here are the varieties you might consider:

  - **Convection:** Circulates air around food. Best for quick and even cooking.

  - **Conveyer:** Heats and cooks top and bottom. Great for sandwiches, burgers, and pizza.

  - **Microwave:** Great for reheating and cooking quick items.

- **Dish machine:** Every bar must have one of these. They are beyond essential. In the bar business, most of your washing will take the form of racks of glassware, rather than stockpots and skillets. Enter the commercial dish machine, complete with crazy-quick sanitizing cycles.

- **Sinks:** You'll need a hand sink for almost every station. Buy the best and have them installed by a great plumber. Check with your local board of health for requirements on what supplies should be stocked near a hand sink.

- **Grease traps or interceptors:** These are passive devices required by municipalities to stop grease, fat, oil, wax, or debris from entering the city's sanitary sewer system.

Leasing versus Buying, New versus Used

Coming up with the cash to buy an entire kitchen and bar full of brand-new equipment isn't easy. Many owners opt to look into other options like leasing or buying used equipment, instead of going with brand-new stuff. In this section, we help you work your way through the process of getting the equipment you need, and also alert you to the pros and cons of leasing and buying, and then deciding to go with new or used equipment.

Don't forget to discuss your options for buying and leasing equipment with your banker and accountant. They have the information about your particular financial situation that can help you make the best decision for your bar.

Looking at leasing

Leasing isn't just for cars these days. Often companies lease equipment for a set period of time and fully maintain the machine during your lease term. After the term of the lease is over, you can choose to renew the lease, but typically you get a brand-new machine to use during the lease period. It can be an ideal situation for many owners.

Here are a few of the brighter points of leasing equipment:

- ✔ Your cash isn't tied up in equipment. By leasing, you have money for working capital and cash flow.

- ✔ Zero repair costs (assuming maintenance and repair costs are included in the contract)

- ✔ No out-of-date equipment. You lease new equipment. When your lease expires, you get to sign a new lease for new equipment. Leasing lets you upgrade your equipment to newer appliances with the latest bells and whistles, so you don't own the same, behind-the-times oven for 10 years.

- ✔ Tax breaks! Leasing also may be fully tax deductible as an operating expense. (Check with your accountant.)

- ✔ More variety of types of equipment. You can lease almost any type of equipment that you need, and you can have more equipment because you're not tying up your cash.

The biggest downside to leasing is that you don't own the equipment. You continue to make payments indefinitely. You can buy some of these appliances used at a very good price. Over time, you can save a lot more money by buying used equipment, even when you factor in maintenance costs. Check out the section "Evaluating used equipment," later in this chapter, for tips on what to look for in used equipment.

In our opinion, leasing is a good option for ice machines and coolers, and dishwashers and coffeemakers in particular. In the case of coffeemakers and dishwashers, many times the company will give you the machine if you buy the accompanying product (coffee and detergent) from them.

Negotiating for new equipment

The greatest thing about new equipment is that it's, well, new. No one has dropped it, dented it, or otherwise abused it . . . yet. The best thing to arm yourself with when looking at new equipment is information. Do your comparison shopping. Know your prices and be ready to negotiate. List price is for wimps!

Know the answers to these questions *before* you buy your first piece of equipment:

- **What equipment do I need for my bar?** Think about the front of the house and the back of the house. We included extensive lists of items throughout this chapter that you need to consider buying for your bar.

- **Who can I buy this from in my area?** Create a list of restaurant supply houses, salespeople, other people in the business, and anyone who can get you in touch with potential suppliers.

- **What do these items cost new and used?** Create a spreadsheet to keep track of prices of comparable items.

Answering these questions before you buy can help you know if you're getting a good deal or being taken for a ride.

When buying new equipment, check all warranties. If you can, buy a service agreement. Make sure the agreement specifies how long it will take for a repairperson to get to your place. This timeline can vary greatly. Does the company guarantee repairs within four hours, a day, or a week? If they can't repair the appliance in three hours or less, you could be losing serious money.

Evaluating used equipment

You can save between 40 and 60 percent of your equipment budget by buying used equipment. But it's only a savings if you don't spend a ton in maintenance and repairs. Voilà! The balancing act begins. We recommend taking an electrician and mechanic with you when buying used equipment. Consult your local phone book and ask around for reliable contractors. Talk to the town engineer, fire marshal, and local builders. Check with your employees and the Chamber of Commerce.

Here's what to do when looking at used equipment:

- ✔ **Visually inspect the equipment.** Missing knobs are usually OK. Warped grill bottoms are not.

- ✔ **Be wary of used electrical items.** These items are more likely to have problems than their gas counterparts, especially if they're not maintained well. Always have an electrician with you to check out anything electrical that he may have to repair. He should advise you about appliances that are beyond repair or always need repair.

- ✔ **Get written guarantees.** You shouldn't expect to get a long time period guaranteed, but you need some assurance that if the appliance stops running next week, you can return it.

- ✔ **Factor moving and installation costs into the total price.** After you figure in these costs, you may be better off buying new with free installation. It's now a matter of money. Is it cheaper to buy new and have it installed, or buy used and pay to have it installed? Get out your pencil and paper and add it up. Now make the decision.

Chapter 8

Setting Up Your Bar's Inventory

· ·

In This Chapter
▶ Creating a home for your inventory
▶ Knowing how much to stock
▶ Figuring out how much to keep on hand

· ·

Knowing what to stock in your bar is sometimes truly a matter of trial and error. (Sometimes more error than we'd like, but that's another story.) But you can start from an in-the-know place by browsing this chapter.

Here we give you some guidelines to help you figure out how many different types of liquor, beer, and wine you actually need to carry to balance your customers' wishes with your bottom line. And we also help you figure out how much to buy and where to put it all.

Creating Your Storerooms

If you're starting from the ground up, God bless you. Your bar needs to be designed so that your *storeroom* (the place where you store extra supplies until you need them) is convenient to every part of the house that needs it, especially the kitchen and bar. You need two basic storerooms:

- ✔ **Dry storage:** Keep your canned goods, dry goods, linens, and cleaning supplies here.

- ✔ **Cold storage:** Here's where you store, um, cold stuff and perishable stuff. It most commonly takes the form of a large refrigerated room, or a *cooler*.

 If it's at all possible, use two separate coolers, one for food items that the kitchen staff has access to and another cooler that liquor is stored in. The second cooler is for bartenders and managers only. It's usually full of expensive inventory, and you need a full accounting of when the items leave and for what reason. If you can keep kitchen and bar stuff separated, you're a step ahead.

Depending on your menu, you may also need a freezer. Some places actually have freezer rooms, but most bars have smaller, reach-in freezers stationed underneath or beside the bar itself.

Make sure your storerooms are both out of the way *and* easily accessible. You don't want them taking up valuable seating or working areas.

Tracking your day-to-day inventory

You need to make an inventory sheet for both of your storerooms. An *inventory sheet* shows who is taking what items when. Whenever someone takes something out of the storeroom, he or she marks down the time and date, item taken, amount, and where the item will be used (bar, kitchen, bathrooms, and so forth). Then the employee has to sign his or her name. This form should be as easy to fill in as possible (and don't forget to keep a pen nearby). Post the sheet on the inside of the storeroom door.

This basic sheet is all you need for your dry storage area. You will need to modify the inventory sheet for your cold storeroom. Add a line at the top of the form that tells your employees that *only* a manager or bartender can take items from the cold storage area. Limiting who has access to the cold storage area helps you keep track of valuable products.

All items should be checked in and out.

Securing your inventory

You can't keep an eye on everything all the time, so invest in a couple of good locks for your storerooms. Locks keep honest people honest. When products go missing, you're hit with a double whammy: You lose the money you spent on the item and the money you could have made on the item.

Keep your cooler locked unless someone is actually stocking or restocking it.

Do not allow everyone to have access to storage rooms. Limit the people who have keys or lock combinations to your managers, head cook, head bartender, and of course, you. When the bar is open, make sure someone has a key at all times. For more advice on preventing theft, see Chapter 14.

Extra keys should be placed in the safe. Always make sure that a set of keys is available during each shift, or you won't get backup supplies when you need them. (Yes, this does happen.)

Keeping Your Inventory Well Stocked

You must keep a backup of all the products you sell or products you need for the kitchen and bar. This is called your *inventory.* If you run out, you're *86* on that item.

Keep your inventory — your entire inventory — in locked rooms. See the "Securing your inventory" section, earlier in this chapter.

Make sure you take a long look at Chapter 14. It gives you tips for setting up ordering and purchasing procedures, maintaining your inventory, and reducing waste to make your product dollars go further.

Stocking your drink items

Choosing what liquors to carry really can help you define your bar. The brands you choose (and don't choose) tell your patrons what kind of place you run and help convey your bar's atmosphere. For example, stocking 40 draft beers sends a different message than stocking 40 types of single malt Scotches.

Stocking a true bar is a different process than stocking a restaurant bar. Stand-alone bars have more brands and varieties of liquors than an average restaurant bar.

Evaluate liquors to determine what fits best with your place. You definitely want variety, but you want your products to move, too. Liquor that sits on a shelf ties up cash, which is not good for your business.

Liquor

Well liquor is the most basic, least expensive type of liquor. It's what your bartender pours when someone orders a "gin and tonic" but doesn't specify, or *call,* a particular brand. *Premium* liquor is a step up from call liquor, and *super-premium* is a step up again. For more about the differences between the liquors, and pricing drinks accordingly, check out Chapter 9.

Some liquors come in more than one flavor. For example, other vodka flavors are definitely available (like blueberry, melon, grapefruit, currant, cranberry, strawberry, peach, watermelon, chocolate, coffee, coconut, grape, apple, cherry, lime . . .). You have to be the judge (and your customers will be the jury!) of how many you need and which ones to choose. If you're looking to create a signature Bloody Mary, consider Absolut Peppar. If you're looking to create something like a Bellini Martini, consider something like Stoli Persik (peach). All the big-name vodka producers have many flavors available these days.

Many histories for "86"

Speculation abounds about the origin of the term *86,* meaning either to run out of something or to cut off someone who's had too much to drink. One story comes from the legendary Delmonico's in New York. The story says the restaurant used to sell out of menu item 86 often, thus a tradition may have been born. Others contend 86 is a reference to article 86 of the New York state liquor code, which defines when a patron should be refused service or "86'd." Yet another explanation is from Chumley's at 86 Bedford St. in New York City during the days of Prohibition. When the cops were going to raid the bar, the bartender yelled "86!" and everyone would run out the Bedford Street door because the cops usually would come in the side door. And finally: The term is just a variation of the slang term *deep six.*

We strongly recommend that you evaluate your reasons for wanting more than five flavors of a particular liquor. If you develop a special drink or drink menu using flavored vodkas, definitely invest in them. But don't keep a bottle of Three Olives Green Watermelon Vodka around for the occasional Watermelon Martini that someone may order. If you invest in a unique liquor, make sure you promote it.

Whether you decide to go with well or premium liquors, Table 8-1 lists liquors we think are essential to stock in your bar. We give you a general category of liquor, recommended quantities to keep at the bar and in inventory, and a list of brand names to consider when choosing what to stock.

When it comes to choosing brands of well liquor for your bar, talk to your liquor sales rep. He likely has a bargain vodka, rum, tequila, and so on that you can use in the well. And as always with well liquor, choose one brand in each category, but keep two bottles of it handy behind the bar.

Table 8-1	Liquor Supply Chart		
Liquor	*Bar Stock*	*Inventory/ Storage*	*Brands to Consider*
Aperitif	3	4	Campari, Dubonnet, Lillet, Fernet Branca
Dry Vermouth	2	2	Martini & Rossi, Noilly Pratt
Sweet Vermouth	2	2	Martini & Rossi, Noilly Pratt

Liquor	Bar Stock	Inventory/ Storage	Brands to Consider
Vodka, super-premium	2	12 (6 of each)	Grey Goose, Ciroc, Chopin, Level, Belvedere, Pravda, Skyy90
Vodka, premium	2	12 (6 of each)	Absolut, Smirnoff, Skyy, Stolichnaya, Finlandia, Glacier, Three Olives, Vox, Fris, Ketel One, Tanqueray Sterling, Imperia, Ultimat, Svedka, SV Supreme, Glacier
Vodka, well	2	12 (6 of each)	Popov, Gordon's, Gilbey's, Lairds, Van Gogh, McCormick, Dark Eyes, Barton, Boru
Flavored Vodka — Orange	1	2	Absolut Mandrin, Stoli Ohranj, Skyy Orange, Smirnoff Orange, Three Olives Orange
Flavored Vodka — Lemon	1	2	Absolut Citron, Stoli Citros, Skyy Citrus, Smirnoff Citrus, Three Olives Citrus
Flavored Vodka — Raspberry	1	1	Absolut Raspberri, Stoli Razberi, Smirnoff Raspberry, Three Olives Raspberry
Flavored Vodka — Vanilla	1	1	Stoli Vanil, Absolut Vanilia, Skyy Vanilla, Smirnoff Vanilla, Three Olives Vanilla
Gin, super-premium	2	3 of each	Plymouth, Tanqueray 10, Bombay Sapphire
Gin, premium	2	3 of each	Beefeater, Bombay, Hendricks, Tanqueray, Damrak
Gin, well	2	3 of each	Seagram's, Gordon's, Gilbey's, Barton, McCormick

(continued)

Table 8-1 *(continued)*

Liquor	Bar Stock	Inventory/ Storage	Brands to Consider
Rum — White, premium	2	3 of each	Ocumare, Mount Gay Eclipse, Bacardi Gold, Oronoco
Rum — Dark, premium	2	3 of each	Mount Gay Extra Old, Gosling's Black Seal, Angostura 1824, Bacardi 8
Rum — White	2	3 of each	Bacardi, Ronrico, Cruzan, Russer's, Whaler's, 10 Cane Rum
Rum — Dark	2	2 of each	Bacardi, Goslings, Myers's Original, Rhum Barbancourt
Rum — Spiced	2	2 of each	Captain Morgan, Cruzan, Whaler's
Rum — Coconut	1	2	Malibu, Cocoribe, Whaler's Coconut, Cruzan Coconut, Captain Morgan Parrot Bay Coconut
Rum — Flavored	2	2 of each	Bacardi (Big Apple, Grand Melon, Limon, O [orange flavored], Razz [raspberry], Vanila, Coco [coconut], Bacardi Ciclon [blend of rum, tequila and lime]); Cruzan Rum (coconut, orange, pineapple, banana, vanilla, and citrus-blended rum called Junkanu); Whaler's (coconut, vanilla, pineapple, banana); Mount Gay (vanilla, mango); Captain Morgan Parrot Bay (coconut, pineapple, mango, and passion fruit)
Rum, well	2	3 of each	Castillo, Ron Llave, Bellows, El Dorado, and McCormick

Liquor	Bar Stock	Inventory/ Storage	Brands to Consider
Scotch, super-premium	2	3 of each	Johnny Walker Black, Gold, Blue and Green; Dimple, Chivas, The Famous Grouse, Glenlivet, Dewar's 12-year-old reserve, Highland Park 12-year-old, Macallan 12-year-old, Bowmore 37-year-old (Wow! A $1,000 bottle behind the bar. That'll start some conversations.)
Scotch, premium	2	3 of each	Cutty Sark, Grant's, Ballantine, J&B, Dewar's White Label, Macallan, Bowmore, Johnny Walker Red
Scotch, others	2	1 of each	Vat 69, Teacher's, Bell's, Whyte and Mackay, Passport, Buchanan
Single Malt Scotches	4	1 of each	Cragganmore 12-year-old, Dalmore 12-year-old, Glenmorangie 10-year-old, Aberlour 10-year-old, Balvenie Doublewood, Glenfiddich 12-year-old, Glenlivet 12-year-old, Glenrothes 1989/1992, Macallan 12-year-old, Macallan 18-year-old, Auchentoshan 3 Wood, Ardbeg Uigeadail, Bowmore 17-year-old, Isle of Jura 10-year-old, Laphroaig 10-year-old
Scotch, well	1	2	Black Prince, Ballantine, John Barr Gold Label, Legacy, McAndrews

(continued)

Table 8-1 *(continued)*

Liquor	Bar Stock	Inventory/ Storage	Brands to Consider
Whiskey, premium (rye)	2	1 of each	Jim Beam Rye, Wild Turkey Rye, Rittenhouse
Whiskey, well (blended)	2	1 of each	Fleishmann's, Carstairs, Imperial, Barton Reserve, Wilson, JW Dant, Philadelphia
Tennessee Whiskey	2	2 of each	Jack Daniel's, George Dickel
Canadian Whisky	2	2 of each	Canadian Club, Canadian Mist, Crown Royal, Seagram's V.O., Tangle Ridge
Bourbon	3	1 of each	Jim Beam 4 and 8 years old, Maker's Mark, Booker's, Basil Hayden, Wild Turkey, Old Crow, Knob Creek, Old Grand Dad, Woodford Reserve, Bulleit
Bourbon – Specialty & Single Barrel	3	1 of each	*Specialty Brands:* Knob Creek, Basil Hayden's Small Batch, Booker's Small Batch, Woodford Reserve Distiller's Select, Elijah Craig 12-year-old Selected Barrel Bourbon. *Single Barrel Brands:* Blanton's Single Barrel Kentucky Straight Bourbon, Evan Williams Single Barrel Vintage Kentucky Straight Bourbon, Elijah Craig 18-year-old Single Barrel Bourbon
Bourbon, well	2	3 of each	Ancient Age, Barton Very Old, Benchmark, Bellows, Early Times
Tequila, super-premium	2	3 of each	Patron, Pyrat Cask 1623, Jose Cuervo 1800, Sauza Tres Generaciones, Sauza Conmemorativo

Liquor	Bar Stock	Inventory/ Storage	Brands to Consider
Tequila, premium	2	3 of each	Jose Cuervo, Jose Cuervo Especial, Jose Cuervo Tradicional, Don Julio, Patron Silver, Sauza Blanco, Two Fingers, Herradura, El Tesoro, Agave Loco
Tequila, flavored	2	1 of each	Reserva del Senor Alemandro (almond flavored), Margaritaville (coconut, lime, passion fruit, mango, tangerine), Jose Cuervo (Citrico, Oranjo, Tropina), La Pinta Tequila Pomegranate, 267 Tequila Infusions (pepper, orange)
Tequila, well	2	3 of each	Montezuma, Baja, Cabrito
Brandy	2	2 of each	Asbach Uralt, Christian Brothers, Korbel, Cornet, Calvados, Cardinal Mendoza
Brandy, well	1	2	E & J, Royal 1889
Cognac, premium	1	1	Remy Martin Louis XIII, Hennessy Cognac Paradis, Hennessy Cognac Richard, Martell Cognac Cordon Bleu
Cognac	1	1	Courvoisier, Delamain, Hennessy V.S., Martell V.S.O.P., Remy Martin V.S.O.P., Alize V.S.
Armagnac	1	1	Sempe, Germain-Robin Alambic, St. Aubin, Salamens
Irish Whiskey	2	1 of each	Bushmills, Jameson, Powers, Tullamore Dew, Clontarf, Michael Collins, Red Breast, and Ray's personal favorite: Midleton

Cordials

Cordials are must-have items for your bar because they're essential for mixing with other drinks to make cocktails or for layering to make popular shooters. Table 8-2 is our list for must-have cordials for your bar (along with appropriate quantities, of course!).

Table 8-2	Cordials to Stock	
Cordial	*Bar Stock*	*Inventory/Storage*
99 Apples	1	1
99 Bananas	1	1
99 Blackberries	1	1
Apple Barrel Schnapps (DeKuyper)	1	1
BluesBerry Schnapps (DeKuyper)	1	1
ButterShots Schnapps (DeKuyper)	1	1
Cinnamon Schnapps (DeKuyper)	1	1
Crantasia Schnapps (DeKuyper)	1	1
Key Largo Tropical Schnapps (DeKuyper)	1	1
Mountain Strawberry Schnapps (DeKuyper)	1	1
Old Tavern Rootbeer Schnapps (DeKuyper)	1	1
Peachtree Schnapps (DeKuyper)	1	1
Peppermint Schnapps (DeKuyper)	1	1
Spearmint Schnapps (DeKuyper)	1	1
Tropical Pineapple Schnapps (DeKuyper)	1	1
WilderBerry Schnapps (DeKuyper)	1	1
Almond Liqueur (DeKuyper)	1	1
Cactus Juice Margarita (DeKuyper)	1	1
Coconut Amaretto (DeKuyper)	1	1
Melon Liqueur (DeKuyper)	1	1
Orange Curacao (DeKuyper)	1	1
Razzmatazz (DeKuyper)	1	1
San Tropique Tropical Rum (DeKuyper)	1	1

Cordial	Bar Stock	Inventory/Storage
Thrilla Vanilla French Vanilla (DeKuyper)	1	1
Wild Strawberry Liqueur (DeKuyper)	1	1
Pucker Strawberry Passion Schnapps (DeKuyper)	1	1
Pucker Cheri-Beri (DeKuyper)	1	1
Pucker Grape Schnapps (DeKuyper)	1	1
Pucker Island Blue Schnapps (DeKuyper)	1	1
Pucker Peach Schnapps (DeKuyper)	1	1
Pucker Raspberry Schnapps (DeKuyper)	1	1
Pucker Sour Apple Schnapps (DeKuyper)	1	1
Pucker Watermelon Schnapps (DeKuyper)	1	1
Tuaca (Italian orange vanilla liqueur)	1	1
Licor 43 (Spanish liquor)	1	1
Celtic Crossing (combines Irish spirits, whiskey, and honey)	1	1
Grand Marnier	1	1
Cointreau	1	1
Triple Sec	1	2
Crème de Menthe, White	1	1
Crème de Menthe, Green	1	2
Crème de Cacao, White	1	1
Crème de Cacao, Dark	1	1
Blue Curacao	1	1
Kahlua/Coffee Liqueur	2	2
Amaretto	1	2
Peach Schnapps	1	2
Sambuca	1	2
Galliano	1	order when needed
Midori	1	1

(continued)

Table 8-2 *(continued)*

Cordial	Bar Stock	Inventory/Storage
Hazelnut Liqueur	1	1
B&B	1	1
Chambord	2	2
Irish Cream	2	2
Southern Comfort	1	2
Irish Mist	1	1
Sloe Gin	1	1
Anisette	1	2
Agwa (herbal liquor with guarana and ginseng)	1	1
Drambuie	1	1
Pernod	1	1
Jagermeister	1	1
Hpnotiq	1	1
Pama (pomegranate liqueur)	1	1
Cachaca (from Brazil)	1	1
Soho (lychee-flavored liqueur)	1	1
Agavero (tequila licor)	1	1
Pisco (the Peruvian national drink)	1	1
Tarantula Azul Tequila (lemony tequila liquor)	1	1
Zenh (green tea liqueur)	1	1
Chartreuse	1	1
Flavored Brandies: banana, blackberry, apricot, cherry	1 of each flavor	1 of each flavor
Crème de Cassis	1	1

Check out DeKuyper's Web site (www.dekuyperusa.com) and register at the "Bartenders Only" area. The site gives you a layering chart that can help you decide what liqueurs to layer where (based on the weight and viscosity of each) to make layered shots for your patrons.

Beer

Beer was among the first beverages served in pubs around the world, and it's sure to be the last. After you've chosen the beer for your menu (check out Chapters 9 and 12 for help), you have to know how much to stock so you don't run out! Table 8-3 is a list of what you need (and how much).

Table 8-3	Beer Inventory		
	Bar Stock	*Inventory/Storage*	*Brands*
Regular, domestic	1 case	10 case	If we have to list brands, open up a coffeehouse (or read Chapter 12). The big three brands are Budweiser, Miller, and Coors.
Light, domestic	1 case	10 cases	Stock the light version of the domestic beers you serve.
Regular, imported	1 case	10 cases	Corona, St. Pauli Girl, Heineken, Guinness, Becks, and so on
Light, imported	12 bottles	5 cases	Corona Light, Heineken Light, Molson Light
Microbrew, domestic	1 case	10 cases	Samuel Adams, Sierra Nevada, Goose Island, and so on
Local brew	1 case	10 cases	Talk to your local distributor for suggestions.
Nonalcoholic	6 bottles	1 case	O'Doul's, Cutter, Haakebeck
Hard lemonade	6 bottles	1 case	Mike's
Red Bull or other energy drinks	6 cans	1 case	Okay. Technically, Red Bull is not a beer, or even a malt beverage, but we usually stock it with the beer, so we mention it here.

You may have noticed that kegs aren't mentioned in this list. There's a good reason for this. While kegs do contain beer, they're a different animal. You need to have one keg connected to each of your taps (preferably with a corresponding tap hand that makes it easy to see what you're pouring), plus at least one backup keg for each kind of beer you sell. Notice we did not say for each tap. (You may be pouring Miller Lite, for example, at three different taps, two inside and one outside, during the warm months. You may not necessarily need to keep three backup kegs if you don't use beer at all those stations quickly.) You'll have to judge how quickly you go through kegs in a week. Most places order beer once or twice a week because they just don't have the space to store more than that.

Wine

To help choose wines for your bar, please see *Wine For Dummies,* 4th Edition, by Ed McCarthy and Mary Ewing-Mulligan (Wiley), and talk to your local reps. There are just too many to suggest specific brands and vintages.

We recommend offering no more than two of each variety (red, white, blush, and sparkling wine). A local wine is always a good choice. Everyone has a favorite, but you're running a bar, not a French restaurant. Keep the selection small (because you have to store it all) and at a medium price. I did know of a bar that had a special: a bottle of Dom Pérignon and a bologna sandwich for $125. It was the talk of the area. Good word-of-mouth advertising!

Keep a case of each wine you serve on hand. And keep it at the right temperature. White wine should be *cold,* very cold. Red wine should be kept around 70 degrees Fahrenheit. You don't need to refrigerate it, but don't store it near the oven.

Mixers and soft drinks

The most efficient way to store most mixers on your premises is with a *bag-in-the-box (BIB) soda system.* Soda water is mixed with concentrated syrup on demand through a fountain system of some sort, most often a soda gun in bars. Fruit juice is also used in many cocktails. Please see Chapter 12 for a list of the typical mixers you should stock.

Talk to your local food supplier for help getting a system. They may install the system for free if you agree to buy all your syrup from the company, with a guaranteed minimum per month.

Keep one backup of each syrup box on hand for easy restocking. If you have several fountains or guns, you may need a couple of extra boxes of your most used items, typically cola, diet cola, and lemon-lime soda. Until you get a feel for how much you go through, consider doubling up on these must-have items.

Also, don't forget the cocktail mixes currently available on the market. _Cocktail mixes_ are the premixed bottles of stuff you add to liquor to give it its identity. They're essential for many common cocktails, including Piña Coladas, margaritas (many different flavors), and Bloody Marys. Popular mixes include

- ✔ Daily's Fruit Mixers (www.dailysfruitmixers.com)
- ✔ Holland House
- ✔ Mr. & Mrs. T's
- ✔ Tree Ripe
- ✔ Major Peters (www.majorpeters.com)

Sometimes these products are sold by food vendors, rather than liquor vendors. Check with your reps to see who carries what in your area.

While you don't need a full case, you should keep a bottle or two around of Rose's lime juice (it's a sweetened lime juice-ish thing) and pomegranate juice. Pomegranate juice is really hot at the moment. If you really want to be ahead of the curve, throw in some Açaí juice for good measure. It's the up-and-coming juice with 30 to 40 times the antioxidants of pomegranate juice. Healthy cocktails — who knew?

Frozen-drink machines make complete frozen cocktails, and many companies will offer you a great beverage program. (We recommend Island Oasis. You can check out the company's products at www.islandoasis.com.)

Water

Bottled water is popular even in bars. It comes in two very broad categories, sparkling (with bubbles) or still (without bubbles). We recommend you choose one of each type. Talk to your sales rep to get the information on where the water comes from, how it's filtered, what minerals are in it or are removed from it, and on and on, assuming you're interested in that. It's good to know, in case someone asks you. People like to know the ins and outs of your business.

A few common brands of still water are Fiji, Poland Spring, Dasani, and Ozarka. Popular sparkling choices are Perrier, Saratoga Springs, and San Pellegrino. Keep six bottles of the two brands you choose behind the bar, and a case of each in the cooler.

Stocking your basic food items

Most liquor will last and last (if you keep it at the right temperature, of course), so when you're getting started, you may have more inventory than you'd like. Ultimately, you sell it, but you tie up your cash in inventory. However, food is a different story. Food is perishable. You buy too much, and it ends up in the trash. You don't want to throw your money away, so buy fresh items judiciously.

Here are a few general tips for stocking food items in your bar:

- Most produce spoils in two to three days, so buy only what you can use during that time. Strawberries, bananas, and pears are prime culprits.

- Produce stays fresher longer if you don't wash it or cut it until you need it.

- Uncut citrus and apples last longer, up to a couple of weeks, if refrigerated properly.

- After produce is cut, use it quickly. Cut bananas, apples, and pears as you need them. Use citrus within 1½ days. Use strawberries the same day.

- Overstocking encourages waste. Stock only what you need.

- For food items, fresh is better. If you can get daily deliveries, do it.

Ultimately, the amount and type of food you need to stock depends largely on your bar's menu (see Chapter 9). For now, though, just make sure to plan ahead with regard to how much and what type of food you need to store, and check out Chapter 14 for tips on using your fresh and staple inventory to your advantage.

Garnishes

Ultimately, your business levels dictate your garnish levels. Because many of these items are perishable, you walk the fine line of making sure you have enough, but not so much that it goes to waste. It's truly a trial-and-error situation. The number of garnishes you have at the ready totally depends on how many customers you have, what they are drinking, and how you garnish the beverages. And your garnish level depends on how labor intensive the garnish is. You may choose to dedicate more caddy space to hand-stuffed olives (which take your bartender some time to make) than to, say, maraschino cherries (which generally come right out of a jar).

But we don't want to totally leave you hanging, so Table 8-4 gives you some help in getting started with figuring out how much you need. And Chapter 12 can help you decide what garnishes to choose for your drinks.

Notice we give you two different par levels, one for weeknights and one for weekend nights. (For more information on *par levels,* or how much of an item you should have on hand at the beginning of a shift, take a look at Chapter 14.) We're assuming that Friday and Saturday are busy nights for your bar; if that's not the case, adjust accordingly. Many bars create par sheets for each and every shift.

Table 8-4	Sample Garnish Par Levels	
Garnish	*Weekday Par*	*Weekend Par*
Oranges slices	1 caddy	3 caddies
Olives	1 caddy	3 caddies
Olives, stuffed	1 caddy	3 caddies
Maraschino cherries	1 caddy	2 caddies
Lemon wedges	5 lemons	10 lemons
Lemon twists	½ lemon	1 lemon
Lime squeezes	3 limes	6 limes
Lime wedges	4 limes	15 limes
Lime twists	½ lime	1 lime

Other miscellaneous foodstuffs that you need

Keep a bottle or supply of each of these items at each well. On a busy night, the last thing you want is for bartenders to be hunting down the small stuff.

- Angostura bitters
- Worcestershire sauce
- Hot sauce
- Superfine sugar
- Salt and pepper

Always have at least a case of each of these in backup, especially the hot sauce; you'll also use this on the tables.

Items for the Back of the House (Like Restrooms!)

Yes, we're mentioning the unmentionables. It's a messy fact of life, but in a bar, stuff happens, and you need to be able to clean it up.

Here's what we think you need:

- Toilet paper: 1 case
- Soap (bar and/or liquid): 1 case
- Hand sanitizer: ½ case
- Paper towels: 1 case
- Feminine items: 1 case
- Garbage bags (all sizes): 1 case of each
- First-aid kit: 2 backup kits
- Cleaning supplies:
  - Floor, oven, stove, glass, and other cleaners: ½ case
  - Polishers (silver, copper, and stainless): ½ case

In most cases, you'll buy your cleaning supplies from a company that specializes in commercial cleaning supplies, like Ecolab (www.ecolab.com). It provides a full range of products (such as floor degreasers, sanitizers, and drain cleaners) that work better on the tough dirt, grease, and grime that bars create.

Chapter 9

Planning and Creating Your Menus

· ·

In This Chapter

▶ Deciding what food to serve

▶ Creating your drink menu

▶ Pricing your menu

▶ Putting it all on paper

▶ Figuring out when to make changes

· ·

A bar is a wonderful gathering place. A place to get away from the world, relax, hang out with friends, or just watch other people. In most cases, people come to your bar to eat and drink, in no particular order. So you, as the owner, need to create *menus* to give your patrons listings of the drinks and food items you serve. Your menus show the world your take on food and beverages. Every bar has a martini, but not every bar has *your* martini. This is truly your chance to let the world see your passion for the bar business. What you choose to highlight on your menus, prepare behind your bar and in your kitchen, and present to your customers is truly the soul of your business.

In this chapter, we give you tips for creating your food and drink menus. We explain what your patrons want and expect from your bar and help you figure out what to charge for it.

Planning Your Food Menu 101

Simplicity is essential when developing a food menu for your bar. Ninety-nine times out of 100, your patrons aren't coming to you for the latest in avant-garde gastronomy. Instead, they want easy-to-understand, familiar items they

can snack on while they're enjoying the beverages you're pouring.

Yours is a bar, not a restaurant. Your menu should reflect that difference.

Figuring out what kind of food to serve

You can take any of these menu ideas and match it with your bar to create synergy. (See Chapter 4 if you need help deciding the type of bar to run.) For example, if your bar specializes in tequila, you can choose a menu category listed in this section and serve foods that enhance your theme. You can stick to appetizers that have a Mexican flavor, you can create a tapas menu that complements your drink menu, or you can offer a full-blown food menu that matches your bar's feel. How you pair your bar and food choices is entirely up to you (and your guests, of course; if they don't buy, you can't sell).

The descriptions in this section aren't hard and fast. They're intended just to help you think about your own menu in an organized way.

Appetizing appetizer

An *appetizer* is a dish that's served before the main meal in a restaurant. In bars, sometimes the appetizer menu is the *only* menu. The owner chooses not to offer full-blown meals to patrons, instead giving them a choice of several appetizers to snack on.

Common bar appetizers include these tasty options:

- Deep-fried jalapeño peppers stuffed with cream cheese
- Beer-battered onion rings with a special sauce
- Nachos slathered in cheese, refried beans, beef or chicken, black olives, tomatoes, and anything else that seems tempting to you
- Chips and salsa
- Fried vegetables, like mushrooms, zucchini, or even dill pickles (one of Heather's personal favorites)
- Buffalo wings
- Fried mozzarella sticks

Are you sensing a theme here?

Appealing pub grub

Pub grub is the affectionate term for typical bar food, such as wings, onion rings, cheese sticks, burgers, and so on. All things deep-fried (or high in saturated fat) usually fall into the pub grub category. If you're interested in serving food, this is usually a good place to start. People expect bars to offer this kind of cuisine.

Pub grub menus can include these filling foods designed to please your patrons' palates:

- ✓ **Hamburgers:** You can create dozens of variations on the basic burger: the bacon cheeseburger, blue-cheese burger, mushroom-and-Swiss burger.

- ✓ **Sandwiches:** Popular ones include the Reuben, grilled cheese, grilled chicken, and so on.

- ✓ **Chili:** Hearty soups and stews are game-day favorites with bar-goers.

- ✓ **French fries:** Some barkeepers include onion rings and hand-cut chips on their menu.

- ✓ **Fried chicken fingers:** You can list these as an appetizer, entree, or both.

- ✓ **Regional specialties:** Every area of the country has a food that's unique to that region, and bars are a common place to find them. For example, in Indiana most bars that serve pub grub serve a fried pork tenderloin sandwich. Many places in the southern U.S. include a po' boy sandwich (fried seafood served on a submarine roll).

- ✓ **Pizza:** This dish — deep, pan, or thin — is always a popular item and can make a great profit. Consider including a small, individual pizza on your menu.

Because people expect bars to have pub grub, giving them something more or something different could be your draw and help you define what you want your bar to be. Giving them something to crave and come back for again and again can make you a success.

Happy-hour fare

Some bars choose to only serve food during *happy hour,* a period of time designed to draw a crowd with special pricing and promotions. Sometimes the food is the happy-hour draw, for instance. Maybe you set up a free buffet from 4 to 6 p.m. Monday through Friday but keep drinks at their regular price. Or maybe you sell two drinks for the price of one (assuming that's legal in your state), and charge $3 per person for the buffet.

If you're considering hosting a buffet in your bar, consider these logistics when selecting your food items:

- ✓ **Ease of preparation:** Choose food that you and your staff can prepare quickly and easily because you'll likely be restocking often. Most happy-hour buffets are made up of appetizer options, simply for ease of eating (the customer can take as much or as little as she wants).

- ✓ **Hold times:** Choose food that can sit for a little while (like 20 minutes) and still taste good.

> ✔ **Safe containers for service:** You need the appropriate serving containers (like chafing dishes or ice baths) to keep food out of the *danger zone* (between 40 degrees and 140 degrees F). Otherwise, food-borne bacteria can grow and make your customers sick. Take a look at Chapter 17 for more help on keeping your customers safe.

Alternatively, you can create special happy-hour pricing (like 2-for-1 deals or $2 off entrees) for items already on your menu. For more tips on special promotions take a look at Chapter 16.

Tantalizing tapas

Tapas are snacks or small plates in the Spanish tradition. Patrons can order several tapas to create their own meal or share them with friends. Often provided free in Spain with the purchase of alcoholic beverages, these small plates make an appearance in many bars in this country. You can provide very simple tapas, like a few olives, complimentary to guests, and make more elaborate offerings, though still small in quantity, available for purchase.

Here are a few examples of tapas Heather recently sampled in bars across the country:

- ✔ Fried new potatoes with chile pasilla aioli
- ✔ Ceviche (assorted seafood in a spicy lime vinaigrette)
- ✔ Cajun shrimp sautéed in a spicy cream sauce
- ✔ Marinated fresh anchovy fillets
- ✔ Manchego cheese croquettes
- ✔ Plato de fiambres (plate of cured meats)
- ✔ Pincho de pollo y chorizo (skewered chicken and chorizo sausage)
- ✔ Pimientos fritos (fried green peppers and coarse salt)

Although the original tradition of tapas is Spanish, many bar owners are experimenting with Mediterranean dishes, Greek cuisine (called meze), Asian flavors, and anything else that strikes their fancy. You can call anything tapas — just think small but shareable quantities.

Tapas food tends to be a bit fancier than your average bar fare, so make sure you have ample kitchen space and culinary experience if you want to undertake this ambitious endeavor.

Full-blown menus

Many "bar and grills" or "grill and taverns" or "grill and bars" have larger menus these days. Owners may start with a pub grub menu (see the section earlier in this chapter for details) but expand their offerings further to include items such as salads, entrees (such as ribs, steaks, and pasta), desserts, and even kids' menus.

Here are some familiar examples of bars with full-blown menus.

- ✔ Bennigan's Grill & Tavern: www.bennigans.com
- ✔ Fox and the Hound Pub & Grille: www.tentcorp.com
- ✔ Fado Irish Pub: www.fadoirishpub.com
- ✔ Buffalo Wild Wings Grill & Bar: www.buffalowildwings.com

Take a look at these Web sites to get a feel for the breadth and depth of their menu offerings.

These places calls themselves bars (or pubs, taverns, and so on), but they really operate more like restaurants. If you're interested in running a bar with a full menu, take a look at *Running a Restaurant For Dummies* by Michael Garvey and Heather and Andrew Dismore (Wiley) for help with managing your food inventory, details on setting up a full-service kitchen, and other topics that are tailored to the restaurant industry.

Just because a bar has a complete food menu doesn't mean it's a family place. Check your local legislation for laws pertaining to allowing children in your establishment.

Considering what hours to serve food

If you decide to offer more than an appetizer menu, consider opening for lunch and dinner. You can continue to get income during hours that the "bar business" is not hopping.

If you serve food, you probably want to limit the hours you serve food, say from 4 to 11 p.m., for example. Your bar can stay open later to satisfy drinking patrons, but you can close the kitchen when customers are less likely to order food. You maximize your labor dollars (which increase with the number of hourly kitchen employees on the clock) during the times you're taking in more revenue from food.

Determining the size of your menu

As we note in the Introduction to this book, we assume that if you're reading this book, you're running a bar or tavern that may or may not serve food. We aren't expecting that your establishment is a restaurant with a bar. Having said that, we recommend that you keep your menu fairly small, with 10–12 items at the maximum.

Take a look at Table 9-1 for our recommendations for how to break down your menu.

Table 9-1	Recommended Number of Selections for Different Types of Menus	
Type of Menu	*Appetizers*	*Entrees*
Appetizer only	12	0
Pub grub	6	6
Happy hour	12	0
Tapas	10	0

Analyzing your kitchen space

Most bars have scaled-down kitchens compared to restaurants, so definitely take into account the size of your kitchen *before* you finalize your menu. If you plan on serving full meals, you need a larger kitchen than if you are simply serving (mostly) fried appetizers. With full meals, you may need an area to put together salads and bread, appetizers, entrees, and desserts, and of course, equipment to cook and refrigerate many different ingredients. If you're, instead, serving eight different fried appetizers you need a few fryers, a prep table, and a cooler, for example. With a smaller menu, you need less variety in equipment and preparation space.

Here's a list of the most common *stations,* or areas where food is prepared, you'll find in a bar kitchen:

- ✔ **Fryer:** The fryer is probably the most common and most frequently used station in the bar kitchen. Things like, er, fries are made here. You can use this station to prepare jalapeño poppers, onion rings, egg rolls, cheese sticks, breaded calamari, and chicken tenders.

Many fried menu items come to you frozen from your suppliers. If you have space, place a small reach-in freezer near the fryer to keep those items handy and close.

✔ **Grill:** You can choose a *flattop grill* (similar to a huge griddle) or a *grated grill* (a bigger version of the tool in your backyard), depending on what you want to cook. A grated grill is essential for making those pretty little checkerboard grill marks on chicken, steaks, and burgers. A flattop grill is great for things like grilled cheese sandwiches or grilled peppers and onions. If you have the space, choose both kinds; you'll have much more flexibility with your menu items.

✔ **Oven:** Depending on your menu, you may not need this particular station. An oven is great if you're making pizza, roasting meats, or baking lasagna.

You may see many different kinds of ovens at your equipment supplier's showroom. Make sure you discuss your specific needs with your salesperson before he or she sells or leases you more oven than you can use. And don't forget to take a peek at Chapter 7 to get tips for choosing your appliances.

✔ **Sauté:** This station consists of a multiburner range, shelving to hold tools and supplies (such as sauté pans, tongs, and plates), and possibly a small cooler (a small refrigerator in kitchen lingo) to hold ingredients. Anything that's cooked in a pan to order (like pasta or a sautéed shrimp appetizer) is made at the sauté station.

In a bar, you may not have an actual sauté station, but more than likely, you need a range with about six burners and someone who knows how to use it.

✔ **Pantry:** The term *pantry* may be too elevated for a bar kitchen, but basically, the pantry is the area of the kitchen where cold menu items are assembled. If you serve salads, ceviche, or cold sandwiches, your kitchen staff assembles them here. In your bar, this station may simply be a small area with a bit of counter space and a cooler.

✔ **Other stuff:** You may also need a decent-size (5 x 3 feet) prep table and a microwave. We wouldn't call them stations, but they're handy to have in most bar kitchens.

Use your kitchen to help you determine your final menu. If you don't have an oven, for example, it will be tough to include pizzas on the menu. Without a fryer, you can't very well make French fries or homemade potato chips. Take a look at Chapter 7 for information on getting the right equipment for your bar.

Thinking about signature dishes

Many bars become known for a specialty. It may be a particular item high-lighted on a particular day, like Friday Fish and Chips. Or it could be that you have the best burgers on the block. Decide what you want your specialty to be and make sure that you can make money on it and produce it quickly. This section shows you how.

Insisting on high profit margins

One of the biggest mistakes people make when developing signature dishes is choosing ones that are too expensive to make or too costly for very many patrons to buy. So opt for signature dishes that are inexpensive to produce, but still extremely tasty.

Take a look at the section "Pricing Your Menus Right," later in this chapter, for help on figuring out what to charge to make a profit.

Requiring easy preparation

If you create tasty, affordable dishes as signature items, your patrons will order them in volume. Do yourself a favor and make them a breeze to pre-pare. After you know how many items you sell on a given night, you'll be better able to handle the volume, but make it easy on yourself when you're first starting out.

Establishing good-quality recipes

Nothing is more frustrating to a patron than to order something in your bar, like it a lot, order it the next time, and receive something different. When patrons become regulars, they will notice variances in your food quality, sometimes before you do. Whatever menu you decide on, make sure your staff can execute it consistently every time a customer orders it.

Employees achieve consistently excellent products when they're trained well. Don't skimp on training them how to execute your menu items your way. Training manuals are excellent tools to give everyone the same message, and they give them something to refer back to as questions arise. Take a look at Chapter 10 for help on training your employees.

Consistency in food and drink is very important; it is a very big complaint in the business. Customers come to your place for *that* item cooked *that* way. Keep a good recipe file in the kitchen and bar. However, in the bar, you will probably hear, "I like the way *Ray* makes my drinks," which you can't do much about.

Planning Your Drink Menu 101

Most bars are fully stocked bars, so patrons can order their favorite cocktails, such as a gin and tonic, Crown and Coke, or margarita. But many bar owners create specialized drink menus to steer patrons toward unique beverages and cocktails that customers can only get at their place. Spend some time thinking about what kinds of drinks you want to be known for, and then create a menu to match.

For details on the types of liquor, wine, and beer available to bar owners, take a look at Chapter 8.

Selecting beers for your menu

Select three local brews, three national beers, three light beers, and three imports. You can choose more or fewer, depending on the size of your place. And of course, if your theme demands that you keep 80 beers on tap, you can disregard our aforementioned advice.

Storing beer at the right temperature is an important factor in maintaining its quality. Beer requires cold storage, so make sure that your *walk-in cooler* (a refrigerated room with proper door seals and a thermostat to regulate the temperature) is large enough to accommodate your inventory.

Creating a signature cocktail menu

When owners concoct signature cocktails for their bars, they often choose to name one of them after the bar or the bar owner (Hymie Lipshitz Great Oversized Martini). In some cases, your signature cocktails match your food menu (like creating special margaritas to go with your happy-hour fajita bar). Whatever you choose, make sure that your signature cocktails are special to your place. You want to create a vibe that says, "You can only get this here."

Martinis are easy to use as a signature cocktail because you can simply change the garnish. You can use house-stuffed olives — filled with blue cheese, anchovies, hot peppers, and other stuffings with a strong flavor — to make a signature impact.

You'll likely sell many signature drinks, so make sure you choose something that's fairly easy to make. Or you can make them up in batches ahead of time for ease of service.

Infusions are a great way to make something truly special to your bar. An *infusion* is a vodka that's been infused with fruits, herbs, candies, vegetables, and the like for three to four days or more. By creating your own recipes for infusions, you can create a one-of-a-kind cocktail.

Here are a few things to keep in mind when making your own infusions:

- ✔ Choose organic produce. Pesticides and vodka don't mix.
- ✔ Clean all your ingredients before you place them in the vodka. Impurities and dirt can ruin the infusion.
- ✔ Choose glass jars with tight-fitting lids to create your infusions. Talk to your liquor purveyor to get free containers.
- ✔ Create and test the first batch of a new recipe in the back of the house (not behind the bar) to make sure that your ingredients don't turn the vodka an unappetizing color. The last thing you want is an interesting bottle filled with brown liquid in full view of your patrons.
- ✔ Create drinks using your infusions that appeal to your clientele.

Think about serving your specialty drinks in specialty glassware. Use a local garnish, a special glass, a special size, or something else that distinguishes them as your signature drinks.

Planning your wine list

Depending on your expertise, clientele, and food menu, you may have a fairly small wine list. Most true bars offer two or three reds, two or three whites, two champagnes, and a blush wine. Consider listing your selections on the menu in flavor categories. For more details on how wines differ, take a look at Chapter 8. And take a gander at *Wine For Dummies,* 4th Edition, by Ed McCarthy and Mary Ewing-Mulligan (Wiley).

If you choose to run a wine bar, you will need many more wines than we've recommended here, with extensive menu descriptions and a knowledgeable staff.

Including nonalcoholic drinks

Don't forget to include signature nonalcoholic drinks on your menu. Designated drivers, expectant and nursing mothers, aspiring athletes, and others enjoy bars without consuming alcohol. Don't miss the chance to dazzle them with something beyond a virgin strawberry daiquiri.

If you're not feeling too creative in the nonalcoholic department, consider serving beverages made by companies such as SoBe, Snapple, or AriZona to help you fill this niche.

Pricing Your Menus Right

The only way money comes into your bar is when patrons purchase your menu items at the price you choose. (Money goes out of your bar in so, so many ways, but that's covered in Chapters 14 and 15.) So you must price your menus correctly to cover your overhead expenses (including things like rent, insurance, and salaries), your costs (like the ice, liquor, and garnish) and incidentals like napkins, stir sticks, and tiny plastic garnish swords.

You can price your menu several different ways. But if you charge more than people are willing to pay, you have a problem. And if your patrons will pay more than you're charging, you're leaving money on the table, so to speak.

Using food cost to price your menu

Your *food cost percentage* (often shortened to simply *food cost*) is the cost of all the ingredients used to make the dish divided by the menu price. This percentage is a guide to help you control your costs and assess your profitability.

Figuring out the cost of a dish

Here's how you figure out how much a dish costs you to make it. We use cheese fries as an example.

1. **Figure the cost of the fries you use.**

   An 8-ounce portion of French fries costs about 30 cents.

2. **Add the cost of the cheddar cheese you melt on top.**

   The cost of 3 ounces of cheddar cheese sauce is about 15 cents. So now you're up to 45 cents.

3. **Add the cost of the side of ranch and the side of ketchup you serve with the dish.**

   Assume you're giving your patron 2 ounces of each, at around 7 cents for ranch dressing and 2 cents for ketchup. You're looking at about 54 cents in food cost so far.

4. **Add 5 to 10 percent for napkins, foil, plastic wrap, and any paper goods associated with the item.**

   To simplify the math, we are going to add 5 cents here, not quite 10 percent of our subtotal, to bring the total food cost for this item to 59 cents.

You also need to figure out the cost of your shortening (or oil), seasonings, and other service items associated with the dish to get the most accurate food costing.

If you serve any complimentary items, such as nuts or popcorn, to guests, make sure you figure in a cost for those items when you're pricing your menu items.

Pricing items based on food cost

Most bars run an overall food cost percentage in the mid-30s. So you should price your food no less than three times as much as it costs you to make.

Here's how you use food cost to set your menu prices:

1. **Find the food cost of the item.**

   See the cheese fries example in the last section to figure this out. Our portion costs us 59 cents.

2. **Divide the cost by your food cost percentage goal.**

   If you want to run a 35 percent food cost, take the 59 cents the fries cost you and divide it by 35 percent (.59 ÷ .35= $1.69).

3. **Adjust the price to make sense when patrons read it on the menu.**

   Basically, $1.69 would be a strange price to see on a menu. Round it up to the next 25-cent increment (like $1.75) or even up to the next dollar amount ($2.00) or near-dollar amount ($1.99). Your goal is to help the patron be able to add the prices in his head.

Table 9-2 shows you how you could price cheese fries at different food cost percentages.

Table 9-2	Menu Cost for Cheese Fries Based on Food Cost Percentage		
Cost of Cheese Fries	**Food Cost Percentage**	**Price at Exact Food Cost**	**Menu Price**
$.59	20	$2.95	$2.95
$.59	25	$2.36	$2.50
$.59	30	$1.97	$2.00

Cost of Cheese Fries	Food Cost Percentage	Price at Exact Food Cost	Menu Price
$.59	35	$1.69	$1.75
$.59	40	$1.48	$1.50

This formula is a guideline, not an absolute rule. If your market will bear cheese fries priced at $3.95 or $4.95, charge it. Your food cost on these items will be lower (meaning they will be highly profitable), which could allow you to charge a lower percentage for more expensive products and still hit your numbers. Take a look at Chapter 15 for more details on running your bar by the numbers.

Pricing your drinks

Pricing is a nuance that comes with experience, which is very tough to explain in a book. Pricing is determined by what you can get, reasonably, from the customer, and by the area and the kind of bar your have. Of course, you would like to deposit more money in the bank, but will Joe customer pay you for it? Difficult question. From the beginning, you have to do comparison shopping in your area and get your bar prices in the right groove, not too high and not too low.

Raising prices is very difficult in bars. Raise the price 5 cents on a drink, and you could have a customer mutiny on your hands.

The majority of your revenue (generally around 80 percent) in the bar business comes from drink sales. Consequently, pricing them competitively *and* profitably is necessary. You'll have to do some math, but don't be scared; we'll help you through it.

We can give you formulas and strategies for pricing your drinks, but ultimately your customers have the final say in what you can charge, simply by their buying decisions.

Your *pour size,* or how much liquor you include in each drink, is critical to figuring out how much a drink costs you and consequently, how much you can charge.

Most bars pour either 1 ounce or 1½ ounces of alcohol in each drink. (If the customer orders a double, you, um, double that amount of liquor in each drink.) So from a liter bottle you get about 30 or 20 drinks, respectively. Take a look at Table 9-3 for details on how much different pour sizes of differently priced liquors cost you.

Table 9-3	Pour-Size Costs from a 1-Liter Bottle	
Bottle Cost	**1-oz. Pour Cost (30 Drinks per Bottle)**	**1.5-oz. Pour Cost (20 Drinks per Bottle)**
$18	$0.60	$0.90
$20	$0.67	$1.00
$25	$0.83	$1.25
$28	$0.93	$1.40
$30	$1.00	$1.50
$32	$1.07	$1.60
$35	$1.17	$1.75
$40	$1.33	$2.00

To complicate matters further (but actually make your life easier, trust us), most bar owners create a tiered pricing structure for cocktails. They categorize their liquors by price (and presumably by quality): well, call, premium, and super-premium. Then they set their prices for each category (even if the cost per bottle within the category varies a bit).

Table 9-4 describes the categories and gives you some examples of brands that fall within each category.

Table 9-4	Liquor Categories	
Category	**Description**	**Brand Examples**
Well	The most basic liquors; least expensive; usually consumed in mixed drinks rather than by themselves; liquors in this category are stored in the *well* (the area where the bartender makes the drinks) for easy access, hence the name.	Local or supplier brands
Call	The most familiar brands of liquor; not too expensive; patrons call the brand when they order a drink ("I'll have a Bacardi and Coke."), hence the name.	Smirnoff Vodka, Beefeater Gin, Bacardi Light Rum, Dewar's White Label Scotch, Jim Beam Bourbon, Canadian Club Whiskey, Jose Cuervo Gold Tequila, Korbel Brandy

Category	Description	Brand Examples
Premium	Better-quality brands; higher price reflects higher quality.	Absolut Vodka, Fris Vodka, Bombay Sapphire Gin, Captain Morgan Spiced Rum, Johnnie Walker Black Label Scotch, Jack Daniels Bourbon Whiskey, Crown Royal Whiskey, Jose Cuervo 1800 Tequila, Courvoisier VS Brandy
Super-premium	Highest quality of spirits; most expensive liquors; liquors are aged longer, distilled in an incredibly pure way, or have elaborate marketing campaigns.	Johnny Walker Red Label Scotch, Belvedere Vodka, Grey Goose Vodka, single malt scotches, Patrón Tequila, Hangar One Vodka, Gentleman Jack Bourbon

We'd love to tell you exactly how to price each category of drinks. But given that we have no idea about the prices in your neighborhood, not to mention the logistical problems involved in printing them all in this less-than-400-page book, we can tell you to do your research. Don't feel greedy because remember, you have to cover way more than just the cost of your liquor with your drink prices. You have to cover ice, garnishes, glassware, rent, salaries — the list goes on and on.

If you stock high-end cordials, cognacs, and scotch, you can pay hundreds of dollars for a single bottle. Set special prices for these special items.

Do not overprice your drinks, or you will have no business. Do not underprice your drinks, or you will go out of business! Balance is the key here. Check out your area for prices because in order to succeed, you must be within the price range of your competitors. So do your homework.

Designing and Printing Your Menus

After you've decided what you actually want to sell to your patrons, you have to decide how you want to let them know what you have to offer. Most bar owners have a few different menu formats, so this section helps you figure out what you want yours to look like.

For help in laying out your menu, take a look *Advertising For Dummies,* 2nd Edition, by Gary Dahl (Wiley). Many of the techniques used to design ads are also used to create menus. Plus, you can get some good ideas on how to advertise your business.

Experimenting with layout

As with choosing your menu items, simple is best when it comes to *laying out* (designing what the physical menu is going to look like) the menu. Make it easy for your customers to decide what they want to order by following these basic guidelines:

- ✔ **Choose formatting carefully.** Use options like *italics,* **bold,** CAPITALIZATION, and <u>underlining</u> sparingly and only for emphasis. Remember: You're creating a menu, not a ransom note.

- ✔ **Separate your food menu from your drink menu.** You can choose to place one menu on each side of the same piece of paper so patrons can just flip the sheet over. Or you can have a separate sheet for each menu.

- ✔ **Group like items together.** Place beers together, cordials together, martinis together, shooters together, and so on. This format makes it easy for patrons to find what they're thirsty for.

- ✔ **Create clear headings that tell patrons what they can find in each section.** This also helps people find what they want. You can even use descriptors as headings, rather than traditional beverage categories. For example, instead of just "Draft Beer," you can have subcategories that describe the different styles of beer and their tastes. So if a patron's in the mood for something "crisp and light," they can look for that description and select a beer to match.

Menu engineering basics

Menu engineering is the strategy of laying out your menu to encourage your patrons to order the items you want them to buy, often the items with the highest profit margins. Choose where you want to place the items on the menu and what fonts, graphics, and formatting you want to use to highlight various items.

The first place patrons look is the middle of the upper half of your menu. Place your high-profit items here to increase your sales. Take a look at Figure 9-1 to see this spot. You can also use graphic icons to highlight signature dishes or other specialty items on your menu. And research shows that in a long list of menu items, the first, second, and last items are typically the most often chosen.

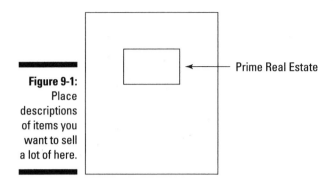

Prime Real Estate

Figure 9-1:
Place
descriptions
of items you
want to sell
a lot of here.

Writing the menu text

Writing menu text is similar to writing a commercial for your menu items. Think about selling the cocktail to your patron. Tell them what's in it (our house-infused, lime-coconut vodka), how it's prepared (shaken with crushed ice and cream of coconut), what it tastes like (crisp and refreshing), and so on. Consider telling them how they'll feel when they're drinking it (refreshed after a hot day).

Descriptive text is always better than a boring listing of drinks. The menu description is your chance to show patrons why your cocktails (and other menu items) are special and something they can't get just anywhere.

Placing your menus in the bar

If you want patrons to use your menu, you have to make them visible. Many times patrons will order something they're familiar with, without ever looking at your drink menu. Make menus easy to access for all your patrons.

Specials boards

A *specials board* is a chalkboard, dry-erase board, or other placard that allows you to quickly write down the, um, specials each day and display them prominently for guests and staff members alike to view. You can post them by the front door, over the bar, or on an easy-to-see wall.

Table tents

A *table tent* is a small menu that stands alone on a table or at various points along the bar, with a listing of menu items. Often, table tents promote specials or list your signature drinks. Unless you have a small menu (like just a few appetizers), table tents are typically too small to list all your menu items.

You can choose table tents made out of card stock that lasts for a while, and then toss them when they get soiled. Or you can buy table tent card holders made of clear plastic. You can easily swap out the cards as you change specials or decide to promote something else. Take a look at Figure 9-2 for an example of a table tent.

Don't forget that your liquor distributors may be willing to give you table tent holders adorned with their logos for free.

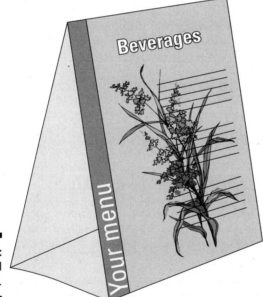

Figure 9-2:
A typical
table tent.

Make sure staff members wipe down table tent covers regularly (at least once per day). These things can get grimy, and nothing is less appetizing than thinking about ordering food, only to pick up a filthy menu.

Drink menus

Many bars have menus that include all their spirits, wine, and beer offerings. Make them available and accessible to all your patrons.

Food menus

Decide how visible you want your food menus. If you want to sell lots of food, make sure you have the menus out where patrons can use them. Consider including a food menu as one side of a table tent.

Making Changes to Your Menu

Every bar changes its menu at some point. So it's not a questions of *if* you'll change your menu, but *when* you'll change your menu.

Here are a few things to consider as you decide to change your menu:

- ✔ **Give your opening menu a chance to work.** Allow at least a month or so to let your patrons try several things and find their favorites.

- ✔ **Avoid a *tiered menu pricing system*** (meaning all menu items in a category, such as appetizers, are priced the same). If you vary your prices, you can offer a wider range of items to satisfy a more-diverse clientele.

- ✔ **Consider seasonal specialties.** You may include chili on your fall and winter menus but remove it during the spring and summer, for example. Maybe a variety of mojitos dominate your menu in the summer, but coffee drinks come into play in cold-weather months.

- ✔ **Commemorate holidays.** You can create a special margarita menu to coincide with Cinco de Mayo. Or develop an all-Irish food menu to commemorate St. Patrick's Day.

- ✔ **Consider what other bars in your area are serving.** Keep a constant eye on your competition. You should know about their happy hours, promotions, food menus, and anything else they are offering their (and your!) patrons.

- ✔ **Stay true to your goals and mission.** Don't veer from your vision of your bar to simply follow the crowd, making your bar like every other bar in town. If you believe in your concept and are running your business well, you will be successful.

- ✔ **Make changes sparingly.** We recommend that you change your menu no more than four times a year. That's really the maximum. Most bars change their menus twice a year at most.

- ✔ **Run specials to try out potential new menu items.** Talk to patrons who order the specials to get their feedback. Consider sending out samples to your regulars free of charge to let them try new drinks or dishes so you can get their opinions.

Never change your entire menu all at once. Change can be very unsettling to your patrons. They come to your place for a reason. They may not come back if they can't get their favorites.

Don't forget that when you change your menu, you have to reprint the darn thing. Save yourself some time and trouble by opting for plastic, leather, or vinyl menu sleeves or holders. Then you can just swap out pages as you need to, instead of reprinting the entire thing. Plus, menus in holders are much easier to keep clean and reuse than the plain paper variety when the beer foam flows!

Part III
Employees, Customers, and Products: Managing the "Right Stuff"

The 5th Wave   By Rich Tennant

Joe's Bar & Grill

"So once I add the floating volume rate to my accumulated reserve assets and divide by the annualized ratio, I'll realize a profit. It still looks like a $6 tip on an $85 tab."

In this part . . .

We help you hire and train the best people, and we show you how to make *the* biggest difference in your business today — by practicing the fine and very necessary art of customer service. Part of providing good customer service is knowing your products, so we cover that aspect in this part, too.

Chapter 10

Hiring, Training, and Keeping Your Employees

. . . .

In This Chapter

▶ Deciding which employees you need

▶ Hiring the right people for the job

▶ Training your new staff

▶ Terminating employees

. . . .

*B*ars tend to take on the personality of the people who work there. So you should make sure that the people you hire match the feel of your bar. If you're creating a fun, high-energy place to hang out, you have to have fun, high-energy people working in it.

In this chapter, we cover different staff positions in the bar and give you tips on how to choose the best candidates to fill them. We explain how to train your new staff members and keep them on your payroll for the long term. And finally, we give you advice for how to end your relationship with employees who aren't working out.

Identifying the Players on Your Team

Most bar owners need several kinds of employees to staff their bars: bartenders, servers, and cooks. Bartenders make drinks. Servers serve drinks. Cooks make the occasional pub grub order. We've expanded this team roster a bit in this section to include a few extra players, just in case you need some additional help. Feel free to read the parts that apply to your bar and skip the rest.

Generally speaking you need one server for every four to five tables in your bar. And you need two bartenders for every 15 stools. That way you have plenty (but not too much) help to make drinks for servers and for patrons sitting at the bar. If you *overstaff* (or have too many staff members on duty), no one makes money and good staff members will leave.

Front of the house: Bartenders, servers, hostesses, and security staff

The *front of the house* in bar-speak is anywhere in your bar that a customer may venture. It includes the bar, any dining areas, the stage, the restrooms, and so on. Employees who work in the front of the house (often abbreviated in written form FOH) represent you and your bar at all times, so they need a few common characteristics.

FOH employees must be

- ✔ **Polite:** FOH employees should generally be "nice." It seems like a no-brainer, but it's important.

- ✔ **Friendly:** They should have a warm smile and be welcoming. They should make people feel comfortable the minute they walk in the door.

- ✔ **Well groomed:** In general, employees should be clean, odor free, and not scraggly. Set your grooming standards and make sure everyone adheres to them. For more help, see the section "Creating standards and keeping them up," later in this chapter.

- ✔ **Able to evoke the feeling of your bar:** This characteristic is probably the most subjective one. Consider, though, would you expect a yuppie bartender at a biker bar, or vice versa? Would you expect an elegant server at a poolside bar? Consider the feel of your bar as you're hiring your staff.

In the next sections we give you details on what to look for specifically when hiring for certain positions in the FOH.

Bartenders

What would a bar be without someone to lovingly tend it? Bartenders make or break bars, without question. Your bartenders are key employees. They must be good with customers. They must project the right image for your bar. And of course, they must be able to mix a good drink.

Bartenders become friends, counselors, and godparents to their patrons. They are the heart and soul of every bar. They can be gorgeous (as in the movie *Coyote Ugly*), they can be entertaining (like in *Cocktail*), and they can become like family (think *Cheers*). All the bartenders in these examples have charisma and charm. They draw people to them, keep them at the bar, and, more importantly, keep them coming back.

Here are a few things to look for when hiring your next bartender. A good bartender should be able to

- ✔ **Socialize while working.** The best bartenders are those who make it look effortless. If an applicant can keep up a conversation with a customer at the bar and make cocktails for the party of ten that just walked in, hire him.

  You don't want bartenders socializing at the *expense* of working. Drinks that are waiting to be made are drinks that are waiting to be drunk. Customers can't order another until they're finished with the first (and that's the whole point, right?). So making drinks has to be the number-one priority.

- ✔ **Develop regular customers.** Regular customers mean repeat business. ("Norm!") Repeat business means more money for you (unless of course you let them run a tab that they don't pay). Look for a bartender who connects with people. She should be able to read people and hold down conversations with anyone who may come into your place.

- ✔ **Handle difficult situations.** Unfortunately, when alcohol is involved, life can get even more complicated than normal. Your bartender should know when to refuse service to an intoxicated patron, anticipate service problems, and be willing to get help from other staff members appropriately.

- ✔ **Make a good drink.** Last but not least, your bartender should be schooled in the art of mixology. He may not know every cocktail ever mixed, but he should be able to make your signature drinks (or have a quick aptitude for learning). Consider whether you want or need creativity in the drink-making department. Some bars benefit from having a creative bartender who whips up nightly specials, while others do better with sticking to the basics.

If you run across a candidate who you think has the potential but not the experience to run your bar, consider the person for a barback position. A *barback* helps a bartender stock and restock the bar, empty the trash, and wash glasses. He typically helps out with everything except making drinks during a shift. This experience can help a new bartender get familiar with the pace of your place before being thrown into the fire of running his own shift.

Servers

Sometimes called waiters or waitresses, servers take orders and serve drinks and food to patrons. Servers need to have all the FOH characteristics listed earlier in this section, and then some. They are responsible for selling your products to your patrons. The revenue you bring in is a direct reflection of how good they are at their job.

Check out this list of server-specific qualifications to look for when hiring:

- **Aptitude for learning your products:** A good server knows your liquors, wines, and beers inside and out. If patrons ask her what's on tap, she should be able to tell them, instead of simply handing them a beer menu. (Of course, if you have 50-plus beers on tap, a menu is quite helpful to your patrons, but your servers should still be familiar with all of them.)

  Knowing the products is the first step; recommending them appropriately is something else. Quality recommendations come with experience and education. Assume your patron is looking for a crisp, hoppy beer. If the server recommends a stout, your patron probably isn't going to enjoy it and may not give you another chance to make him happy.

- **Ability to develop regular customers:** Many servers, like bartenders, develop customers who come back to see them again and again (whether they like it or not). Customers are drawn toward happy, positive people. Look for upbeat, friendly people to fill these positions.

- **Organized and efficient:** In a bar atmosphere, servers experience different demands than they do in a restaurant. In a bar, a server may have drinks for six separate tables on a single tray. In a bar, patrons move around more than in a restaurant, so being able to keep track of who ordered what and where they've moved to is a requirement. A good bar server remembers faces, orders, and who has paid for what.

Hosts, hostesses, and greeters

These employees greet your customers as they come in the door and show them to their seats. You're more likely to employ these particular people if you run a tavern or bar and grill.

Helpful qualities in a greeter include:

- **Friendly and approachable:** If a person doesn't smile easily and genuinely, you probably don't want her. A greeter may be the first and last person your customers see in your establishment, so you want a greeter who will give them a warm welcome and heartfelt so long.

✔ **Effective at communicating:** To keep a busy bar running smoothly, all employees need to be able to work together to handle their areas. As the first link in the chain, a greeter should communicate well with customers and other employees. Greeters can inform guests about drink specials, upcoming promotions (like a special live band), or discuss seating options (like outdoor, at the bar, or pub tables). They can also help servers by giving them seating updates on new guests in their sections.

✔ **Excellent organization skills:** Greeters often answer phones, take to-go orders, coordinate seating with managers, and handle minor customer concerns simultaneously. They must stay organized and composed during the organized chaos.

Security staff

Club security or bouncers have long been hired for their larger-than-life size and their physical intimidation factor. Owners hoped that by hiring huge body builders, they would reduce the number of incidents because people would be afraid to mess with them. That theory is changing somewhat as more bars and clubs look for improved communication and problem-solving skills in security personnel.

Security guards, first and foremost, control who gets into your bar. They must be able to recognize and identify fake identification, keep underage people from getting in, and screen incoming patrons for potential problems. In a worst-case scenario, they help you handle any problems.

An effective bouncer can help you head off incidents before they become big problems. A good security person has

✔ **Effective communication skills:** This idea may be new to some people who have been in the bar business for a while, but the ability to talk to customers, including those who are intoxicated or potentially violent, is the best first step in avoiding a fight or other incident.

In a worst-case scenario, a guard who has effective communication skills can help discuss the details of a bad situation with the authorities, should the need arise. You need complete documentation of any incidents, from calling a cab for a patron to breaking up a fight, so make sure your guards can recall and accurately record the details. Take a look at Chapter 3 for details on what your documentation should look like to protect yourself.

✔ **A quick wit:** It may seem strange, but having a sense of humor can help diffuse tense situations. Although you don't want someone who is extremely sarcastic and will alienate patrons or cause a situation to escalate, someone with quick one-liners can often keep things on an even keel. ("Yes, I know the owner too. In fact. he pays me to keep relatives and friends out!")

✔ **The ability to make appropriate decisions:** Throwing someone out of the bar is not always the answer. A good security guard needs to have other tools in his repertoire. Ask the potential guard about how he's handled difficult situations in the past. How has he resolved them? Does his solution match your philosophy? Also, ask him about a few scenarios to see how he would react.

Here are a few scenarios you can use as examples to get started:

- A patron hands you a fake ID. What do you do?

- A couple is engaged in a heated argument in the bar. What do you do?

- A potential patron offers you money to get into the bar without waiting in the long line. What's your reaction?

- A patron may be using illegal drugs in your establishment. What do you do?

✔ **Physical presence:** Presence doesn't mean the guard has to look like they spend 15 hours a day lifting weights and taking steroids. But the guard should have a cool confidence that tells people, "I am in charge. Don't mess with me because you won't win."

Don't hire bullies or showoffs. Watch all new security staff members closely for a week. Check them all out with the local and state police. If you have complaints about them from customers, investigate the complaints immediately. If you have to replace them, replace them.

✔ **A neat, clean appearance:** A great security person will not have long hair or lots of *bling* (flashy necklaces or jewelry). These items can be used against a security person and a good one knows it.

Unless you have a security background, it's very hard to train a security person yourself. Retired police, fire, and security people are the best choice to train others and keep on your payroll.

It's your name, reputation, money, and liquor license on the line, so make sure any guards or bouncers you hire properly represent you and consistently act in your best interest.

Back of the house: Cooks and dishwashers

The *back of the house* (or BOH) describes any part of your bar where guests can't go. Typically, it refers to the kitchen and the office. Employees who work in the BOH can be less friendly than your FOH (front of the house) staff, but they should still be focused on customer satisfaction.

Most bars can do without a chef. If you feel like you need one, take a look at *Running a Restaurant For Dummies* (Wiley) for details on hiring the right chef for your business.

Cooks

In bars, the kind (and number of) cooks you need greatly depends on your type of bar. (Take a look at Chapter 4 for help deciding what kind of bar you want to run.) Assuming you have a standard pub grub menu, you'll likely need a couple of line cooks. *Line cooks* prepare food as guests order it. You may also need a *prep cook* (a cook who comes in before busy shifts to chop vegetables or make soups, for example). Your menu (see Chapter 9 for help with this) and your type of bar will dictate how many cooks and which types you need, but the requirements for hiring them are similar.

Here's what to look for in a good bar cook:

- ✔ **Punctuality:** You need someone who will be there on time, every time.

- ✔ **Willingness to learn:** You need someone who is open to doing things the way you want them done. Ideally, look for someone who eventually wants to take on some responsibility for what goes on in the kitchen. Ultimately, he may be able to order food supplies and write new menus.

- ✔ **Previous experience:** If you have a small kitchen, you have to have qualified employees. You should hire cooks with experience, unless you're willing to spend a lot of time training them.

- ✔ **Positive attitude:** Cooks don't have to be "people people," but they have to be able to deal with the stress and chaos that goes with working in a bar kitchen. They'll need to be able to deal with misordered food, quickly replace dropped and spilled items, and respond to a whole host of other problems. Having a naturally positive attitude goes a long way in this business.

Dishwashers

Despite the lack of glamour, dishwashers are essential if you serve any food whatsoever. You need someone who can keep the dirty plates from stacking up, the trashcans from overflowing, and the floors from becoming slippery.

When you're looking for a dishwasher, pay attention to these characteristics:

- ✔ **Good work history (if they have a work history):** This position can be a great starting place for someone who wants to get into the bar or restaurant business, so don't discount someone because she doesn't have a lot of experience. But if she does have a work history, make sure it's a positive one.

✔ **Punctuality:** Again, your dishwasher needs to be on time, every time.

✔ **Necessary physical attributes:** Dishwashing is a physically demanding job. A person must be able to stand for long periods of time, lift heavy loads, and carry stacks of dishes without dropping them.

Managers

Depending on the size of your restaurant, you may be the only manager, at least for a while. But we recommend that you get at least one other person to help with these duties as soon as you possibly can, just so you can have some semblance of a life. Managers supervise employees, ensure the bar is running smoothly, and communicate with customers. They manage schedules, inventory levels, purchasing practices, and sanitation policies. They are essential to keep your business running well. If things are going right, the owner's doing his job; if things are going wrong *the manager* is to blame.

When you're ready to take the plunge and hand over some of the control to another manager, here's what you should look for:

✔ **Punctuality:** Okay, this may seem totally obvious, but sometimes the bar business gets a little lax on this particular point. But remember, a manager sets the expectation, and employees don't deal effectively with the "do as I say, not as I do" mentality.

✔ **Integrity:** You need someone you can trust to take care of your bar the way you want it taken care of. You should be able to trust the person with your money and your business while you're away.

✔ **Positive work history:** Definitely check references and make sure anyone on your management team has glowing reviews.

✔ **Previous experience:** Anyone in management should have extensive experience in a bar, restaurant, or hotel. Now, having said that, some hospitality schools are cranking out qualified candidates who may not have management experience but could be considered for management-trainee positions.

Finding the Right Employees

Staffing your bar with quality people isn't easy. In this business, you're not just competing for the public's drinking dollar; you're also competing for the best staff. You have to sort through lots of candidates to find the ones who best suit your business. In this section, we show you how to find, interview, and choose the right employees for you.

Sourcing potential employees

Never has the hospitality industry had so many ways to find employees at all different levels than it does now. Gone are the days of hanging a "Help Wanted" sign in your window and waiting. You have Web sites, recruiters, and organizations all dedicated to hiring and training hospitality workers. In this section, we give you the inside scoop on finding the right candidates for your bar today.

The newspaper

The newspaper is still a great way to get local applicants who want to work today. You can advertise for any position in the newspaper, from dishwasher to manager, and get a decent response. The day you place the ad, be ready with a stack of applications because lots of restaurant and bar people are constantly looking for greener grass at the bar around the corner. Even if you don't have tons of positions, you're likely to get swamped with applicants when you first open.

Feel free to hang on to applications and resumes for candidates who are qualified for positions you don't currently have open. There's always a chance that someone you hire may not work out, so it's nice to have a backup plan. But, remember, the would-be employee is looking for a job *now* and if they're a good candidate for you, they're likely a good candidate for someone else too. Don't wait too long (more than 3–6 months) or so if you really want them.

The Internet

Consider placing an ad or searching for applicants through job placement Web sites. Although these services are usually free to applicants, they're not free to employers. Don't let that discourage you though. Good help is hard to find, and you just may need to pay a little for it.

Here are a few of our favorites Web sites for finding qualified candidates:

- ✔ **Hcareers, `www.hcareers.com`:** As of this printing, this online database has nearly 400,000 subscribers and charges a maximum of $375 for a single, 45-day job posting. Rates are discounted for multiple postings and resume searching.

- ✔ **Hospitality Career Network, `www.hospitalitycareernetwork.com`:** The network currently boasts 58,000 active job seekers on its Web site and charges $200 for a single job posting for 90 days.

- ✔ **CareerBuilder, `www.careerbuilder.com`:** Many local papers are hooked into Careerbuilder.com, so if you place an ad in the paper, your ad goes to this online site as well. The price for these ads varies based on your location.

✔ **Monster, www.monster.com:** Possibly the best-known job hunting Web site, Monster is a good choice for the hospitality industry, too. Many job seekers are looking for a career and start in bars and restaurants until they can find a "real job." They end up bringing career drive to their part-time job and staying because they truly love it. Monster is a good way to reach people who may not realize the bar business could be just what they're looking for.

You can place ads and search for applicants through these Web sites. Separate fees apply, of course, but it may be a good idea to actively search for candidates who meet your requirements rather than wait for them to find you.

If you live in a larger metro area, take a look at the Web sites for your local TV stations. Some allow you to place free job postings online. Also consider online community bulletin boards, such as Craigslist at www.craigslist.org, if you live in a city with listings. In some cities, you can post jobs for free!

Recruiters

Recruiters are a great way to find high-end hospitality talent. Recruiters, sometimes known as headhunters, scour the country looking for applicants to fill specialized positions. They often charge 10 to 25 percent of the candidate's starting salary in exchange for their services. If you're looking to simply staff standard positions in your bar, skip this method and choose another.

Bartending schools

Many wanna-be bartenders attend a school to learn the basics. Most programs consist of about 40 hours of classroom and bar experience. Students are tested on cocktail recipes, opening and closing procedures, and other must-have bar skills, and they usually complete any required alcohol safety certifications during their class time.

Most bartending schools offer placement services for their students upon graduation. Contact a school near you for details on its programs and fees, if any.

Here's a list of nationwide bartending schools that may offer training to students in your area:

✔ **ABC Bartending Schools:** www.abcbartending.com

✔ **Bartending College:** www.bartendingcollege.com

✔ **Professional Bartending Schools of America:** www.pbsa.com

Word of mouth

As with many other businesses, in the bar business, people network with each other. Because bar and restaurant people work similar hours, they socialize with each other. Ask other bartenders or waitstaff for their recommendations for new staff members. If one of your best servers recommends someone to you, you can expect that she knows the person is qualified.

Liquor-company representatives are very good sources of potential employees. They are in other bars and taverns all day and are more than willing to help you. They are the best; they know which bartenders and servers are leaving or unhappy with their current situation.

Interviewing candidates

After you have a good selection of applicants, decide on your system for interviewing candidates. If you're hiring several staff members at the same time, like when you're first opening a bar, you may conduct a first, brief interview just to screen out who not to hire. Then, use the second round to get down to more details about individual candidates.

The interviewing process generally goes like this:

1. An applicant comes in and fills out an application.

2. Assuming the applicant looks good on paper, you, as the manager, meet with him and screen him, asking general questions about experience, goals, and schedule availability.

3. If you think the person is a good fit for your place, you can ask some more-specific questions during this interview or schedule another. For great second-tier questions, check out "Selecting the best applicants for your bar" later in this chapter.

If you have the time to spend with each candidate, you can have more-extensive conversations, role-play if necessary, and consolidate steps 2 and 3 into one interview.

Testing bartenders and servers before hiring them

Assuming you want experienced bartenders and servers, we strongly recommend that you give them a written test during the interview process. Although testing is not a silver bullet to definitively choose the prime candidates, it can weed out some posers. Take a look at Figure 10-1 and Figure 10-2 for sample screening tests for bartenders and servers, respectively.

1. What kind of liquor is Dewars? _____
_____

2. Name two drinks you'd serve in a snifter.
_____
_____

3. What does "añejo" mean? _____
_____

4. What style of beer would you recommend if a patron wants something "rich and creamy"? _____
_____

5. Describe the following drink instructions.
Dirty _____
Tall _____
Double _____
Dry _____
Blended _____
Up _____
Presbyterian _____

6. Name two glasses you could serve a martini in. When would you choose one over the other? _____
_____
_____

7. What's in a Mojito? _____
_____

8. List three liquors (or liqueurs) often paired with coffee.
_____
_____
_____

9. What's the difference between a Kir and a Kir Royale? _____
_____

10. If you add Grand Marnier to a cocktail, what flavor do you impart to it?
_____

Figure 10-1:
Sample
bartender
screening
test.

1. Name common garnishes for the following drinks.
Wheat beer _____
Mojio _____
Margarita _____
Bloody Mary _____
Gin and Tonic _____
Amaretto Sour _____

2. What's the difference between a Gibson and a Gimlet? _____
_____

3. What two drinks combine to make a Boilermaker?
_____   _____

4. Your customer orders a martini. Name three follow up questions should you ask?
_____
_____
_____

5. Name three premium gins.
_____
_____
_____

6. Name a liquor that goes well with Red Bull. Why would someone drink this?
_____

7. Define these terms:
Rocks _____
Float _____
Virgin _____
Up _____
Dirty _____

8. What's the difference between a Bloody Mary, a Bloody Maria, and a Bloody Bull?
_____
_____

9. Name three brands of bottled malt beverages on the market.
_____
_____
_____

10. What's in a Tom Collins? _____
_____

Figure 10-2:
Sample
server
screening
test.

Selecting the best applicants for your bar

If candidates pass the screening interview and the written test, the next interview gets down to the nitty-gritty. During an interview, you obviously ask prospective staff members questions about their experience and availability. But also pay attention to their body language, communication style, and ability to carry on a conversation. You want employees in your bar to be engaging, interesting, and comfortable speaking to people.

Here's a list of detailed questions you can ask potential candidates to get that next level of detail about them and how they might fit with your place:

- ✔ Name a difficult situation you've faced at work. How did you resolve it?
- ✔ How do you handle difficult customers?
- ✔ Why are you the right person for this job?
- ✔ What bars do you like to hang out at? How is this one the same or different?

Never, ever ask candidates about their religion, marital status, sexual orientation, age, gender, race, political affiliation, nationality, or whether they have children. To do so invites a lawsuit. You can't ask them about their disabilities, but you can describe the physical requirements of the job and ask if they have any concerns about their responsibilities. Check out the Equal Employment Opportunity Commission's Web site at www.eeoc.gov for details about what may constitute discrimination. Make sure that everyone who hires in your organization is familiar with the EEOC requirements, too. You're responsible for their actions on your behalf.

Making the job offer

When you think you've found the right employees, extend them an offer. Discuss their pay, regular schedule, a start date, and their training schedule with them. Make sure they know what they need to wear when they come in on their first day.

Pay is not typically negotiable for FOH staff members. Servers typically make one-half of minimum wage plus tips. In most cases, servers make minimum wage while they're in training and take no tips. It gives them an incentive to get up to speed quickly so they can run their own shifts. Bartenders make minimum wage plus tips. You may negotiate different hourly rates for BOH staff members, based on the experience level and requirements for your kitchen, but a general range is minimum wage for dishwashers and $8–$10 per hour for cooks.

In most cases, restaurant employees start on the first Monday (assuming you're open then) after they're hired. Start them out during your slowest times to give them some time to get used to the pace of your business.

Must-have forms for hiring staff members

As soon as you hire your staff, give them a copy of your employee manual with all of your policies and procedures (see the "Creating standards and keeping them up" section). Have them sign a document confirming that they received a copy and agree to follow the rules of your place. Have them complete any other necessary paperwork before their first shift.

We recommend you keep these forms on hand for new employees.

- ✔ **I-9:** Also known as the Employment Eligibility Form, every employee must complete the I-9 in order to work legally in this country. Employers must keep these documents on file for three years after hiring or one year after the end of employment. We think it's a good idea to keep them on file for every employee at all times, no matter how long they've been employed by you.

- ✔ **W-4:** These forms tell the IRS how much tax to withhold from each paycheck. The fewer dependents that an employee claims, the greater the amount of tax that comes out of her check.

- ✔ **Attendance calendar:** This form isn't a government requirement, but it helps you have a place to quickly jot down sick days, vacation days, days off, late arrivals, and early departures. If your computer system synchs up with your time clock, you may be able to keep track of this more easily on the computer.

- ✔ **Emergency contact card:** Also not a requirement but very handy in case of, um, an emergency. You also get a backup number to track down an AWOL employee.

Create a separate file for each employee. Keep copies of all these forms as well as their employment application, résumé, notes from their mom, and any other documentation that may come up in the course of business.

Training New Employees

In the world of bars and restaurants, there are as many ways to do things as there are owners and managers. Even when you hire experienced employees, you need to train them to do things the way you want them done. Hiring experienced employees generally cuts down on the time it takes them to learn your specific systems though.

When you start training, assume your employees don't know anything about your business. Tell them exactly how you want them to do things.

We recommend you give new employees

- ✔ Written materials to read and refer back to
- ✔ Hands-on experience to practice and hone their skills
- ✔ A mentoring structure to have someone to go to with questions

Training is expensive but necessary. Do it right the first time and hopefully you'll keep your people around and not have to train another batch right away.

Creating standards and keeping them up

Written standards are the most foolproof way to maintain consistency. If someone can look up your vacation policy and see it written in black and white, you're likely have fewer discussions about the rules and exceptions to them.

Using an employee manual

An *employee manual* describes your company's rules and procedures for every employee. This documentation is the same for all employees, whether they work in the FOH or BOH (front or back of the house, respectively) and are a supervisor or staff member. An employee manual is the best way to communicate your expectations for behavior, dress, level of service, and more to your newest employees. Make sure each new employee gets a copy of the manual on Day 1. Have them sign a form agreeing that they received a copy of the manual to review.

Standard items that make an appearance in many employee manuals include

- ✔ Welcome letter
- ✔ Mission statement
- ✔ Company history
- ✔ Orientation period
- ✔ Communication policies
- ✔ Performance and job standards
- ✔ Code of ethics
- ✔ Confidentiality policies

✔ Emergency procedures

✔ Drug and alcohol policies

✔ Antiharassment policies

✔ Customer-service program

✔ Problem-solving procedures

✔ Safety issues

✔ Training meetings

✔ Performance evaluations

✔ Performance rewards

✔ Food-safety procedures

✔ Other policies

The employee manual is your best tool to communicate all the rules to every employee in a consistent way.

Training for job-specific functions

In addition to understanding how things work in your bar, your new employees need to know how to do their jobs in your bar. An *operations manual* helps you train employees to perform specific duties for each position. Thoroughly explain each position, including the duties, standards, and objectives. Tell them what they're here to do, how to do it, when to do it, your quality standards, and so on.

Be as detailed as possible when creating your operations manual. Employees can refer to it during and after training for questions that come up.

Here are some examples of what you should include in your operations manuals for different positions:

✔ **Bartenders:** Bartenders need the details on your recipes for cocktails, inventory procedures, opening and closing procedures, standards of service, cash-handling procedures, comp drink policies, responsible alcohol-service guidelines, and anything else you need them to know.

✔ **Servers:** Detail for your servers information about the products you sell (including all liquor, wine, beer, and spirits). Include copies of all food and drink menus. Give them detailed opening and closing procedures.

✔ **Kitchen staff:** Unless you have a very large kitchen with many different positions, you can probably have a single operations manual for your kitchen. Include opening and closing procedures, details on using different pieces of equipment, and food-safety information.

Providing on-the-job training

In the bar business, you can memorize all the drink recipes, practice carrying trays, and pretend to be doing the job all you want. But until you actually do it, you don't really know how to do it. There's just no substitute for doing the job itself. So training staff members while they're actually working is a fact of life in the hospitality business.

Consider having new recruits shadow experienced employees for several shifts until they get the hang of the inner workings of your place. In most places, a new employee *trails* or shadows an experienced employee for a week. By the last shift in the week, the experienced server is trailing the newbie just to make sure they have the systems down before they're running their own section.

Developing a mentoring program

Many successful bar owners develop their staff by creating a hierarchy. For example, giving one bartender the title of "Head Bartender" and making him the primary contact for new bar staff members helps you in several significant ways:

- ✔ It develops supervisory skills in your experienced bartender, possibly preparing him to take on more responsibility as your business grows and expands.

- ✔ It gives new staff members an immediate resource to get answers to their questions.

- ✔ It keeps training consistent because all trainees are hearing the same information the same way.

- ✔ It frees you up to handle the millions of other things that are constantly going on in your bar.

You can develop trainers in every area of your bar, as you need them. Choose people who handle the ebb and flow of business well, handle their own responsibilities with ease, and are willing to help other people practice their skills.

Improving Employee Performance

A successful bar is staffed by happy, hardworking people. Keep them in the know and constantly challenged to keep them satisfied. You can motivate them by providing opportunities for improving their skills and rewarding their performance.

Growing employee skill sets

Your bar's success depends on keeping staff members informed about your business, products, changes, specials, and promotions. You can keep employees happy and satisfied with their job through ongoing opportunities to learn more about their jobs, their co-workers' jobs, and the industry.

Here are some simple ways to help your employees improve their skills and knowledge:

- ✔ **Hold regular staff meetings:** Set aside time to communicate with your staff regularly. Many restaurants use a daily premeal meeting to discuss what's going on that day. You can implement a similar schedule in your bar. Discuss drink promotions, nightly entertainment, and any special events (such as conventions, for example) going on in your area that may affect business that day. Have monthly meetings to discuss more global issues that affect your bar's systems and processes, menu changes, or staff changes.

- ✔ **Encourage cross-training for other positions:** The most valuable employees are those who can do several different jobs. They can jump in and help out when another employee doesn't show up. They provide scheduling flexibility for vacation time, limited schedules, and *swing shifts* (that is, shifts that stretch beyond a single "normal" meal period like 11 a.m. to 9 p.m., for example).

  But more importantly, to the employee anyway, cross-training offers additional opportunities for exposure to different parts of the business. For example, servers often want to learn to be bartenders. It may take them awhile to get up to the speed of the most experienced bartender on your staff, but cross-training them can help them understand more about mixing drinks, how spirits differ, and what flavors work together (and what don't), and open up new worlds to them.

  One of the greatest benefits of cross-training employees is the empathy that develops. If a server has an idea of what it's like to be behind the bar with servers impatiently demanding drinks, she's less likely to be so demanding when she's on the other side.

- ✔ **Encourage continuing education:** Unless you run some megabar corporation, you probably can't offer full tuition reimbursement for a complete four-year degree in bar management for every staff member. But you may be able to help students and lifelong learners in other ways:

  - • Post information on your staff bulletin board about relevant seminars and classes. Look to your local community colleges for personal enrichment classes in bar-related topics, such as "Wine tasting for beginners."

  - • Schedule training for staff members with your liquor, wine, and beer salespeople.

- • Develop a library of professional resources that staff members can check out. Include books on customer service, bar management, and mixology, among others.

✔ **Offer advancement opportunities:** Give employees a goal to work toward and they often will. Of course, you need more Indians than chiefs in any organization, so you can't promote them all, but if your employees see that you reward hard work with increased responsibility, it gives them incentive to keep reaching.

Motivating your staff

Motivating your staff is essential to keeping them. And ultimately, giving them respect is the best way to motivate them. People who feel that they are heard and appreciated are much more likely to stay in a position than those who feel insignificant and disrespected.

Here are a few specific ideas for keeping your staff motivated:

✔ **Encourage staff communication with you:** Don't just say you have an open-door policy. Actually mean it. Be willing to listen to their concerns and ideas.

✔ **Offer constructive criticism in private:** Almost all employees need to work on some aspect of their performance at some time or another. Make sure your criticism is constructive and discreet. So instead of saying, "Your drink service is way too slow," privately give them tips on how to speed it up.

✔ **Praise them often in public:** Find something positive to say to every employee publicly every shift. If you're having a hard time finding something positive to say, then you likely need to do more training with them.

✔ **Know your staff and their strengths and weaknesses:** All staff members are not gifted equally. Set them up to succeed by tailoring their responsibilities to match their talents. Have new staff members fully develop skills before throwing them into the mix on their own.

✔ **Be friendly (not friends) with your staff:** Know about their interests and life outside work. If your bartender is a student, ask about his courses. If your cook plays drums in a garage band, ask how rehearsal is going.

Balance your interest with their comfort level. If you're too friendly, they may be uncomfortable. And don't get so involved with the drama that you lose the supervisor-employee balance. Nothing good ever comes from it.

✔ **Encourage camaraderie among your staff:** Make sure staff members are respectful to each other. Encourage them to help (rather than alienate) newcomers. If your core staff is a closed clique, you'll have trouble keeping your new hires. Everyone doesn't have to be friends, but they must be friendly and respectful during working hours.

✔ **Don't lose your cool:** Easier said than done some days in this business. When you see tables full of empty glassware, peanut shells littering the floor, wrecked restrooms, and empty ice wells, you may want to scream. Stress and tension are incredibly infectious. If you lose it, your staff will, too. Keep your composure when handling the inevitable chaos, and you'll win the battle.

✔ **Develop incentive programs:** Bar and restaurant employees love swag and perks. Coordinate contests with staff training events. Say you've just done a training of top-shelf vodkas. Give a preferred parking space to the employee who sells the most on Friday night. If you roll out a new appetizer menu, give a gift certificate to the employee who sells the most in a weekend. Reward kitchen staff members if they hit certain ticket times. Hold a mixology contest and reward the winning bartender with an extra day off.

Incentives don't have to cost you a lot. They just need to be valuable to the people receiving them.

When It Doesn't Work Out: Dismissing Employees

Unfortunately, rules do get broken and consequences ensue, which may include terminating an employee. For your own protection, include a clearly worded policy in the employee manual on how you handle infractions, and follow it to the letter.

Here's the standard sequence of escalating action to follow when problems arise:

1. **Issue a verbal warning:** Make a note in the manager's log and in the employee's file that you discussed the situation.

2. **Issue a formal written warning:** This warning typically describes the behavior, includes a plan for resolving the situation, and details the next steps if the behavior doesn't cease (or improve) immediately. You should have a conversation with the employee, and then have them read the warning, agree to the terms, and sign it. Place the warning in their file.

3. **Suspend the employee:** A suspension may last from a single shift to a week, typically. If you're considering any additional time, you should likely terminate the employee.

4. **Terminate the employee:** If the behavior continues beyond suspension, fire the employee.

You have to decide (and write down for everyone to see) what types of infractions warrant these discipline steps. I've worked in places where this type of a policy is in effect for punctuality and at other places where it's reserved for only very serious breaks in the behavior code.

It may seem obvious, but we're saying it anyway. Do not, we repeat, *do not* discuss any disciplinary situations with nonmanagement staff *ever*. If you do, you risk opening yourself up to a whole lotta drama (including potential lawsuits) if the employee catches wind of your indiscretion. What happens in the office stays in the office!

Looking at causes for immediate termination

Some situations, especially those involving illegal activity and violence, are causes for immediate termination. When the safety of your staff, patrons, and property are involved, you can (and should) skip the multitiered discipline policy described in the previous section and go straight to termination.

Here's a short list of our recommendations for immediate dismissal:

- ✔ Violence toward you, a customer, or another staff member
- ✔ Theft
- ✔ Flagrant rudeness to a customer
- ✔ Drug or alcohol use at work

Considering the legal issues involved

Definitely talk with your attorney before you open your bar to review the basics of employment law in your area. He can help you get the specifics on the regulations related to "termination with cause" and "termination without cause" to make sure you're covering all your bases.

Your best defense is a good offense. Make sure you have clearly written policies that you (and any managers working for you) follow consistently. Document all infractions, training, and disciplinary situations so you can clearly show patterns and present evidence if the need arises.

Changing staffing levels during a business slowdown

In some areas, particularly seasonal resort areas, *staffing up* (or hiring additional people for your busy season) is a given. If you run a bar at an East Coast beach resort, you may hire extra staff between Memorial Day and Labor Day, for example. If your bar is located at a ski resort, your staffing levels may be higher between Halloween and April 1.

Communicate your temporary staffing schedules to staff members when you hire them. Explain the nature of your seasonal business and let them know how long they can expect to work for you. You can avoid the uncomfortable conversation of "you're a great worker, but we don't need you anymore" by being upfront from the beginning.

Chapter 11

Rule #1: Practicing Good Customer Service

. . . .

In This Chapter

▶ Understanding why service makes a difference

▶ Training your staff with an eye toward service

▶ Handling situations when things don't go as planned

. . . .

There's a business adage floating around estimating that it costs you five times more to gain a new customer than to keep an existing one. Although it's a tough statistic to calculate in the bar business, it certainly feels true. Ultimately, you want your customers to be regular customers. Not only that, you want them to bring their friends in and have them become regulars, too.

In this chapter, we unlock the secrets of the elusive art of customer service. We show you why it's more important than ever, even though fewer places practice it consistently. We give you help in forming your own customer service plan from Day 1. And we help you resolve customer service problems with style and grace.

Why Customer Service Is So Important

Customer service is the ability to satisfy your customers' needs and wants. It isn't just important, it's everything! And great customer service is more than just handing your patrons the drinks or food they order with a smile and a "thank you." That's the minimum. You have to exceed their expectations on a regular basis to keep them coming back for more.

With a little luck (and a lot of management), your bar will turn into a great meeting place. People will come in to meet other people and share great food, a great beer, outstanding cocktails, and good conversation. That's what it's all about. You and your staff have to make this happen! After all, as the saying goes, "If you aren't taking care of your customers, your competition will."

A big step toward good customer service is to create an atmosphere of excellence in everything you do. Use the best products. Keep your bar exceedingly clean. Create and maintain standards for food presentation. Require spotless uniforms, clean wait stations, and impeccable service. Don't accept anything less. Check out Chapter 10 for more information on setting standards for your bar.

Making people feel important

Every time a customer walks into your bar, he or she should feel welcomed and wanted. No one should ever feel like you (or any staff members) are doing them a favor by letting them sit at your bar. It should definitely be the other way around.

"Hello" and a smile are the best business card you have. Greeting people by their first or last name makes everyone feel like they belong; it gives them a sense of "This is *my* place."

Here are a few things you can do to help make customers feel important:

- **Listen to your customers.** They want to tell you something because they want you to succeed. Listen and say thank you.

- **Do not start rumors or be a part of a rumor.** If you don't have anything nice to say about someone or something, say nothing.

- **Be prepared to settle arguments.** Always keep a sports almanac, a copy of *Guinness World Records,* or your computer on Google to check facts. Don't take sides. Just fix arguments. If you take sides, you're sure to make two enemies.

- **Be hospitable.** Get regular customers to schedule group luncheons at your place. Try to get their softball team, the local Rotary, Kiwanis, or any service group to have their luncheon meetings at your place. It makes the regular feel special to say, "Come to my bar."

Building customer loyalty

Building customer loyalty means creating regular customers, making people feel like your bar is their bar. Feeling welcomed and appreciated is the key to creating this experience. Everyone who works for you can add to this experience by remembering past orders and experience, calling guests by name, or in a genuine and sincere way, telling them they're glad they stopped in.

One of Heather's friends has a philosophy specifically against using drink specials to build relationships and loyalty with his clientele. He charges regular price for drinks, but then selects people each night to buy drinks for. He walks around talking to people, making sure they're having a great time. Then he offers "the prettiest table he's seen" a round of drinks and thanks them for coming in. (Yes, he is an outrageous flirt, but his customers love him.) Incidentally, he doesn't just buy drinks for women. He buys them for couples, men, and anyone else he'd like to see come back to his place. He says he goes for an intimate experience "that appears to be from the heart." After he gives them that, he claims, "they're mine forever."

It's more special to a patron to buy them a drink personally than to offer $1 off longnecks to everyone who walks in the door. Your customer feels like "Wow, they actually care that I'm here, not just that *someone* is sitting in this bar stool." Personal attention builds customer loyalty.

All I really need to know I learned bartending

About ten years ago, I had a cover on *BARTENDER* magazine. Now you can use it as a customer service plan. This is for you: Make a copy and hang it up for your employees to see. Please don't forget to give me credit. Thanks. Ray Foley

Everything I really need to know about how to exist in this world, personal or business, I learned bartending. This knowledge was shared with me by owners, managers, salesmen, waitresses, waiters, bartenders, and customers. Most of these teachers were successful in life's everyday challenges. These tips you cannot spend; they are the tips you keep for life:

- Give everyone a fair shot.
- If you haven't anything nice to say, don't say it.
- Use the *best* premium products and you'll be the *best*.
- Serve.
- Be the solution to the problem, not part of the problem.

- Don't drink and drive; don't let others.
- Respect salesmen; you're one.
- Don't take sides. You'll make two enemies.
- Be neat.
- Wear a clean shirt every day.
- Don't cheat or steal.
- Smile!
- Keep your hands and fingernails clean.
- Use Mr., Sir, or Ms., when talking to strangers.
- Don't be a part of a rumor.
- Keep your space clean.
- Don't waste.
- Be on time.
- Help others when they're busy.
- Don't use the easy way. Use the right way.
- Don't give up. Follow your dream.

Here are a few other ideas for creating customer loyalty:

✔ Move beyond patron-owner mode, into friend mode. Get to know your customers' families and what's going on in their lives.

✔ Know their business. (Not their personal business, mind you, but their actual profession.) Be ready and able to discuss something you saw on the news that made you think of them.

✔ Buy small, but thoughtful, presents for special occasions, like the birth of a baby, wedding, or anniversary.

✔ Ask about their vacation or business trip.

✔ Know who their significant other is so you can ask about them. Be careful though, as not everyone is in a monogamous relationship. You don't want to be in the middle of relationship discord.

Heather walked into one of her favorite places recently with a friend. Her favorite bar owner greeted her warmly, as always, and then became uncomfortable when he saw her guest (a man he knew was not her husband). She introduced her friend and mentioned that her husband and her guest's wife would be joining them shortly. The bar owner immediately relaxed and stopped eyeing the new patron suspiciously.

✔ Special order a product for them. Maybe you've had a discussion with two of your regulars about their recent trip to Italy. They absolutely fell in love with limoncello (lee-MON-chel-o), a thick lemon liqueur served well chilled in a cordial glass. Special order a bottle for the next time the patrons come in and share a glass with them.

✔ During Friday happy hour, tell your regulars that the first cocktail is on the house.

✔ Have special glasses or mugs for your most loyal patrons with their names on them.

✔ Put your regulars' names on the bar stools or at the bar rail where they normally sit.

✔ Name a cocktail after them: Mike's Martini.

Of course, you can't do all of this for everyone, every day. Start small, and then build into long-lasting relationships. Take a look at Chapter 16 for more information on building a permanent clientele.

You're only as good as the customers who come to your place. Customers are first and foremost. Do something nice and they will tell 10 people; do something wrong and they will tell 100. There is no substitute for good service!

Training Your Team in the Art of Customer Service

Customer service must be something you live, not just something you say. It absolutely starts from the top down. Your employees take their cues for how to treat your customers from you. If they see you practicing good customer service, they'll follow suit. And you can help your employees practice good customer service in other ways, which we explore in this section.

Hiring people with a service mind-set

Some people enjoy making other people happy and making someone's experience a great one by making their day. Others sincerely care about making sure people enjoy themselves and go out of their way to ensure that every patron they take care of has a wonderful time. They may not be super-bubbly or have the ability to talk to anyone about anything, but their desire to make sure your guests are happy is their number-one priority. These, of course, are the types of people you want working for you, to ensure that your bar is providing the best customer service possible.

Here are a few things to look for to get service-oriented employees:

- **A smile:** This smile should be what your patrons see the entire time they're in your bar.

- **Sales experience:** Often people who are in sales in other industries can be fantastic bar employees. They bring their experience helping people buy products in a retail store, for example, and use those skills in your bar. Different product, same basic idea.

- **A problem solver:** Problems arise because things don't go as planned. (Really, who plans for problems?) Hiring employees who can think on their feet and come up with solutions that work for you and the customer is a terrific bonus to your bar.

- **Organization:** An employee's ability to stay organized during the chaos that is a day in the life of a bar is essential to heading off problems before they happen.

- **Empathy:** A service-oriented employee sees the world from the customer's point of view. Taking the time to look at a burger and say, "Would I want to eat this?" can stop a less-than-perfect plate from leaving the kitchen.

Empowering your staff to make things right

Your bartenders and servers will be the first people to hear about something that's wrong in your bar, so you need to give them some authority to make things right. Of course, you don't want every complaint to end up in free drinks for a party of four every night. But the easier you make it for a server or bartender to make sure your patron's experience is terrific, the chances are higher that their service will pay off for you in the long run.

You have to balance how much authority you want employees to have, of course, but here are a few ideas to help you establish your policy:

- ✔ A server or bartender should be able to *immediately* get a replacement drink or food item if it doesn't meet a patron's standard. The longer a patron waits, the more difficult the situation becomes.

- ✔ Consider giving staff members a certain number of drinks they can give away at their discretion each night.

- ✔ Service means service. Your employees need to understand that they will have to make decisions on the spot; they cannot call the manager every time there is a problem. When employees must replace a cocktail or a meal item, tell them to write down what they replaced and an explanation. Then you can solve that problem after the customer leaves. Don't get into an argument with the customer. The customer is always right. Remember, though, that some problems should only be handled by a manager (like cutting off patrons or handling sexual harassment). Take a look at "Dealing With Difficult Customer Situations," later in this chapter, for more help.

Knowing exactly how to handle difficult situations takes time and experience. Your staff members will learn from their mistakes. Don't hold it against them if the situation doesn't turn out perfectly. Each time they tackle a tough situation they gain skills to make it work better the next time.

Look for positive coaching opportunities. Anyone can go over what an employee could have done better in a situation. But also take the time to praise positive customer service situations.

Keeping your employees in the loop

The more your employees know about your business, the more they feel like it's *their* business. And when they think of it as *their* business, they're more invested in seeing it succeed. They, in turn, can spread the information and enthusiasm to your customers.

You can keep them up-to-date in all kinds of ways like scheduling brief meetings each shift, holding longer weekly meetings, putting notes in their paycheck, or posting memos in a centrally located place (like by the time clock, on a bulletin board, or in an employee locker area). Make sure all staff members are getting the same information consistently.

Consider letting your staff in on these important things going on in your bar:

- ✔ Upcoming promotions
- ✔ New menu items
- ✔ Live entertainment schedules
- ✔ New game leagues

Take the next step, and get input from your staff about what they think customers want to see. They're in the trenches day in and day out. They may have another point of view you hadn't considered. Or maybe your customers have made suggestions to your staff. Encourage them to share those ideas with you. You can offer your employees bonuses for new ideas or promotions.

Dealing With Difficult Customer Situations

In every business, customer service problems arise. In the bar business, you often combine a problem with alcohol, and then you have a real recipe for trouble. In this section, we give you some advice when things just don't go the way you'd like them to. We show you how to keep your cool and diffuse the situation before it becomes a scene.

Handling unhappy customers

People are in a bar to have a good time. In a restaurant, they may be there to actually eat, trying to get in and get out, to get on with their busy day. But in a bar, most people have come to unwind, relax, and hang out a bit. A bar is not a necessity; it's a luxury to be able to take time out of a busy life and take a load off. As the bar owner, you can't survive if you can't keep your customers happy. But you will encounter unhappy customers from time to time. In this section, we give you some tips for handling these situations.

Take a look at Chapter 16 for help in turning customer service problems into repeat business.

Beware of providing freebies: Complimentary food and free drinks

Don't just reach for the *comp* (complimentary) button on your register if you have a customer service problem. It's a very dangerous precedent. Each situation has to be handled differently. Yes, the customer is always right (that's why they're called customers, not people), but comping food or drinks for bad service does not usually bring the customer back. If the customer doesn't want to pay because his steak was overcooked, make sure he tells you before he's eaten three-quarters of it. If the problem is the house's fault, take the item off the bill and say, "I am sorry. I hope you will come back and give us another chance to serve you." Giving free cocktails to people who weren't pleased with their meal does not help you. Try to get them a meal that they love before they leave, rather than just comping things off their check. Some customers do this for a living!

On the other hand, it's also a dangerous precedent to assume your customer is trying to cheat you. Do what's right by the guest, and then make sure you're not overcooking your steaks. Sometimes it *is* your fault, and if you are sincere in your apologies and in correcting the problem, you can have a customer for life and a raving fan.

The bartender should never give free cocktails. If you buy a drink for someone, always ring it up on the register. If you're the owner, have the bartender give you a check for the patron's drink, and then pay for it. This step stops people from saying, "When do I get a free drink? When does the house buy me a drink?" When they see that you have to pay for it, they change that cry!

Problem-solving policy: Timely and private responses

Problems should be taken care of *as soon as possible.* Don't let the customer steam. If the customer is exceptionally agitated, take the person out of the room to your office and solve the problem. You don't want to make the situation worse by causing a scene in front of other customers and your employees. Remember, you want to solve the problem, not be part of it! Listen to the patron's explanation of the problem and ask, "What would you like me to do?" or "What can I do to help?" The person usually has a solution in mind. You can go·with the patron's solution or offer your own.

Avoid telling the patron "No." If you can't comply with the request, explain what you can do. "How 'bout if we get you a new server who probably won't spill a tray of beers on you, and get you a complimentary T-shirt because yours is wet?"

Handling intoxicated patrons

Preventing intoxication is everyone's responsibility. All FOH employees should feel responsible and accountable to check IDs, watch for signs of intoxication, and prevent drunk driving. Individual staff members may be added to any lawsuits filed against the bar if they were involved in serving a patron who was harmed or harmed another as a result of drinking. People who do not practice responsible alcohol service can face criminal charges and civil-court battles, resulting in fines and possibly jail time. This is serious!

The National Restaurant Association (www.restaurant.org) also has a new "ServSafe" program for alcohol, which will likely become the industry standard.

 Consider getting your staff members TIPS certification (www.gettips.com) to help them practice responsible, yet customer-friendly, alcohol service. TIPS stands for Training for Intervention ProcedureS, and the organization teaches bar and restaurant employees how to prevent intoxication, underage drinking, and drunken driving. If TIPS doesn't offer workshops in your area, you can sign up for online training. In some states, your insurance company may give you a discount if your employees are certified.

Watching for signs of intoxication

There's no magic formula for how much a person can drink before he or she is intoxicated. Sure, guidelines based on gender, height, and weight have been established, but they're just guidelines. Many things (such as food, medication, sleep, and so on) can affect how we process alcohol. So, as a bar owner, you have to resort to the tried-and-(mostly)-true method of observing your patrons.

Here are the most common signs of intoxication to help you identify potentially intoxicated patrons, but for the most part, you need to use common sense and judgment to determine who's had too much to drink. The Cheat Sheet at the front of this book includes a more-extensive list of behaviors.

- Loud speech
- Ordering drinks rapidly
- Slurred speech
- Stumbling
- Spilling drinks or missing their own mouth when drinking
- Aggressive behavior

Many people who don't exhibit the common signs of intoxication may, in fact, be legally intoxicated. You must know the laws in your area, monitor your staff members, and execute good judgment to serve your clientele and your community safely.

Intervening with a potentially intoxicated patron

No one likes to be told they're "drunk." Before you totally cut a patron off, consider slowing down alcohol service to the patron.

If a server or bartender is taking steps to slow down service to a patron, make sure they include you or another manager in the loop. The manager needs to begin keeping a close eye on the situation to decide the appropriate next steps.

Here are some ideas for slowing down service:

- ✔ Offer the person some food. Food can slow down the absorption of alcohol.

- ✔ Remove an empty glass or bottle before coming back with the next one.

- ✔ Make yourself scarce. Obviously you don't want to avoid the person, but a bartender or server can find ways to take a little longer to make or serve a cocktail when necessary. Great excuses include "They're changing the keg" or "We have to grab _____ in the back" or "He's restocking the cooler." Any reasonable excuse is usually accepted.

- ✔ Coach your staff to offer water or nonalcoholic beverages. "Let's slow down a bit."

Cutting off service entirely

If your bartender or server has just a slight feeling that the customer has been overserved, they should call the manager. Always get the manager involved before service is stopped. Managers should have experience in handling what could be an explosive situation. Also, they can bring a level of objectivity to the situation. A customer may not think that a "lowly" employee, especially a server, has the authority to cut him off. A customer is more apt to show a manager some level of respect. Definitely let the manager make the final call and have the awkward conversation with the patron.

Keep these tips in mind when refusing service to a customer:

- ✔ **Do not cut anyone off in front of others.** The manager should invite the person to the office, or pull him or her aside, to break the news. Keep it factual, not accusatory. "I think you should call it a night."

✔ **Quietly give the person's friends the same information.** Tell whoever the person is with that you're not serving that customer anymore. Do not get into any negotiation about it.

✔ **Make sure the patron has a ride home.** If the person doesn't, call a cab and make sure the person gets into it.

✔ **Do not make a big deal out of cutting someone off, but be firm.** "Your last call has come early." And last call is last call, after all.

Only cut a customer off away from other customers, even his or her friends. *Always.* Be discreet; avoid embarrassment. Stop the drinking before it gets to be a big deal. Only if the customer won't cooperate should you walk away and refuse to serve him or her. Check out "What to do with troublemakers," later in this chapter, for help.

If you're having trouble cutting a person off, consider offering to pay for the person's drinks, as long as he or she leaves immediately. Make sure the patron has a way home, either in the form of a cab or a friend. If someone who's been drinking gets into a car accident after leaving your bar, you can be held legally responsible if you or your employees have overserved them.

What to do with troublemakers

Occasionally, when you add alcohol to a good time, it can turn into a not-so-good time for some patrons. One guy jumps in front of another at the pool table, or spills the other's beer, or dances with someone else's girlfriend. A host of problems can arise at any time.

Warn the troublemakers fairly amicably. "You guys need to settle down. We're having a good time, but we need to stop (insert problem behavior here)."

Sometimes, despite your best efforts, you have to *86* someone (or kick the person out of your bar). Do it as quietly, but forcefully, as possible.

Here are the steps we recommend.

1. **Present the tab. Ask the patron firmly, but politely, to pay it and leave.**

   If the person resists (which he or she probably will), proceed to Step 2.

2. **Firmly explain the person's options.**

   "We can part ways amicably, or I will call the police." If you know the person is intoxicated, call a cab.

3. Assuming the troublemaker pays and leaves, you're done. If the person doesn't leave, call the police.

Again, you want to be discreet and avoid embarrassment. One customer is a lot less likely to get feisty if you're not making a big deal of it in front of others. Ask the guest to follow you outside and explain to him there that he was being asked to pay his tab and leave.

The police can diffuse the situation before anyone gets hurt.

If you kick out someone who's causing trouble, never let the person back in your place.

Only touch a customer in self-defense or to break up a fight. You may restrain a customer, but you can't hit him. You can only stop a patron from harming someone else, or, believe it or not, you could be the subject of a lawsuit. Whenever possible, avoid touching, pointing at, or pushing anyone in your bar. Call the police if you need to.

Chapter 12

Boning Up on Bar Beverages

· ·

· ·

The old saying in the bar business was: "They eat you poor and drink you rich." We hope this chapter will get you rich, both in knowledge and the bar cash register.

Choose your products carefully; would you use cheap meat in the kitchen? It's important to use quality and recognizable brands at your bar. Irwin Shaw said in his short story "The Monument," "Build a monument to your customer and your bartender by using only the best for them. Would you give your best friend inferior products?"

The heart of any bar is the products you pour. The liquor, beer, and wine flow. People have their favorites, but you, the bar owner, choose what to pour. We hope to help you make choices about what items fit your bar better.

In this chapter, we get you started with the basics of wine, beer, and spirits. We help you understand how you pour is as important as what you pour. And we show you why the details, like ice and garnishes, matter.

Knowing the Bar Basics and Then Some

Every good bartender or bar owner worth her salt rim knows lots about liquor. Maybe too much in the personal-experience category, in fact, but we digress. If you don't feel like you have yet mastered all you need to know about the products you sell in your bar, this section is a great place to start.

Wondering about wines

Wine is a beverage made of fermented juice of any kind of fruit. Most popular wines are made exclusively from grapes. In fact, most wines are named after the variety of grapes they are made from.

Although wine has been around for thousands of years, it's been enjoying a new popularity in the last 30 years in the United States. It's no longer reserved for special occasions. And more important to you as a bar owner, wine is enjoyed by people across all socioeconomic lines, not just a select few. Thirty years ago, a bar owner could get away without serving wine, but these days, you should include it on your menu.

A few things contribute to this new era of wine savviness, including increased disposable income (wine isn't always cheap, though many good wines are available at reasonable prices) and greater access to information (like interesting wine lists in local restaurants and books like *Wine For Dummies*). As more people eat out more often, the interest in drinking wine will continue to grow.

In most cases, we recommend you select one or two wines from each category to stock your bar. Take a look at Chapter 9 for more help in putting together your menus. And don't bother with the old rules about serving wine (like white wines with fish and chicken, red wines with beef). Today, it's about what wines stack up against spicy and strong, or flaky and delicate, regardless of color.

Wines today are very trendy; today's Merlot is yesterday's Chardonnay. (That is to say, Merlot, the hot red wine for years, is being replaced by Pinot Noir.) Read your local paper and wine magazines, and of course, talk to your customers to keep up with the changing wines and trends.

For more details about wine than we can possibly include in this chapter (or this book, for that matter), take a look at *Wine For Dummies*, 4th Edition, by Ed McCarthy and Mary Ewing-Mulligan (Wiley).

White wines

Sweet, dry, crisp, light, and fruity all describe various white wines popular today. Many good wines are available at low prices, so work with your sales reps to find the right ones for your patrons at a price that works for you.

Here's a list of some of the more popular white wines with brief descriptions.

- **Chablis:** In the United States, this sometimes inexpensive "jug" wine (literally, wine that comes in a jug) with a high acidity is made from a blend of whatever grapes happen to be available. But in the last ten years, Chablis more often has been made solely from Chardonnay grapes in the Chablis region of France.

Winemaker Carlo Rossi (actually the company that uses his name) is trying to gain a new foothold with young, would-be wine drinkers. They've commissioned artwork and furniture made out of recycled jugs of wine. You can check out their creations (with how-to videos and downloadable project instructions) at www.jugsimple.com and submit your own designs at www.myspace.com/carlorossi.

- ✔ **Chardonnay:** This is among the most popular white wines in the U.S. today. It tends to be a heavier, buttery white wine and can have oaky, smoky, or sweet tones.

- ✔ **Pinot Grigio:** This Italian-style wine is made from the Pinot Gris grape. It's light-bodied and light in color with a fairly neutral taste, bordering on the crisp and acidic.

- ✔ **Riesling:** Riesling is a sweet wine traditionally produced in the Alsace region of France, Germany, and Austria. Chile, South Africa, New Zealand, and the United States now produce good-quality Rieslings as well. Although it's definitely on the sweet end of the taste spectrum, many winemakers put their mark on Riesling by balancing the green flavors with the acidic overtones by choosing when to harvest their grapes.

- ✔ **Sauvignon Blanc:** This is a crisp, dry, and refreshing white wine grown all over the world, most notably New Zealand, South Africa, and Chile. It's gaining increased popularity as white-wine drinkers look for Chardonnay alternatives.

- ✔ **Verdicchio:** This Italian-style wine is known for its high acidity and a characteristic nutty flavor.

For more information, we recommend *White Wine For Dummies* by Ed McCarthy and Mary Ewing-Mulligan (Wiley).

Red wines

Red wines vary greatly in terms of flavor, body, and finish. Taste several to find some that pair with your food and your place. Check out wines at many different prices to find what best fits your menu and pricing structure.

Here are a few common styles of red wines that you may want to find a home for in your bar.

- ✔ **Cabernet Sauvignon:** This strong, robust wine features heavy *tannins* (acidity) and a strong *finish* (or lingering flavor). Cabernets age well, often improving the longer you keep them. Many countries make cabernet sauvignon, including France, the U.S., Chile, and Argentina.

- ✔ **Merlot:** Plummy, berry flavors define this more medium-bodied wine. Because the Merlot grape is mild, it's often blended with stronger grapes. Italy, California, and France are the most notable Merlot producers, but more winemakers in Australia, New Zealand, Croatia, and Slovenia are jumping into the ring.

✔ **Pinot Noir:** This wine is at least 2,000 years old (the type, not the actual bottle) and originated in the Burgundy region in France. Although wines can have vastly different flavors depending on the soil and climates the grapes are grown in, in general, Pinot Noir is a light- to medium-bodied wine with an aroma reminiscent of black cherry, raspberry, or currant. Pinot Noir is a current favorite among red-wine drinkers.

✔ **Shiraz/Syrah:** Called Shiraz in New Zealand, Canada, and Australia, in France and the U.S. it's known as Syrah. This wine is gaining popularity among red-wine drinkers thanks to its excellent aroma and blackberry and chocolate tones. The wine changes substantially based on the soil the grapes are grown in. So the same grape grown in New Zealand and Oregon may taste very different.

✔ **Zinfandel:** (No, this is not the same as the sweet, pinky-white zinfandel, although they are made from the same grapes.) Zinfandel is primarily found in California, though a similar style is available in Europe under the name Primitivo. It's a fruity, but not sweet, wine with a full, lush mouthfeel.

Sparkling wines (commonly called Champagne)

All Champagne must be cultivated and fermented in the Champagne region of France. If it's made anywhere else, it's called a *sparkling wine* instead. Your average bar patron will still ask for champagne when referring to any sparkling wine. For more information, we recommend *Champagne For Dummies* by Ed McCarthy (Wiley).

Champagne is wine that is fermented a second time after bottling. This second fermentation produces the fizzy bubbles associated with this celebratory beverage.

Here are a few terms related to Champagne that may be helpful when you're choosing some for your bar.

✔ *Vintage* means all the grapes included in the wine are from the same year.

✔ *Nonvintage* refers to Champagne that is made from a blend of different years. Most Champagne is nonvintage.

✔ Terms like *brut, extra dry, sec, demi-sec,* and *doux* refer to the sweetness of the Champagne, brut being the driest and doux being the sweetest.

✔ Some Champagne has a pinkish tinge to it, developed as the fermenting wine spends more time with the grape skins (or *tannins*). This blush Champagne can be called *blanc de noirs* or even *rosé.*

For most bars a nonvintage brut champagne is your best bet. It's what people who don't drink a lot of champagne expect champagne to taste like. If you're more of a trendy bar with a clientele that would be interested in a higher-end Champagne, consider adding a sec or demi-sec to your list.

Appreciating beer

Beer is among the most popular beverages consumed in bars in this country. It is brewed from malted barley, hops, and water. Yeast is added, which converts the natural sugars to alcohol and carbon dioxide. The carbon dioxide gives beer its carbonation.

Here's a list of some beer terms you may have seen on labels or heard in beer commercials:

- **Ale** is *top-fermented beer* (meaning the yeast collects on top of the fermenting vat). Pale ales are usually a little bitter, usually taste hoppy, and generally have a higher alcohol content. Amber ales are sweeter and milder with less hops.

- **Bitter** beer is a strong ale, usually English, with a higher-than-normal alcohol content and as the name implies, a bittersweet taste.

- **Bock** beer is a dark, strong, slightly sweet lager beer brewed from caramelized malt.

- **Ice** beer is brewed at colder-than-normal temperatures and then chilled to below freezing, forming crystals. The crystals are filtered out, leaving a smoother-tasting beer with a slightly higher alcohol content.

- **Lager** is a *bottom-fermented beer* (meaning the yeast collects at the bottom of the vat or even the mug after its poured) that is stored at very low (cold) temperatures for a long period of time (several months). *Lager* is the German word for *to store.*

- **Lambic** beer is brewed in Belgium. Ingredients such as peaches, raspberries, cherries, and wheat are added during the brewing process.

- **Light** beer has fewer calories and less alcohol.

- **Low-carb** beer has less sugar and fewer calories than its regular counterpart.

- **Malt liquor** is fermented at a higher temperature than other beers, which results in a higher alcohol content.

- **Pilsner** is a light, hoppy, dry lager.

- **Sake** is beer brewed and processed from rice. (Some consider sake a wine.) Sake is served warm or at room temperature.

- **Stout** is an ale produced from heavily roasted barley. It is darker in color and has a slightly bitter flavor, reminiscent of coffee or dark chocolate.

- **Trappist** beer is brewed in Belgium or The Netherlands by Trappist monks. It contains high levels of alcohol and is usually dark in color.

- **Wheat** beer is made from, um, wheat. It's usually garnished with a lemon or orange wedge. Some people add a little raspberry syrup.

Unless you plan to use a huge beer selection as a draw, we recommend choosing about 12 beers to keep on hand. Select three local brews, three national beers, three light beers, and three imported beers. Don't forget you need adequate cold-storage space to store them all. And definitely take a look at Chapter 8.

Demystifying distilled spirits and liqueurs

The term *distilled spirits* is a catchall term for liquor with an alcohol content of 35 percent or more with a low sugar content. Spirits include liquors like gin, tequila, and whiskey. If a liquor has a 35 percent alcohol content *and* a high sugar content, it's usually known as a *liqueur*. Grand Marnier, crème de menthe, and amaretto are familiar liqueurs.

Who made the first cocktail?

The true answer is lost to history, but many stories abound. Most people agree that it's an American invention. The earliest printed use of the term that we can verify was found in the Hudson, New York, newspaper *The Balance and Columbian Repository* on May 6, 1806. The editor received many questions about the new term, present in a concession speech from a losing political candidate, and here was his response:

> Cock tail, then is a stimulating liquor, composed of spirits of any kind, sugar, water and bitters — it is vulgarly called a bittered sling, and is supposed to be an excellent electioneering potion inasmuch as it renders the heart stout and bold, at the same time that it fuddles the head.

Here are some of the more colorful stories surrounding the creation of this now ubiquitous beverage:

✔ Rumor has it that early in American history, bartenders used to pour remnants of drinks and almost empty barrels into a single container, selling swigs from this mixture to patrons at a reduced price. "Cock" was another name for spigot, and "tailings" is the last bit of alcohol, so this drink was called "cock-tailings," quickly shortened to "cocktail." A similar story recollects a bartender who poured his dregs into a container shaped like a rooster (or cock) and the tap was set at the cock's tail, hence cocktail.

✔ Some believe that an apothecary in New Orleans served his guests a mix of brandy, sugar, water, and bitters in an eggcup, or *coquetier* in French, which was quickly shortened to "cocktay" and then "cocktail."

✔ Alcohol was often used as a medical treatment, rumored to be applied from the tip of a feather from a cock's tail; then, when people started to drink or gargle the medicine outright, the name "cock's tail" was still used.

✔ Betsy Flanagan ran an inn in Yorktown that was frequented by American and French soldiers after the American Revolutionary War. To impress her patrons one evening, she stole chickens from her neighbor and served mixed drinks with the chicken feathers sticking out as garnishes. As her guests became drunken and rowdy, they continued to call for more "cock tails."

Hard liquor brings the people in. In this section, we give you a brief explanation and list of products available for your bar. You should consult with your managers and bartenders about which brands to have available.

- ✔ **American whiskey:** Whiskey distilled from grain or grains. It has a warm, spicy flavor that warms your whole body on the way down.

- ✔ **Bourbon:** A whiskey that must be made from at least 51 percent corn and aged in new white-oak barrels. Its flavor is more pure, but still spicy, than a scotch that's aged in barrels previously containing other spirits (like port or sherry).

  Tennessee whiskey differs from bourbon in that it's filtered through sugar-maple charcoal before it's aged. The sugar-maple charcoal makes the difference. Jack Daniel's is a sour mash whiskey, not a bourbon.

- ✔ **Brandy:** Made by distilling wine or fruit and then aging in oak barrels. Brandy can be American or from other parts of the world. The flavor of brandy varies based on the wine or fruit used, but it tends to be a bit sweeter than a whiskey but not as sweet as a liqueur.

- ✔ **Canadian whisky:** Whisky from Canada. No "e" in whisky. Canadian whisky tends to be a little less strong in flavor than American whiskey.

- ✔ **Cognac:** Brandy from the Cognac region of France. Its flavor fully depends on the wine used to make it.

- ✔ **Cordials/liqueurs:** Made from infusing the flavors of fruits, herbs, spices, and other plants with a spirit such as brandy, whiskey, schnapps, or other mildly flavored liquor. There are hundreds of cordials.

- ✔ **Gin:** A distilled-grain spirit flavored from different plants, mainly the juniper berry. Its flavor reminds us of chewing on pine needles, but in a good way.

- ✔ **Irish whiskey:** Triple-distilled from barley and other grains, sometimes in pot stills, and aged between five and ten years. Its flavor is smooth and mellow and slightly sweet with honey overtones. The Irish have been distilling whiskey for at least 600 years. God bless 'em!

- ✔ **Rum:** Distilled from sugar cane, it's closely akin to vanilla. It's much less flavorful than vanilla but accepts flavoring easily. It comes in light, dark, spiced, and flavored.

- ✔ **Scotch whisky:** Whisky (no "e") from Scotland. It must be distilled in Scotland, not necessarily bottled there. Its flavor varies widely based on where it's distilled, for how long, and how. It's traditionally aged in barrels that previously contained other liquor, like sherry or wine. Most quality scotch is described by connoisseurs as smoky and smooth. Scotch comes in many different varieties. Look for *blended* (a combination of malt and grain whiskies) and *single malt* (from one barrel) scotch.

✔ **Tequila:** Produced from the heart of one species of the agave plant. It's a tart liquor with a bit of a bite at the finish. Just as Champagne must come from the Champagne region in France, tequila must come from Mexico. Tequila not made in Mexico is mezcal.

✔ **Vodka:** Distilled from grain, wheat, potatoes, rye, or corn. It's known to be flavorless and pairs well with almost any mixer. It is the most called-for spirit in America.

For more information, sneak a peek at Ray's *Bartending For Dummies*, 3rd Edition (Wiley).

Musing over mixers

The term *mixers* is the classification given to the endless variety of stuff you add to liquor to make cocktails. The mixer itself isn't alcoholic, but many mixers are manufactured solely for the purpose of mixing with alcohol. We give you more information about how to mix cocktails later in the chapter, but for now we're discussing the mixers themselves.

The precise definition of cocktail is debatable. Purists claim that it takes more than simply mixing alcohol with something else to make it a true cocktail. Things like ice-cream drinks, even though they contain alcohol, don't make the cut with purists. In most cases, bartenders agree that a drink prepared by mixing liquor with juice or mixers is a cocktail.

Here's a list of the most common mixers used in cocktails today:

✔ **Club soda:** The original neutral fizzy drink.

✔ **Cola and diet cola:** Mixes with anything. Most bars choose either Coke or Pepsi products, but local favorites like RC are getting some shelf space.

✔ **Ginger ale:** Familiar brands include Canada Dry, Vernors, and Schweppes.

✔ **Lemon-lime beverages:** Familiar brands include 7-Up, Sprite, and Sierra Mist.

✔ **Milk or cream:** Several common cocktails (like toasted almonds and white Russians) require milk, half and half, or cream. Keep a pint of vanilla ice cream behind the bar for very creamy cocktails.

✔ **Juice:** Common cocktail juices include tomato, orange, pineapple, cranberry, grapefruit, cream of coconut, lime juice or Rose's Lime Juice, and lemon juice or sweet and sour mix. Some purists will suggest fresh-squeezed juice; of course, it's better, but much more expensive.

✔ **Tonic water:** Some bars keep both tonic and diet tonic in stock.

We recommend that you include these beverages (at least the soft drinks) on soda guns at your bar. A *soda gun* system allows you to dispense liquid mixers, such as sodas and juices, at the touch of a button. It keeps most of the regularly used mixers handy in one location so you don't have to manage any more bottles. Take a look at Chapter 7 for more details on how to get equipment for your bar.

Don't forget the other must-have bar essentials, such as bitters (Angostura brand is our recommendation), Worcestershire sauce, hot sauce, superfine sugar, and salt and pepper. Many recipes call for these ingredients.

✔ **Bitters:** For use in Manhattans, Old Fashioneds, and other cocktails that call for bitters or for cocktails you would like to add a little bitter flavor to.

✔ **Worcestershire sauce;** Mainly for a Bloody Mary or other tomato-based cocktails.

✔ **Hot sauce:** For any cocktail that you want a little spicy or hot! (See www. tabascofoodservice.com.)

Making sense of the never-ending stream of "new" liquors

What this world needs is another vodka. New products seem to come out every week. We used to say, "If something falls off a tree, they'll make it a flavored vodka or schnapps."

Liquor companies are always doing research and testing new flavors and products. Sometimes they reintroduce old products with new labeling and bottles. The bar business is an ever-changing industry, and that's what makes it interesting and challenging. Because there will always be new products, hot new food items, and innovative cocktails, you will never be bored in the bar business!

But every time a new product is introduced, the liquor companies want placement. You can use this to your advantage by holding an introduction party at your place. The liquor companies will give you T-shirts, key chains, stickers, and other promotional items for your customers. Everyone likes something for free, and a new-product launch is a great way to get people in the door. The more new products, the better for your place. Work with your sales representative and let him know you're interested in promotional nights and tastings for his products.

Mixing and Pouring the Best Drinks in Town

If you use the best liquor, the finest juice, and quality mixers, you make the best cocktails. There is no substitute for quality. But — here comes the but — you can't always use premium ingredients because of cost. You have to figure out whether your customers will pay what it costs you to make the very best. So in most cases, you have to balance quality and value.

Remember, you're in this business to make a profit. You will have to charge according to cost! If your customers will pay, then use only the best of all products. If your customers won't pay for the best of the best, you must price according to cost. That is why they have well, call, premium, and super-premium products! You get what you pay for. For more information on pricing your drinks, take a look at Chapter 9.

When you're ready to start mixing drinks, pick up a copy of Ray's *Bartending For Dummies,* 3rd Edition (Wiley). It includes hundreds of recipes for popular cocktails and unusual mixed drinks, as well as recipes for nonalcoholic beverages.

Choosing your pouring strategy

Some bar owners are rigidly insistent on measuring every *pour* (how much liquor goes into a drink) and watching every drop, while many customers think anything less than free pouring every drink is chintzy. Again, it's all about balance and consistency. Measuring equals consistency. But there are several ways to measure your pours without getting out the old jigger every time. (A *jigger* is a double-ended measuring cup usually with a ½-ounce cup on one end and a 2-ounce cup on the other.)

With technological innovations, you can measure your pours without counting the seconds (two counts = two seconds = about 1 ounce) while you're pouring or using a shot glass every time. Here's a list of tools you can use to help you pour perfectly measured drinks every time:

✔ **Metered pour spouts:** These spouts fit right into your bottles and dispense precisely measured shots each and every time. Take a look at Precision Pours's Web site (www.precisionpours.com) for more information on this easy-to-use tool that can help you control your product costs.

✔ **Computerized liquor-control systems:** Check out Easybar (www. easybar.com) for controls that integrate with your *POS* (point of sale) system (or computerized cash register system). Easybar has tools that can portion, measure, and dispense beer, alcohol, wine, and mixers while adding the purchase price to guest checks automatically.

 The Warning icon here may be a little too strong, but we want to mention that using these tools cuts down on the speed of service a bit. Your bartenders can't make drinks as quickly with some of these systems in place. And you'll always have some customers who complain, "Is that all?! Fill it up!"

Pouring the perfect beer

Although your customers choose a beer based on its taste, you can impress them by serving an attractive glass of beer. How that glass looks depends on two things: how clean the glass is and how you pour the beer into the glass.

Following are a few tips for obtaining a *clean glass* of beer; that is, an eye-appealing glass filled with a beer with a clear color and a good, tight collar of foam. A three- or four-sink setup is ideal for getting glasses beer clean; a three-tank setup is most common. The first tank is for washing, followed by two rinsing compartments.

A beer glass should be washed each time it is used — unless the customer requests that his glass be refilled. Proper cleaning and drying can be accomplished in four simple steps:

1. **Used glasses should be emptied and rinsed with clear water to remove any foam or remaining beer that will cause dilution of the cleaning solution.**

2. **Each glass should be brushed in water containing a solution of odor-free and nonfat cleaning compound that will thoroughly clean the surface of the glass and rinse away easily in clean water.**

3. **The glass must then be rinsed twice in fresh, clean, cool water — with the proper sanitizer in the last tank.**

    Proper and complete rinsing is most important for a "beer clean" glass.

4. **Dry glasses upside down on a deeply corrugated surface or stainless-steel glass rack.**

    Never towel-dry glasses. Store air-dried glasses away from sources of unpleasant odors, grease, or smoke that is emitted from kitchens, restrooms, or ashtrays.

The right head of foam gives a glass of beer that essential eye appeal. You control the size of the head by the angle at which you hold the glass at the beginning of the draw. If you hold the glass straight so the beer drops into the bottom, a deep head will result. If you tilt the glass sharply so the beer flows down the side, the head of foam will be minimized.

For most beer glasses — and to please most customers — the head should be allowed to rise just above the top of the glass without spilling over and then settle down to a ¾-inch or 1-inch head of frothy, white foam.

Another secret to serving a perfect glass of beer: Rinse the glass with cold, fresh water just before filling with draft beer.

Maintaining your draft beer equipment

To make sure you're selling perfect "brewery fresh" draft beer, you also need to pay attention to proper refrigeration, cleanliness of the dispensing equipment, and proper pressures.

Because draft beer is perishable, it must not be exposed to warm temperatures. The retailer must preserve it by providing equipment that will maintain the temperature of the beer in the barrel between 38 to 42 degrees Fahrenheit. When you're storing and pouring your beer, you must also maintain these temperatures throughout your dispensing equipment so the beer that you serve to your customers will also be 38 to 42 degrees Fahrenheit. This temperature range seems to satisfy the majority of tastes and is too small a variation to affect its flavor or quality.

Just as it's important to keep your beer glasses clean (see the previous section), you have to make sure your dispensing equipment stays free from dirt and buildup. You need to thoroughly clean the beer faucets, tubing, hose, coils, taps, and vents, including direct-draw systems, on a regular basis.

You need to keep beer that's on tap at the proper pressure to maintain its brewery-fresh taste and natural carbonation. The pressure of the dispensing equipment must correspond to the normal carbonation of the beer at its temperature in the barrel. The size and length of the coil in the dispensing equipment will determine what pressure you should use.

Considering the importance of ice

Ice matters more than you may think. To get good ice, you need a good water purifier and a cube shape and size to your liking. Take a look at Figure 12-1 to see a few varieties of ice cube sizes.

Figure 12-1:
Different ice
cube sizes.

Full Cube	**Half Cube**	**Cubelet**
1 1/4″ x 1 1/4″ x 1 1/4″	1 1/4″ x 1 1/4″ x 5/8″	5/8″ x 5/8″ x 1 1/4″

Some purists (often people who've never owned bars or worked at a busy bar) think you should chop your own ice to make cocktails. Don't believe the hype. It's slow and impossible.

A small, crushed-ice machine can be handy if you make a lot of blended or frozen cocktails. At a minimum, you need an ice machine in the back. Don't make your cubes too big. But for shaking cocktails, many bartenders will tell you big is better. Honestly, it's a matter of opinion.

You can find ice machines that make ice in many sizes: full, half, cubelets, nuggets, flakes, and crushed. Two of the best ice-machine manufacturers are Manitowoc (www.manitowocice.com) and Kold-Draft (www.kold-draft. com). Take a look at Chapter 7 for more help on choosing equipment for your bar.

You should, if possible, have one ice machine behind the bar that can make ice *and* be used for storage, and one machine in the back of the house that can be stacked (or have additional units stacked on top of the existing unit), so as your business grows you can make more ice by stacking.

Shaking versus stirring

The main reasons for *shaking* a cocktail is to make the ingredients cold, combine them all, and maybe put a head on the cocktail. *Stirring* a cocktail mixes the ingredients but doesn't create any foam in the drink.

As a general rule, you shake cloudy drinks and stir clear ones. Obviously there are exceptions, because 007 likes his martinis (clear!) "shaken, not stirred."

Shake cloudy cocktails and stir clear cocktails. Never, *never,* shake a cocktail with any type of carbonation (soda, champagne). It will spray foam everywhere. It can be a great way to welcome a new bartender to your crew.

Prettifying Drinks with Garnishes

Garnishes, those little decorations that add color or flavor to a drink, can make or break a cocktail. What's a Bloody Mary without a crisp and cool celery spear? Or a gin and tonic without a lime or three? In some cases the garnish defines the cocktail (the difference between a Gibson and a martini is the cocktail onion, after all).

The most important point to remember about your garnishes is that they should be fresh and clean. We talk about different types of garnishes in the next sections. Use your imagination to decide what garnish you put with what drink, but always consider price and freshness. It may be a great idea to garnish every Bloody Mary with a skewer of marinated vegetables and deli meats, like a little antipasto on a stick. But if the cost of the garnish eats into your profit margin, you can't serve it for long! For more on pricing your drinks (and covering all your costs), check out Chapter 9.

Having fun with citrus fruit

Citrus fruits can garnish anything from a Long Island Iced Tea to a wheat beer. Here are a few common cuts of many of your favorite citrus fruits and how to use them:

> ✔ **Wedges:** A *wedge* is a section of a citrus fruit, usually one-eighth of the fruit, sliced lengthwise. Take a look at Figure 12-2 to see how this looks. Here are the basic steps to create wedges:

1. **Slice the fruit in half the long way.**

   If you commonly hang your wedges on the edge of a glass, go ahead and cut a notch in them now. Make a small cut the short way across the inside of each half at this point. Make sure you don't completely cut through the fruit's peel or you'll cut the wedges in half, rather than notching them.

2. **Lay the cut halves down (peel side up) and halve them the long way again.**

3. **Cut each of those halves the long way to create eight wedges total.**

✔ **Wheels:** A *wheel* is a full circle of fruit, placed on the edge of a glass. You make wheels simply by cutting the ends off the citrus fruit, then slicing the fruit the short way to the desired thickness. Make a cut from the middle of the fruit slice to one side to create a slit to hang the fruit on the rim of the glass.

✔ **Squeezes:** A *squeeze* is very similar to a wedge, but smaller. In fact, it's half the size. Make wedges as pictured in Figure 12-2, and then cut those wedges in half the short way. Rather than hanging on the side of a glass, a squeeze is squeezed into the cocktail by the bartender, and then dropped in the drink.

✔ **Twists:** A *twist* is a small piece of the peel of a citrus fruit. Take a look at Figure 12-3 for tips on how to cut these.

1. **Cut off both ends of the fruit.**

2. **Insert a sharp knife or spoon between the rind and the meat of the fruit and carefully separate them.**

3. **Cut the rind into strips.**

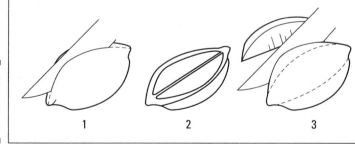

Figure 12-2: Making citrus wedges.

1   2   3

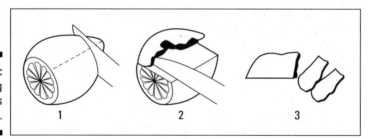

Figure 12-3:
Cutting
citrus
twists.

Other must-have garnishes

To make a perfect cocktail you must have the perfect garnish. Many garnishes are traditional, but innovative barkeeps can use their creativity to exceed the patron's expectation. Add the ribbon on the package; it always helps to garnish your cocktail because it upgrades the appearance and makes for a complete presentation.

Here's our list of other basic garnishes and how you can use them:

- ✔ **Flags:** A flag is a maraschino cherry wrapped in an orange slice and then stabbed with a sword to hold it all together. Use them to garnish things like Amaretto Sours.

- ✔ **Olives and olive juice:** Olives are the traditional garnish for martinis. Add a little olive juice to make a martini "dirty."

- ✔ **Celery:** It's a garnish and stir stick in one! Use these to garnish Bloody Marys and the host of related drinks like Bloody Bulls, Bloody Caesars, and so on.

- ✔ **Onions:** This garnish is the differentiating factor between a martini and a Gibson.

- ✔ **Mint:** Whether you muddle it for a Mojito or use it to top off a Razzberry Lemonade, this herb is becoming a must-have for many bars.

- ✔ **Cherries:** When all else fails, toss a cherry in it.

- ✔ **Strawberries:** Notch these superfoods and hang them on the edge of anything fruity.

Rimming: Why, when, and how to do it

Rimming is coating the rim of a glass with a granular or crumb-like substance as a garnish. It adds a decorative touch that improves the presentation of the cocktail and complements its flavor. The most basic example of rimming is using salt on the rim of a margarita.

Bartenders are becoming much more creative with rimming choices (like cocoa, graham-cracker crumbs, or shaved coconut), but the most common rimmers are sugar and kosher salt. Prime cocktail candidates for rimming include margaritas and martinis, but that's not an absolute rule. You can used toasted coconut to grace the rim of a Piña Colada, salt on a Bloody Mary or Salty Dog, or superfine sugar on the edge of a Screwdriver. Your imagination is your only limitation.

Here are the basic steps for rimming a glass:

1. **Moisten the rim of the glass.**

   Choose a complementary flavor to enhance the cocktail. Many people choose a lime wedge or Triple Sec to rim a margarita, or Kahlua to rim a Chocolate Martini, for example.

2. **Dip the moistened rim into whatever you want to coat the glass with. Gently turn the glass as you coat it to ensure you coat it evenly.**

3. **Shake off any excess.**

4. **Fill the glass with your cocktail.**

Chapter 13

Getting Ready for Your Grand Opening, Step by Step

*E*very bar is different, and every bar owner goes through a slightly different process of getting ready for the grand opening. However, bar owners tend to follow a series of steps when preparing for the big day. Sure, you can figure out these steps through trial and error, but there's nothing wrong with being prepared and making your grand opening as smooth and successful as possible.

In this chapter, we give you a series of steps to follow to help you plan for your bar's opening, with a detailed timeline of all the tasks you need to accomplish and keep track of before you open the doors and serve your first drink. Everything in this chapter is covered in detail somewhere else in the book, but here we give you an idea of how the information in those chapters fits together to get you ready for opening night. From deciding what your signature cocktail might be to choosing a new logo, if it's important in the startup cycle of a new bar, it's in this chapter.

Every bar is different, so every opening timeline varies. If you're building a bar from scratch, you have more steps (and a longer timeline) than if you take over an existing place. This chapter is intended to be a guideline. Check with all relevant state and local government and regulatory offices to determine how long it takes to get the paperwork you need to open the kind of bar you want . . . keeping in mind that the processing time may be longer than quoted. Take a look at Chapters 2 and 4 in particular for help in getting started.

Figuring Out How Much Time You Need to Prepare

Early in the planning stages, you may need to adjust your timeline and go with the flow, accepting the fact that timelines aren't always set in stone. You may not need to have your business plan completed nine months before your opening if you're taking over an existing, established restaurant and don't want to make any changes to it, for example. As you get closer to opening day, you need to create and stick to a firm schedule to get everything completed on time.

If you're terrible at keeping a timeline, pad your schedule. This approach is similar to setting your clocks 15 minutes ahead to be on time. But in this case, time is money. If you hire the chef a month earlier than scheduled, it's an additional expense you'll absorb before you're even open. You may have a very good reason, and it may be the right thing to do. Just make sure that you factor the additional time and money into your schedule and expense projections.

In the sections that follow, we group together similar tasks at each time interval. Use these categories to stay organized and eventually to delegate to the person in your organization who will handle the functions permanently.

Remember, you won't have tasks in every category at every point on the timeline. In fact, depending on your concept you may decide to skip some categories (like construction if your physical layout is already perfect) altogether. Pick which tasks are necessary for you to complete your bar.

Here's the list of categories we use, shown in the order they appear in each time interval:

- **Administration:** Administration tasks include paperwork, phone calls, planning activities, and so on.

- **Construction:** Construction tasks consist of work related to designing and building your restaurant.

- **Human resources:** Anything concerning hiring, training, or managing your employees falls in this category.

- **Purchasing:** Purchasing tasks include buying equipment, supplies, and just about anything else your restaurant needs to get up and running.

- **Front of the house (FOH):** Tasks in this category include organizing your bar, establishing your hours of operation, and all forms of customer service.

- **Back of the house (BOH):** BOH tasks include organizing your storeroom and placing and receiving your first food orders.

✔ **Advertising and promotion:** This category includes any publicity, advertising, and public relations duties you should do.

✔ **Research:** Research is ongoing and forever. We list ideas to help you stay competitive and to reform and refresh your plans as you go along.

One Year Out: Planning!

Planning, planning, planning. Just by picking up a copy of this book you've started the planning phase. Use this time early in your schedule to thoroughly research your ideas, articulate your concept and vision, and put together a comprehensive plan for achieving it. At this point in the process, your main concerns should involve administrative duties and, yes — believe it or not — research.

Here are the issues that you should address at this time:

✔ Construct a detailed and professional business plan. Consult Chapter 5 for details on creating an effective business plan for your bar.

✔ Get the details for what it takes to get a liquor license in your area. Because it's essential *and* the requirements vary widely from state to state, county to county, and city to city, get the lowdown on what *you* need to run *your* business well in advance. Take a look at Chapter 3 for help getting started. And Appendix A gives you a listing of all the state liquor control boards.

✔ Develop your logos, trademarks, and brand identity. Chapter 4 helps you figure out exactly what you want to be. Consider hiring a graphic artist at this stage to help you create marketing images for your bar. Chapter 6 gives you tips on choosing a name for your place.

✔ Put together your team of advisors, including an accountant, an attorney, and an insurance agent. Take a look at Chapter 3 for details. Get your architect and designer on board, if you're using them.

✔ Check with the local governing agencies to confirm timelines for your permits (beyond your liquor license). Requirements and schedules vary greatly, so get the details as soon as you can and account for them in your schedule. See Chapter 3 for details on how to get started.

We mentioned doing research earlier. What kind of research, you ask? Well, research really should be an ongoing habit as long as you're a bar owner, but at this point, the purpose of the research is to take advantage of your bar's market potential.

You really should create a plan that ensures that your bar takes advantage of everything that could affect it — accepted pricing structures, for example — and stay on top of the competition. Study other bars in your area to know what they're doing and how it's working. Watch how customers respond (both positively and negatively) to specials, entertainment, and menu changes to help you figure out how to improve on your own ideas. In other words, you need to formalize your process for conducting market, trend, and competitive research. See Chapter 5 for suggestions on watching the competition and Chapter 16 for tips on building and keeping a bar crowd.

Nine Months Out: Finding Funds, a Location, and POS Systems

At the nine-months-and-counting mark, you should have your business plan in hand and be shopping for money. You can also begin researching specifics for your business, such as looking at prospective locations and getting information about computer systems.

Start meeting with potential investors. Explain your concept, business plan, and financial forecasts. Check out Chapter 3 for more information about financing your business, and see Chapter 5 for help creating your business plan.

You should also research *point of sale (POS) systems.* Much more than a simple cash register, a POS system can help you track and analyze just about any type of data you can think of. Some of the super–high-end machines can actually control your liquor pours too. Check out Chapter 12 for info on controlling your costs with measured pours.

You also need to start shopping for the perfect location for your bar (see Chapter 6).

Seven Months Out: Signing the Lease and Setting Up Finances

Around seven months, your plan starts to become reality. Finalize your choice for a location and sign your lease. Get your money together and set up your bank accounts, look into credit card processors, and develop your other financial systems.

Here are the administration issues that you should address at this time:

✔ Sign a deal with the landlord. But take a look at Chapters 3, 4, 5, and 6, first to make sure that your location meets all your objectives and requirements for your concept and sales projections.

✔ Finalize your financing. Check out Chapter 3 for the full story.

✔ Set up business bank accounts to pay deposits, rent office space (if you need it), and deposit all your investors' money. See Chapters 3 and 15 for help.

✔ Decide how you will get cash from the bar into your bank account. You can use an *armored car service* (a service that comes to you to pick up your deposits complete with armed guards and an armor-plated vehicle) or make a daily deposit at your local bank.

✔ Establish your plan for regular financial reporting. Create the format for your P&L (profit and loss) statement and any other reports you'll create on a regular basis. Check out Chapter 15 for the story on what numbers to watch and why.

Don't forget your ongoing research duties! Here's what you should do now, in terms of research:

✔ Research credit card processing systems. Kindly turn to Chapter 15.

✔ Check out potential payroll companies. Weigh your options for contracting with a company or doing it yourself. Chapter 15 can get you started.

Six Months Out: Getting Organized!

Your biggest task at this point is to get — and stay — organized. Get your permits, licenses, and other legalities straightened out. Set up your temporary base of operations. And do your homework to figure out what equipment you need and whom you should buy it from.

Here are your administration issues for now:

✔ Set up water, electricity, gas, and other required utilities. Make sure that the billing is set up and the utilities are on *before* construction begins.

✔ Complete paperwork for permits and licenses. Figure out which permits your contractor will handle and which you must apply for on your own.

Depending on the laws in your area, you may need to apply for your liquor license sooner. Most governing boards require that you have the bar's permanent location before they issue the license. If you change locations, you'll likely need to reapply for your license. And in some places, a finite number of licenses are available; once they're gone, they're gone. Definitely take the time to find out the specifics on what you need in your area. Check out Chapter 3 for details on liquor licenses and other legalities.

✔ Set up your temporary office space. You can use a space in your bar that's somewhat secluded or away from the construction noise. You may choose to work out of your home or even a trailer outside the bar while it's under construction. You need a space with electricity, lights, some form of climate control, desk space, a land-based phone line, and Internet access.

Get a fax machine earlier rather than later for exchanging plans with architects, designers, and so on. You can also use it to send and receive certain documents, such as specifications for equipment and résumés from management candidates.

And if you don't already have a computer, now's the time to get one. A computer is essential for doing research, ordering, creating all the manuals you'll need, and developing your menu.

Another issue you have to start working on now, particularly if you're building your bar, is construction! Here's what you need to do:

✔ Interview your contractor candidates. Check out Chapter 4 for information on working with a contractor.

Make sure that you give your contractor your full specifications and your schedule. Make him or her commit to a detailed schedule in writing to confirm a completion date, with a financial penalty attached for not meeting the deadline. If your contractor gives you any resistance, consider adding a graduated incentive bonus if they finish early.

✔ Review your plans for the BOH, FOH, and exterior of your bar to make sure they fit your actual space. Take a look at Chapter 6 for help.

You also need to start researching equipment suppliers and sourcing equipment. Make sure to consider new versus used equipment and buying versus leasing options. Chapter 7 can help you.

Five Months Out: Building and Buying

Construction begins on your new site! Interview candidates for your key positions, such as your managers or head bartender, assuming that you're not either or both of them. Use any available time to work on manuals, job descriptions, and anything else you can get out of the way early.

If you're building your bar, or remodeling an old one, here are your construction issues at this time:

✔ Begin construction. This schedule may be too soon or too late, depending on your operation. Make sure you've researched all your permits and they're in place when they need to be. Chapter 3 can help.

✔ Make sure that you and your contractor are still on the same page regarding the concept, the design, and the schedule and that anyone else involved with the process (such as designers) shares your thoughts in these areas.

You knew that at some point you had to start buying the stuff that goes into your bar, right? Well, now's the time to get started. Here's what you should do at this time:

✔ Order your bar and kitchen equipment. Chapter 7 has all the details.

✔ Order your tables, chairs, and fixtures. Specify delivery for 30 days before opening. This schedule gives you time to allow for shipping and delivery delays. Take a peek at Chapter 6 for help in choosing your décor.

✔ Purchase the POS system.

It's also time to start hiring people! Here's what you need to do now:

✔ Interview manager and head bartender candidates. Flip on over to Chapter 10 for more info.

✔ Develop job descriptions and pay rates. Take a look at Chapter 10 for help.

Also be sure to investigate phone systems and phone service companies at this time, and remember that all systems are not created equal.

Four Months Out: Manuals and Menus

Construction is well underway. Use this time to work on employee and operational manuals and finish up your drink menus. Check out the sidebar "Things to do in your free time," later in this chapter, to find tasks that you can complete now to save yourself time later. Four months out, here's everything you need to do:

- ✔ Check in with your contractor to make sure that construction is proceeding according to schedule.
- ✔ Finalize exterior construction.
- ✔ Create employee and operational manuals. Spend some time in Chapter 10 for some direction on what to include in your manuals.
- ✔ Finalize job descriptions and pay rates. Chapter 10 can help.
- ✔ Finalize your drink menus. Take a look at Chapter 9 for tips.
- ✔ Finalize your hours of operation. It's best to get this out of the way before you hire your staff so they can immediately coordinate their schedules with the bar's schedule.
- ✔ Research pest control companies. Set up a regular schedule for treatment after you're up and running. Take a look at Chapter 17 for help running a safe bar.

Three Months Out: Supervisors, Suppliers, and Vendors

During this period, most construction should be finishing up. You can start looking at supervisors and managers now. Research your suppliers and vendors at this stage of the game. You're still planning, but the planning really becomes a reality now. Here's what you should do:

- ✔ BOH construction should be complete. FOH construction may be ongoing.

  Don't install your FOH floor until the end of construction. Putting off the floor installation until as late as possible in your construction cycle minimizes construction-related dirt and damage.

- ✔ Review résumés for supervisors and managers.
- ✔ Start sourcing food and beverage purveyors. Check out Chapter 8 to know what to order and Chapter 14 for tips on managing your inventory.

✔ Revise the advertising and promotion plan you developed for your business plan. Work with any outside public relations professionals you're hiring. Check out Chapter 16 for advice on getting the word out and growing your business.

✔ Research your music options. Chapter 6 can get you started.

Two Months Out: Preparing to Hire, Attending to Details

It's time to turn your attention to hiring your staff. At two months, you need to create your plans for hiring, training, scheduling, and retaining your new team. Here's what you should do:

✔ Hire any other supervisors or managers.

✔ Create a blank interviewing roster for both the FOH and BOH. Look to Chapter 10 for details.

✔ Create a schedule for these hiring milestones:

- Initial interview

- Second interview

- Hiring

- Orientation

✔ Create a training schedule

- Steps of service (greeting, drink orders, offering food menus, and the like)

- Product training (menu, beverage, theme, and so on)

- POS

- Menu tastings

- Equipment training (dishwasher, blender, food processor, coffee machine, and any other equipment you have)

✔ Finalize employee manuals. Chapter 10 is a great resource for this information.

✔ Coordinate outside trainers (most likely liquor salespeople) as necessary.

✔ Order any merchandise (like T-shirts, hats, or beer mugs) you plan to sell to customers. Order any customized uniform items, such as aprons or shirts.

Another serious thing to keep in mind two months out — you should have your liquor license in hand. You should also be working on any purchasing tools, like ordering procedures and forms, that you'll use after you're up and running.

Here are other things you should do during this stage:

- Make the final food menu adjustments. See Chapter 9 for help making the hard decisions on what to tweak and what to cut.

- Follow up on any outstanding permits or licenses. Check out Chapter 4 for info on licenses, permits, and other legalities.

- Finalize your music program. See Chapter 6 for details.

- Review and approve your drink menus. Let Chapter 9 be your guide.

- Finalize your operational manuals. Chapter 10 gives you the scoop on setting up manuals to operate your bar with ease.

- Set up your trash service, including dumpsters and grease removal, recycling, and pest control services.

- Activate the phone lines in your bar. You may choose to do this later in the month, especially if you have office space somewhere else. Choose an on-hold message.

- All FOH areas should be completed at this time.

- Create purchasing sheets with exact specifications of all products. Chapters 8 and 14 give you a head start on selecting and organizing your inventory.

- Review all printed materials, trademarks, and proprietary marks. Approve the specifications on all signage, business cards, menus, advertising, takeout bags and containers, letterhead, matches, beverage napkins, and stirrers.

- Finalize all purchasing agreements with purveyors.

- Work with BOH to finalize smallwares order list and quantities. Take a look at Chapter 7 to figure out what you need.

- Create your purchasing forms. Check out Chapter 14 for examples.

- Create your purchase order for linens.

- Finalize your promotional campaign. Look at Chapter 16 for help.

- Create a guest list, ready invitations, and finalize plans for your preopening party.

Six Weeks Out: Finalizing All Paperwork

Use this time to make sure that you have all the paperwork, training materials, and schedules ready when your prospective employees walk through the door. Set the expectation that you operate a professional, organized, and well-run business and that you expect nothing less from them. Here's what you need to do:

- ✔ Create a *construction punch list,* or a list of unfinished items that must be completed before opening.

- ✔ Print and collate your final employee manual.

- ✔ Make sure that you have all hiring paperwork in house, including applications, government-required forms (such as the I-9 and W-4s), uniform agreements, emergency-contact cards, training materials, and so on. Check out Chapter 10 for the details.

- ✔ Review controls for maintaining optimum inventory levels while maximizing cash flow and for minimizing your risk of theft. Take a look at Chapter 14 to get the full story.

- ✔ Design and lay out your physical menu. See Chapter 9.

Thirty Days Out: Navigating the Final Month

The last month is a hectic one. You clean every square inch of your new bar. You set it up exactly the way you want it to look. Take pictures because you'll be setting the standard for how both the BOH and FOH should look before and after every single shift. You hire and train most of your opening staff during this crazy time, so make sure that you've set up your interviewing and hiring systems in the weeks beforehand to minimize the chaos and maximize the information transfer.

Here's your list of things to do:

- ✔ Follow up on outstanding punch-list concerns.

- ✔ Start the hiring process for general employees. Place your ad and set up interviews at your location. Chapter 10 guides you through the process of hiring and training your employees.

- ✔ Place food orders for delivery two to three weeks before your opening. Coordinate the delivery so you have time to train employees on food prep and menu tastings.

- ✔ Thoroughly clean all FOH spaces, including restrooms, dining areas, the patio, the lobby (if you have one), the bar, and the lounge to get rid of any lingering construction dust and dirt.

- ✔ Set up all furniture and fixtures.

- ✔ Set up the managers' office.

- ✔ Finalize the table settings. See Chapter 7 for more info.

- ✔ Run a final test of all equipment (assemble it as it comes in).

- ✔ Thoroughly clean the kitchen, storerooms, and coolers to get rid of any lingering construction dust and dirt.

- ✔ Unpack, wash, and store all smallwares.

- ✔ Set up all storerooms.

- ✔ Get your signage in place.

- ✔ Send invitations for your preopening party.

Ten Days Out: Fine-Tuning

T minus ten days means more of the same. You may be "just" the project manager at this point, overseeing the schedule to make sure that everyone is doing his or her job (rather than doing any of the jobs yourself). All employees should be hired by this point. Engage your staff's help in setting up your bar and assembling your menus. Continue to train and test your staff to make sure that they know your menu and processes in time for opening day.

Here's what you need to do now:

- ✔ Follow up on outstanding punch-list concerns.

- ✔ Continue setting up new-employee files.

- ✔ Continue adding new employees to the POS and payroll systems.

- ✔ Continue training and testing your employees on products, processes, and procedures. Test all FOH employees on menu knowledge, steps of service, table numbers, and so on, and test all BOH employees on station-specific menu items, station setup and tear down, and sanitation procedures.

> ✔ Place your beverage order.
>
> ✔ Receive your beverage order.
>
> ✔ Set up your bar.
>
> ✔ Print and collate your final menu.

Three Days Out: Dress Rehearsal!

Are you getting excited? Your bar should be in full working order by this point. All your employees should know your drink and food menus inside and out. Each line cook should know how to make everything on her station.

Here's what to do:

> ✔ Follow up on outstanding punch-list concerns.
>
> ✔ Continue setting up new-employee files.
>
> ✔ Continue adding new employees to the payroll systems, including time clocks.
>
> ✔ Conduct your first *trial run.* Some people call them dry runs, soft openings, or a host of other names. Before you actually open, you invite employees' families, friends, investors, advisors, consultants, and others to try out the bar.
>
> You treat them just like regular diners, only they eat and drink for free. We recommend a two-drink maximum and one entree or appetizer per person. This is a chance for you to go through a practice shift and see how everything works together. You'll likely have a few things to iron out between your trial run and opening day, which is exactly why you do it. Trial runs aren't cheap, but they're well worth the money.

The Day Before: Relaxing before the Big Opening

Hopefully, you're having a fairly relaxed day. If you've followed the steps in this chapter and kept everything on schedule, everything should be under control at this point. You can even have a little celebration tonight to congratulate your team for a job well done. Make sure you don't let it go on too late; you want them fresh for the big day.

Here's all you should have to do today:

✔ Follow up on outstanding punch-list concerns.

✔ Continue setting up new-employee files.

✔ Continue adding new employees to the payroll systems, including to time clocks.

Most importantly, give yourself a pat on the back — your bar is ready, and so are you!

Things to do in your free time

Okay, we know free time in the bar business doesn't happen, but some tasks associated with opening a new bar can really be done earlier or later in the process, depending on when you have time. It's simply a matter of choice. Consider getting some of these out of the way early in your timeline. Your to-do list can quickly become unmanageable if you leave them all until the last couple of months.

✔ Set up your training schedule. Rough out how many days you plan to have employees in the restaurant and what they might do on those days. Because you're setting up a bar rather than a restaurant, your staff probably doesn't need as much training as they otherwise might. Usually a week total is more than enough.

✔ Establish your procedures for handling cash, ordering, requisition, and receiving.

✔ Set up your credit card agreements.

✔ Figure out how you're going to get your money into your account. Are you going to schedule an armored-car pickup or deposit it yourself every day?

✔ Develop any reports and forms you'll use. Take a look at Chapter 15 for help in figuring out which numbers to watch and why.

✔ Research your music program. Take a look at Chapter 6 for help in deciding which musical choices best fit your bar.

✔ Interview pest control companies. They're one of those unmentionable necessities.

✔ Investigate phone companies and phone systems.

✔ Research printers for letterhead, advertising or promotional materials, matches, napkins, and anything else you'd like to print with your logo.

✔ Develop your employee manual. One of those must-dos that can mostly get done early.

✔ Write job descriptions and establish pay rates for job classes.

✔ Develop your payroll processes. Decide whether you're doing it yourself or hiring an outside service.

Part IV
Managing Your Inventory, Revenue, and Future

The 5th Wave   By Rich Tennant

"Cooked books? Let me just say you could serve this profit and loss statement with a fruity Zinfandel and not be out of place."

In this part . . .

After you have everything you need for your bar and you get your business going, how do you make the most of it? This part is your guide to making sure your bar is financially sound and then some. We give you tools to help you turn bottles of liquor into buckets of cash. We help you create things like procedures, reports, and processes to track and control your inventory and purchasing. (Trust us, it's not as painful as it sounds!) And, most importantly, we show you how to keep your patrons happy, bring in new customers, and turn them into regulars.

Chapter 14

Controlling Expenses and Operating Efficiently

*Y*our biggest ongoing, controllable expenses in the bar business are your food and beverage products. You can make or lose money simply by managing these expenses, so you need to make sure you do so effectively.

In this chapter, we help you keep control of several key areas of your bar business to maximize your profits. We show you how to buy your products effectively. We help you keep track of the products after they make their way to you (along with tips on what to do if they get lost along the way). And we help you make sure that your products reach your patrons without ending up in the trash or in someone else's pocket.

Perusing the Power of Purchasing

Purchasing means buying anything you need for your bar, including liquor, wine and spirits, other beverages, equipment, paper goods, tables, silverware, and everything else. Paying the lowest price possible for the highest-quality products ultimately makes you more money.

Because you typically buy equipment fairly infrequently, most of this chapter focuses on buying food, beverages, and paper goods. (If you need help buying equipment, take a look at Chapter 7.) If your bar is like most restaurants, you spend not only lots of time but also lots of money buying these types of supplies. But you can definitely apply these same principles and tips to negotiating for and purchasing anything else you need for your place.

 Appoint only a few key personnel to buy products for the bar (like the head chef, head bartender, manager, and yourself). You all must work together on this. The more people who are buying for your bar, the more likely that you will lose control. It can cost you a bundle in unnecessary or wasted products.

Putting together your list of supplies

Just like you make a shopping list before you head to the grocery store, you need to put together a comprehensive list of what items you need to run your bar before you can start buying. Take a look at a sample list in Table 14-1. Please also refer to Chapter 8 for items that you should keep in stock.

Here are some tips for setting up your own list:

- ✓ **Include all the liquor you need (including brand name and bottle sizes).** Chapter 8 gives you details about specific types and brands of liquors that can work for your bar. We also cover recommended quantities in that chapter.

- ✓ **Add all the ingredients necessary to make your menu items.** Be as specific as you can. If you need your mozzarella cheese for pizza to come to you already shredded, specify it.

- ✓ **Include everything else your bar needs, such as paper goods, light bulbs, and glassware.** Make sure that you know what paper towels fit your dispensers, which light bulbs fit your fixtures, and whether you need to buy ashtrays. If you run a smoke-free bar, ashtrays are a waste of money.

- ✓ **Group like items into categories.** Most suppliers group products with common classifications, like baked goods, dairy products, and so on. This step makes it easier to keep your purchasing and inventory systems in synch.

- ✓ **Estimate how much you think you'll need.** Based on your recipes and menu items, and how much you think you'll sell of each item during a week, create your projected weekly sales volume. This number tells you how much of an item to order.

Table 14-1	Sample Supplies List (Abbreviated)		
Item	*Category*	*Unit*	*Projected Weekly Sales Volume*
Pizza dough balls, 20 oz.	Baked goods	Case, 24 ct.	3
Bread, 3-ft. loaf, Italian	Baked goods	Each	6
Cheese, mozzarella, shredded	Dairy	Case, 14 lb.	2
Cream, sour	Dairy	Case, 8 lb.	.5
Chicken, breast, 4 oz. raw, 15%	Meat/poultry	Case, 10 lb.	2
Beef, burgers 3:1, 80/20	Meat/poultry	Case, 10 lb.	5

Don't worry if you can't fill in every detail on your list, like the unit size, *before* you speak to your first sales rep. Start with your menu specifications and your projected sales volumes to figure out how much of the specific items you need. Then you can work with sales reps to get the best prices for your specific quantities, in a volume that is realistic for your business. When you're first starting out, you have to be flexible and follow a trial-and-error approach.

Use your supply list to create your inventory control sheets and save yourself some time. Take a look at "Maintaining Your Bar's Inventory" later in this chapter for help.

When you're drawing up your supply list, consider prep time as a factor. Many bars don't have a huge kitchen staff to spend hours and hours preparing every item on the menu from scratch. And your patrons and concept likely don't require "from scratch" quality in all things. For example, the local Italian joint down the street may hand-bread mozzarella triangles before deep-frying them and serving them with freshly grated parmesan cheese and house-made marinara sauce. But you may decide to go with a terrific, commercially prepared cheese stick that goes right from the freezer to the fryer and is served up with a canned marinara sauce. Both products are quality products from the patrons' standpoint. The Italian joint's version probably costs them less in raw goods but is more expensive in terms of the labor dollars to create it. Your version is more expensive from your distributor, but you save money in preparation time.

Finding the best suppliers for your bar

Now that you know what you need, find out what's available from different suppliers. Because food-service brands are typically not mentioned on menus, you have quite a bit of flexibility in deciding whom to buy food products from. No one knows what brand of canned tomatoes goes in your chili. Liquor is a bit trickier.

In most areas, a single distributor is available for specific brands of liquor. So, if for example, you want to carry Bacardi rum, you must buy it from one particular company. It's a little trickier to negotiate great deals, especially if you have to keep certain brands in your bar because the company has a monopoly on a particular brand. You may not be able to say, "Forget it. I'm going to buy Ronrico Rum instead," if your customers really want Bacardi.

Setting up supplier relationships

Whenever possible, figure out what you need before your sales rep tells you what you need. Sales reps can be a great source of information, but don't rely on them as your only source. Remember, they are in the business of selling you products. The more you buy, the more money they make.

Here are some tips to keep in mind when working with suppliers:

- ✔ **Talk to other bar and restaurant owners to see where they buy their products.** For the most part, this business is made up of people willing to help each other out.

- ✔ **Be aware enough about your business to know whether something is good or bad for your business.** Easier said than done, we know, but it gets easier with time and experience. You have to be smarter about your business than the salespeople. Salespeople often get bonuses for selling certain products over others. Those products may still be great for your business, so it's not necessarily a bad thing. Just know what you want and why you want it, and stick to your guns.

- ✔ **Invite your sales reps to your bar to see your setup.** Show them your kitchen and its limitations. Go over your menu with them. Show them your supply list (like the one in Table 14-1, only longer). Talk to them about your expectations. Show them your delivery area and storerooms so they get a feel for any logistical challenges.

Get the supplier's sales rep *and* her boss into your bar for the meeting, if at all possible. This step can shave time off the negotiating game. Often, the real power in negotiating prices doesn't lie with the sales rep. Usually her boss (or boss's boss) has the final say. If they know that you're professional and organized, with specific needs and wants, the whole process goes much smoother and quicker.

- ✔ **Buy quality products, always.** Quality products rarely disappoint customers. Depending on how you price your drinks, people may not feel like they're getting a value, but we recommend that you maintain a high quality and charge appropriately.

- ✔ **Shop for the best price.** Don't shop around for the best price on individual items from separate suppliers. Instead, contact potential vendors with the full list of products you want to purchase, like the list in Table 14-1, and look at the overall best price. Suppliers have more leverage to give you better pricing when you do a larger volume of business with them.

If suppliers aren't interested in getting your business, they aren't going to be interested in servicing your business. Make it clear to them that you want them to understand your business and how you want it to work. You're setting up an ongoing relationship, not just buying groceries for the week.

Request your sales rep's office, cell, and home phone numbers. Ask for her boss's office and cell numbers, too, but make sure that the sales rep is aware that you've asked for the boss's contact info. That way, she's not completely surprised if you call her boss for some reason, and it keeps the pressure on because she knows that you may call if you have reason.

Keeping the good vibes going

The best sales reps understand their clients' business and bring them ideas, new products, and opportunities in the marketplace that can benefit their business. They must understand your goals, business, costs, and order and delivery requirements to do their best job for you. Always ask about return policies and get them in writing. All suppliers will have one before you buy, and then might conveniently forget it afterwards.

At the end of the initial meeting, send the sales rep on her way with your list and an understanding of your goals. Give the rep a specific deadline to get back to you with a price quote. Be upfront and let her know that you're requesting quotes from other companies; you can even mention the competitors by name. This step shows the sales rep that you know what you're doing and you're confident in your research. Remind her that the purveyor who can meet most of your needs will get the majority of your business.

If you develop a good working relationship with your sales reps, they can personally deliver small quantities of must-have goods when you run out midshift. You shouldn't count on this service, however, because it gets old fast.

Using purchase orders (POs)

A *purchase order,* or PO, is a form that the person in charge of purchasing fills out and leaves for the person who receives the order. The person in your bar who accepts delivery of the order compares the stock he receives, the purchase order, and the actual invoice that accompanies the delivery, looking for things that don't match. That way, if you know that you got the wrong chicken, you can fix it before someone starts thawing it and marinating it.

A purchase order includes the details of the products you need in your bar. After you've figured out exactly what items and their sizes you need for your recipes, you definitely want them to arrive in your bar that way. If you're buying wine, and you order a particular vintage of wine but receive another, it makes a difference in quality, price, and the value to your customers. Maybe you order 5 pounds of salami, but instead you get 50 pounds; it may spoil before you can use it. If you want 5-ounce bottles of hot sauce to put on every table and instead get a case of pint-size bottles, you'll have to fix the problem.

You may think these kinds of things don't happen, but it's a regular occurrence in the food-service industry. The problems get worse when the person who does the ordering doesn't do the receiving. A purchase order can help you minimize the problems, or at least catch them before they become bigger problems. Check out Figure 14-1 for a sample purchase order.

You can e-mail (or fax) the purchase order to your supplier, and then print a copy for the receiver. Or you can complete the PO, and then call in your order to your rep. They may never see the form, but it still helps you communicate your order accurately. Some suppliers will let you place orders through a secure Web site and then print a copy of your order for receiving purposes. It's an informal purchase order, but it definitely serves the same purpose.

For information about dealing with problems that occur when ordering goes wrong, check out the next section, "Reordering your supplies."

Reordering your supplies

These days, most suppliers can give you next-day turnaround on your order. We recommend that you place orders for delivery of perishable goods, such as meat and produce, twice a week, once on Tuesday and once on Thursday. You should be able to order liquor once a week.

Date _____ Your Company Name _____ Order No. _____
Account No. ____(your account with the supplier)_____ Page ____ of _____
Salesperson _____

To: _____(Their Company Name)_____
Fax Number: _____
Email: _____

Please send the following: _____
Deliver Via: _____(your transportation requirements)_____
Deliver By: _____(date and time you need it)_____
Special Instructions: _____
_____
_____

Quantity	Size of Unit	Item	Unit Price	Extended Price

Page Total _____
Order Total _____

Receiving Supervisor: Please complete the following information:

Rec'd by _____ Condition of order _____
Date rec'd _____ Other info _____

Figure 14-1:
Sample
purchase
order.

Because your business levels increase over the weekend, your Thursday orders are larger than your Tuesday orders.

Require deliveries before 10 a.m. or between 3 and 4 p.m. Refuse deliveries at any other time because with a bar full of customers, you can't accurately check in your order. You're the buyer; you make the rules.

Only time will prepare you for the quantity of what you need. This is a guessing game until you have experience and are in business for two or three months. Keep your eye on your inventory. And take a look at Chapter 8, where we give you our recommendations for the initial order of your most expensive items, your liquor. This information should get you started until you can establish how much liquor you actually use.

Using requisition sheets

Only a few people should have the power to spend money on behalf of your bar. But your bartenders, cooks, and servers will use the actual products more than you will and may know when you need something before you do. Use *requisitions sheets* to give them a written way to communicate ordering information to you.

Requisition sheets are kind of like POs (purchase orders; see the "Using purchase orders (POs)" section), but they can be less formal. Take a look at Figure 14-2 for an example. Any form that you use to track requests for supplies can be a requisition sheet. Your bartender can use a copy of the beer menu to identify needed stock, for example. Whatever system you use, make sure that it's a written system, understood by everyone involved. (We recommend that it's not a collection of sticky notes hanging by the telephone.) A written system provides an excellent way to communicate requests and start a paper trail for your supplies. And make sure your employees sign and date the request, so the purchaser knows how old the request is and who to talk to if they have questions about the order.

Receiving your products

When a delivery truck pulls up at your back door, check everything in immediately, before the driver leaves your building. Your *receiver* (the person from your bar who is checking products in) should have a PO to compare the *invoice* (a form that the supplier sends with the goods that lists the items, quantities, and prices) and products against. The receiver and the delivery driver both should sign for the shipment.

Use whatever tools are necessary to make sure you get what you intended to order. (We recommend written tools like purchase orders and requisition forms.) You can't assume that the process will work on autopilot. You have to steer it. More often than not, no one's trying to cheat anyone out of what they order. Instead, mistakes are made and are truly accidental. And mistakes happen on both ends of the telephone. Don't just assume that your supplier is at fault. Double-check your documents to confirm that you didn't order the wrong stuff.

Requisition Form

Today's Date _____

Completed by _____

Date needed _____

Quantity	Size of Unit	Description of Item

Special Instructions _____

_____

_____

Receiving Supervisor: Please complete the following information:

Date Requistion Rec'd _____
Date ordered _____
Requested Delivery Date _____

Figure 14-2:
Sample
requisition
sheet.

When trouble occurs, how do you resolve it? Get on the phone ASAP to your sales rep. Often, she can personally resolve a problem for you, even bringing you the missing product. If you have the right products, but are charged the wrong prices, you still want to let her know right away, so she can get your billing straightened out.

Maintaining Your Bar's Inventory

Your *inventory* is the stock of supplies you have on hand at any given time. It's an investment, and you get no return on that investment until that product sells. It's truly a balancing act: You want as little money as possible tied up in inventory, but you want to have enough to efficiently do business.

Taking inventory refers to counting your stock to find out how much money you have invested in it and confirm how much product is actually making its way to patrons and translating into dollar bills in your pocket.

Inventory is also a warehouse of your cash flow. Excess inventory ties up money that you can't use for other necessities until the products sell. Not managing the balance between cash flow and inventory is the failing of many a bar. In this competitive business, you want your money where it can work for you, not tied up in the skid of swizzle sticks you got for half price and that is now taking up space in the storeroom.

Salespeople love to come up with incentives for you to buy in bulk, but always examine their offers with a keen eye. For example, they may say, "If you buy 100 cases of tomato juice today, you'll save $3 a case." Take a look at that deal. If you buy 100 cases of tomato juice at $40 per case, you've invested $4,000 in tomato juice. Suppose that it takes you five months to sell this juice, even with your famous Sunday Bloody Mary Bar. Let's also assume you have to pay the $4,000 invoice 15 days from receipt of the goods. In the meantime, at your margin of 50 percent (which means when you sell a Bloody Mary for $4, $2 goes to cover the cost of the ingredients, one of which is tomato juice), you have to sell more than 2,000 Bloody Marys to break even on that great deal. All the while, you "saved" $300. And until you break even, you're in the red.

Here are a few ideas to keep in mind when a kind-hearted salesperson tries to lure you into buying more of something than you need:

- **Buy quantities that you can realistically use while the item is fresh.** Watch out for deals and large volumes of produce and other perishables. If you're throwing out half of what you buy, are you really saving money?

- **Balance volume purchases of nonperishable items with the cash flow you tie up in inventory.** It's great if you're getting a good deal on three cases of an expensive, 40-year-old Scotch. But if it takes you four years to move it, you'll have lost investment opportunities for that money in the meantime. Find the balance that works for you.

- **Understand that you only bring money in when you sell food and beverages.** You have to build all your costs (rent, taxes, insurance, wages, food costs, and so on) into the prices on your menu. For more on developing and pricing your menu, check out Chapter 9.

Par levels: Consistently keeping enough product on hand

Most bars and restaurants resort to the tried-and-true process of manual counts for inventory purposes. In most cases, food and beverages are counted on a shift-by-shift basis, using par sheets. *Par sheets* are lists of items that restaurants and bars keep on hand during a shift to help them make food and drink orders quickly. A *par level* is the actual number you write on the par sheet to communicate how much of something your staff should make ready.

Here are some examples for ways to use par sheets and par levels:

- ✔ Set a par level for the number of domestic bottled beers in the reach-in cooler. (Remember, you will have more bottles in the cold storage in the back; par sheets help you decide what to keep handy during a shift.)

- ✔ List par levels for garnishes. Bartenders can get these items ready before their shift begins to ensure they have extra lime wedges or stuffed olives close by when they need them.

- ✔ Decide how much house-made margarita mix you need to have ready and waiting before your business picks up for the night.

- ✔ Estimate how many pizza crusts should be thawed out before your lunch rush.

A par sheet gives you a place to count what you have on hand, compare it to what you need to have ready, and communicate to your staff how much to prepare before the next shift. Take a look at Figure 14-3 for an example of what a par sheet looks like.

Par levels are a good guide, but they shouldn't replace thinking entirely. When ordering and prepping, you must consider the weather, holidays, the day of the week, and so on, or you run the risk of over- or underprepping.

Keeping par levels and doing *shift counts* (counting your products before or after every shift) helps you stay on top of your inventory. Don't wait until the end of the month to find out you're missing supplies.

Taking your bar's inventory

Knowing how much product you have on hand at any given time is essential so that you

- ✔ Can order product when you get low

- ✔ Know where and how your inventory dollars are being used

- ✔ Make sure that your inventory is actually making it into your menu items and out to your paying guests

- ✔ Assess the cash value of stock on hand for accounting purposes

Daily Par Sheet

DATE _December 12, 2008_   DAY OF WEEK _Friday_
POSITION _Bartender_

Menu Item / Product	Amount on Hand	Par Levels Mon - Wed	Par Levels Thu - Sat	Amount to Prep	Shelf Life	Comments
Margarita mix	1/2 container	1	3	3	3 days	
Miller Lite	12	36	48	36	2 weeks	
Lime wedges	1	2	4	3	2 days	

Figure 14-3:
Sample
daily par
sheet.

Everyone seems to have their own way to track inventory. Most bars use one of these methods (or a combination of several methods). They generally fall into a couple of categories:

- **High-tech systems:** These computerized systems include scanner guns and bar codes and practically update themselves as products come in and go out of your business. Some systems are fully integrated, tracking products from the time they're delivered, through the preparation process, to the time they make it to the customer. Other systems can automatically count down your inventory as you use products. If you're missing a single can, it shows up. The systems work well if you're planning on having an exceptionally stable menu. If you're planning any kind of a change, completely automated systems can be more work than they're worth. And these systems are more expensive than low-tech versions.

   To use this kind of a system effectively, you have to have someone who accurately enters all data in a timely manner. This *only* happens in a business with sufficient staff to devote the necessary time to this detailed process. In an independent (rather than a corporately run) bar, these systems usually end up being scrapped, or underutilized at best.

- **Low-tech systems:** These rely on paper and people: purchase orders, requisitions forms, and you or one of your employees physically counting your stock, each shift, each day, each week, and each month.

Even if you use an automated system, you still must physically count your inventory on a regular basis (monthly, at a minimum, more if you need it) to account for everything and catch any discrepancies, including simple human errors and theft. Yes, it's a big job. Yes, it takes a lot of time. But it's absolutely necessary to ensure that your profits are not ending up in a trash can or in someone's home pantry.

As part of your monthly P&L (profit and loss statement, which you can read all about in Chapter 15), you count your inventory. This count is a full and complete account of all the food and beverage items in your bar. Your goal here is to *reconcile* (or match up) your assets on hand (your inventory) against the liability of the invoices (the bills you must pay).

Take a look at Table 14-2 to see what a snapshot of an inventory worksheet looks like. We use the same products from Table 14-1 where we decided which supplies we needed to order.

Table 14-2	Sample Monthly Inventory Worksheet			
Item	*Unit*	*Unit Price*	*On Hand*	*Value*
Pizza dough balls, 20 oz.	Case, 24 ct.	27.34	.3	8.20
Bread, 3-ft. loaf, Italian	Each	2.49	1	2.49
Cheese, mozzarella, shredded	Case, 14 lb.	18.52	.2	3.71
Cream, sour	Case, 8 lb.	9.37	.5	4.69
Chicken, breast, 4 oz. raw, 15%	Case, 10 lb.	16.43	3	49.29
Beef, burgers 3:1, 80/20	Case, 10 lb.	18.56	2	37.21
Total Value of Inventory				*$105.59*

Here are some general guidelines for taking your monthly inventory count:

- **Conduct your inventory late at night or early in the morning.** This way, you minimize the likelihood that you count something twice because someone moved it while they were working.

- **Split up the process over two days.** Do dry storage and food one day, and liquor another. Do not try to do them both on the same day; it's a lot of work.

- **Enlist the help of several employees.** It's a great lesson to help them become aware that you have put controls in place.

- **Make sure you create and use a complete and consistent format for your inventory worksheets.** Including the unit is essential for getting an accurate count. The "Unit" column helps everyone know how you want them to count each product. For example, in Table 14-2, look at the line for pizza dough balls. If someone went into the freezer and counted 7 balls of dough and wrote "7" in the "On Hand" column, the "Value" column would reflect the dollar value for 7 *cases* of dough (or $191.38), rather than the value for 7 dough balls, or roughly .3 cases of dough (or $8.20). That's a significant difference.

- **After you have your count, use a spreadsheet program, like Excel, to help you calculate the value of your inventory.** Multiply the amount of each item you have on hand by the price you paid for the item.

✔ **Add up the total of all the items in your inventory to get your total value of inventory.** You need this number for your monthly P&L reports discussed in detail in Chapter 15.

✔ **If at all possible, and to keep people honest, rotate the items that individuals inventory.** In other words, have people inventory things they are not responsible for. If the bar manager is responsible for the liquor and the kitchen manager is responsible for the food, have them inventory each others' area. Otherwise, they may have incentive to fudge the numbers.

Remember to conduct inventory at the end of a period, like the end of the week, month, or year. That way you can reconcile all your invoices and statements with the actual physical count to get a true and accurate picture of your bottom line.

Having too much inventory is as bad as running out. Inventory is money, and too much money sitting on a shelf is poor planning. Keep records on when you buy product and when it moves. A good *turn* on your inventory is 1½ times a month, which means you go through your entire inventory 1½ times each month.

Paying Attention to What Goes On in Your Bar

Being present in your bar is the best way to manage it. It may sound simple, but when your staff members see you putting in the time, closely watching what's going on, they will start to model that behavior. Being aware of what's happening can go a long way toward keeping everyone on their toes, which helps you manage your business the way you want it run.

In this section, we focus on saving you money by managing your business every minute of every day. We show you ways to reduce money suckers, such as waste, breakage, and theft, to help you keep more of every dollar.

Reducing waste

Waste costs money, plain and simple. Waste occurs in many places: perishable food, utilities, labor, and so on. Spend some time analyzing your operation. Identify areas where waste occurs.

Kitchen waste will be the number-one area to check. Almost everything can be saved in the kitchen (assuming it's not spoiled). Have a great stockpot for vegetables, bones, and the like (talk to your chef), and you will have a great (and inexpensive) base for all your sauces.

Talk about waste with all the kitchen help. Most people don't intend to waste and won't once they know they are throwing away money. Ultimately, if they do waste money, you will have to close the bar, and they will have to find a new job. It's a team thing!

Let everyone know you're watching for waste and abuse of food, liquor, linen, and paper products. You can stop the waste and abuse of these items by your employees, but stopping the customers, that would be another book.

Looking at the most-common wasted items

The easiest way to reduce waste is to be organized and be vigilant. It starts from the top down. When you're visible, your employees are less likely to leave the water running, steal something, forget FIFO (first in, first out or using the oldest products first). Train your staff to have your eyes for waste. Financially motivating your employees based on controlling expenses benefits you immediately and forever.

Here are a few key areas to be vigilant about:

- **Watch your utility bills.** Close the cooler doors and turn off the inside lights when no one's working in them. (Are you air conditioning the neighborhood?) Don't open windows when you've got the AC cranked and it's 95 degrees out. Turn off unused burners on your ranges on a slow night. Turn off lights in vacant storerooms.

- **Stay on top of your office supplies.** Sticky notes, pens, paper, and menus add up. Office supplies are the most stolen items in any business. They're small, aren't usually tracked, and everyone can use them. Plus, many people don't feel like it's really stealing if an item or two just happens to make it home with them in their purse or pocket. Keep them locked up in the office on a strictly need-to-use basis.

- **Ration your linens.** Although you want a clean bar, employees can clean more than a single bar top with a single towel. Remember, every towel has to go out to the cleaners after it's dirty, and that's another expense. Even if you wash the linens yourself, it's more work (and water and detergent and wear and tear) than you need.

Consider rationing your towels. Give each bartender or cook one towel to last them the whole day. Also, clean up floor spills with dirty linens, not clean linens. It may seem gross at first, but it's much more efficient to clean up half a gallon of ice water with dirty linen, and then sanitize the floor with a mop, than to do the same exercise with fresh-from-the-package linen.

✔ **Watch portion and pour sizes.** Though unintentional, giving away an extra half shot in each drink adds up quickly, ultimately subtracting from your bottom line. Dishing up an extra 2 ounces of fries with each 1-ounce order is like giving away two free orders. Standardized portions and pour sizes give you a way to monitor use and reduce waste.

When good food goes bad: Eliminating spoilage

Food products have a much shorter shelf life than liquor, especially those that fall into the perishable category, such as fresh fruits and vegetables, dairy products, and meats. Canned foods and frozen foods tend to be more forgiving of time.

Spoilage in a food-service establishment, like a bar, takes on a whole different perspective when you consider the volume. If you've ever been grumpy about tossing out a rotten head of lettuce at home, think about tossing out an entire case in a bar. Ouch!

The good news is that spoilage can be prevented. Begin with an attitude that spoilage is unacceptable. Keep your staff working on the first in, first out (FIFO) rule. Train them from Day 1 that they need to use the oldest products first. Notice we didn't say *spoiled* products. No one is advocating that you serve your patrons rotten food. But you don't want a carton of sour cream to continue to get buried behind newer ones and then expire in the cooler before you can use it.

If you're ordering in the proper quantities, your staff shouldn't have too much extra product to manage.

Believe it or not, beer and wine are perishable. Those little "born on" dates aren't just for show. If these products aren't stored at a consistent, proper temperature, the perishing process speeds up. If you buy ten cases of wine and your storage room temperature is fluctuating, you had better be going through your stock quickly, or the wine's quality will be affected.

Battling breakage

Accidents will happen. But the root of breakage is disorganization. If your staff is organized and working together, your food is coming out of the kitchen on time, and your dish area is tidy, you're much less likely to sustain breakage than if everything is chaos.

Breakage is an expense that you probably can't eliminate, but you can take steps to control it.

- ✔ Install magnetic flatware catchers on your trash cans in the dish area. You'd be amazed at the amount of flatware that gets thrown away in bars and restaurants. You can also put a sign near the garbage cans: "What are you throwing away?"

- ✔ Only buy glassware with the appropriate washing rack. (Take a look at more glassware advice in Chapter 7.) Using the wrong racks invites breakage, especially if the glasses have long stems.

- ✔ Organize your dish area so that plates, china, flatware, and so on are neatly stacked coming in and going out.

- ✔ Use rubber mats in the dish area and storerooms where glass items, from stemware to liquor bottles, are stored. A simple thing can go a long way in getting more bounce for your buck.

- ✔ Hire, train, and communicate with quality employees. Educate them about your values. Reward them for following the rules you set up.

Assess what hard goods (such as plates, glasses, and the like) you're buying on a regular basis. Some items are more delicate and prone to breakage than you may have originally thought. If the breakage is too much, you may have to change what you're serving in.

Another form of breakage amounts to theft. Verifying that a broken bottle of liquor really was broken is important. Otherwise employees may "drop" bottles right into their lockers. Make sure you save all broken bottles, and know your suppliers' return policies. Some will credit your account if you produce the unopened (albeit broken) top of the bottle. If the seal is intact, you may be in luck.

Reducing and eliminating theft

Theft means stealing, pure and simple. If a dishwasher pockets silverware from the restaurant, that's theft. If a bartender gives a drink away to a customer without ringing it up, that's theft. If a prep cook loads a couple of steaks into a cooler in his car while he's stocking the cooler, that's theft. You can't possibly be everywhere at once, so it's good to have systems in place to help deter the problem.

Check all your supplies in, lock them up in the correct storeroom, and check everything out to the correct stations (back of the house, bar, and front of the house). Keep tight security measures. If you fail to put controls into place, you will lose good help, and it will be your fault. People are only as honest as you let them be! Do not give them any temptation. Remember, even churches are locked.

Using a measuring system (even as simple as a shot glass) can help you get a consistent pour on your drinks. You can buy systems that mount right on your bottles, or you can get a computerized liquor control system that works with your POS (point of sale) system. For more on controlling the amount of liquor your bartenders pour, see Chapter 12.

Many years ago, Ray learned "There is always one more cocktail in the bottle." Pass that mantra along to your bartenders often. Every ounce is money.

Establish a policy on when the house buys drinks. Some owners buy the first drink on Friday or offer a special happy-hour rate for regulars. Whatever your policy is, require all drinks to be rung up on the register. Have a *house check* (a check you keep each day to ring up drinks the house buys) because it keeps everyone honest and slows down the buying of drinks. As staff members see the total creeping up for the day, they're less likely to ask you to add more to it. Giving a cocktail to a customer for free is like giving away money from the register.

A great policy is that when the owner buys, you take the money out of your pocket and pay. This way the customers see you paying with your money, and your gesture makes them feel that you're giving them money, not a cocktail.

Watching out for your staff's sticky fingers

Yes, it's a sad fact of life. Some people will steal from you. Not all — just a few dishonest jerks. People are only as honest as you let them be. It's your job to keep them honest!

The most important step you can take to prevent theft is to hire smart. ("Hire smart, fire seldom" is a good hiring policy.) Check out potential employees' references. You asked for them, now call them. Take a look at Chapter 10 for more tips on hiring the best employees.

Here are other suggestions to keep your staff from stealing from you:

✔ **Use a ticket system.** For every food item and drink, the server must give a *ticket* (a piece of paper with the order and the table/check number on it, also called a *dupe* in bar lingo) to the employee preparing the order. Nothing leaves the kitchen or the bar without a dupe or order slip — nothing!

✔ **Make sure that every customer gets a check, including you.** Everyone sitting at the bar should have a check in front of them. Don't place the check behind the bar. Write the customer's name on the back of the check. And if you buy someone a drink, ring it up. Everything has to be rung on the register, even if you comp it later.

✔ **All employees should leave and enter by the same door, and all coats and bags should be left in an employee area with a closed door with a camera installed outside or near the door.** The employees must have a place to keep their purses, valuables, and coats. A dishonest person will steal from anyone, even her co-workers. If people question your motives, tell them that you're stopping people from stealing from you and them.

✔ **Never let a bartender work with an *open register* (a register that you simply push a button to open). The register should open only to close out a sale.** Everything has to be rung on the register. If you use an open register for some reason, watch out for too many "No Sales" on the register tape. A "No Sale" is a sign that the bartender opened the register drawer without ringing something in. The register should only be opened to settle a bill. Install a change maker to keep the bartender from having to make change from the register.

✔ **Don't let a bartender count the money at night.** Instead, have him bring it to the office with a time of closing, the dupes, and any slips documenting any money taken out and with the specific reason it was done. (For example, if the bartender has ten $100 bills in the drawer in the middle of a shift, you may decide to pull that money out and move it to the safe in the back for safe keeping. If you do that, you need to replace the money with a note saying who's taking the money and why. Only a select few people should ever have reason or authorization to do this.)

✔ **Keep a daily diary behind the bar.** It should list the time your bar opened, the time it closed, and any other facts that are important for each shift. Managers and supervisors complete the log, and should keep log entries factual and professional. This tool will be extremely valuable when you have to reconstruct events for any reason. These documents can be subpoenaed and read in court, so make sure they accurately represent your business.

✔ **Watch or have your manager watch employees leaving at night.** You don't have to pat them down or make them declare their 3 ounces of liquids, but make sure they are not leaving with the store.

✔ **Do not place tip cups next to the register.** Have a big tip cup, placed behind the bar, at least 6 feet from the register.

✔ **Put locks on doors.** This suggestion sounds simple, but if you want to keep people out of something, lock it up. You can lock up coolers, storerooms, offices, bar wells, liquor cabinets, and just about anything else. Locks don't keep out thieves, but they keep honest people honest. If you don't give people the opportunity to steal, most people won't. If people want to steal, they'll figure out a way, but locks are your first line of defense.

✔ **Give keys to as few people as possible.** The fewer people with keys, the easier it will be to find out what's going wrong. And in this case, keys are a deterrent to the few people who do have keys — they know that it's usually not hard to figure out what happened.

Chapter 15

Keeping Your Bar's Bottom Line from Hitting Bottom

In This Chapter

▶ Checking out forms to keep your business in line

▶ Setting up payroll parameters

▶ Keeping your information safe

*I*n lots of ways, running a bar is like running any other business. You have inventory to manage, employees to manage, taxes to pay, invoices to pay, and customers to keep happy. Many people mistakenly focus on one (or maybe a couple) of these details at a time. So they miss many opportunities to dig a little deeper and investigate whether or not they're making money, and they spend even less time figuring out why. Without keeping control of the money and products, you will be out of business fast. (Heather's dad is a successful accountant and entrepreneur. His mantra is, "Watch the nickels and dimes and the dollars take care of themselves.")

In this chapter, we help you apply standard accounting practices to your bar. We get you started with understanding some bar- and restaurant-specific forms that help you analyze your prices, costs, and inventory. We give you the details about setting up your payroll systems. And finally, we help you keep all your information safe.

Keep up with your business on a shift-by-shift, daily, weekly, and monthly basis. Don't let the details sneak up and surprise you after it's too late. Don't miss the opportunity to make corrections. Use the worksheets, reports, logs, and other tools in this chapter and throughout the book to keep up with your numbers and the real dollars they represent.

Reading Your Income Statement

An *income statement* (sometimes called a *profit and loss statement* or *P&L* for short) summarizes your expenses and sales for the month. Then it allows you to compare these two figures and determine your bottom-line profit (or loss) for the month. Take a look at Figure 5-5 in Chapter 5 to see what an income statement looks like. You must look at this report to see whether your bar is profitable. If the income statement doesn't match your expectations, check your math; errors do happen. But if the actual numbers are correct but not what you need them to be, start looking for the causes.

Here are just a few examples of what symptoms an ailing income statement might have with ideas on how to investigate further:

- ✔ If your cost of goods sold (COGS; see "Creating a cost of goods sold (COGS) report" later in this chapter) is a higher percentage than you had hoped, look at your past invoices to make sure you haven't over-paid for the goods you received.

- ✔ If your beverage costs are high, investigate waste and theft.

- ✔ If your sales are low, go back to your daily business review to see whether you can isolate which days and shifts were below normal and start piecing together the problems to find a solution.

- ✔ If your marketing expenses are high, evaluate whether sales are increasing at the rate you hoped they would. If not, figure out why.

- ✔ If repair costs are high during a period, consider looking at leasing newer equipment without maintenance fees.

Some establishments create (or run) income statements and other financial reports to span different periods of time, like quarterly or annually. Feel free to add these to your must-have financial documents list, but make sure you're staying on top of your business on a short-term basis, too.

Deciphering Your Balance Sheet

A *balance sheet* is a financial tool that compares your assets (like your inventory, furniture, and bank accounts) to your liabilities (your debt, including invoices you owe). See a sample balance sheet in Chapter 5.

Ultimately, a balance sheet gives you a snapshot of where your business stands at a specific point in time. Potential investors and creditors look at these reports to assess your financial health. Watching these reports over time can help you understand how your business is growing. Keep an eye on this tool every month, even though it's the least dynamic report you run.

We strongly recommend getting an accountant, preferably one with a bar or food-service background, to help you create and analyze these financial forms. He can help you with the ins and outs of accounting (like the scary words *depreciation* and *accruals*) that are beyond the scope of this book. And take a look at *Accounting For Dummies,* 3rd Edition, by John A. Tracy (Wiley) to get familiar with accounting terms and practices.

Analyzing Reports in the Bar Business

Your business levels and sales will change from day to day and shift to shift. Getting the most-current information available is essential to help you adjust your purchasing plans, preparation schedules, and even staffing schedules. (For example, if you have an extremely busy lunch that lasts well beyond the normal for your 1:30 p.m. drop-off, you might consider calling in an extra staff member or two to help you restock your depleted supplies.) Because this business is extremely fast paced, you need reports that keep up with you. This section gets you started.

We strongly recommend doing as much of this reporting as possible using a computer. It saves a ton of time and tends to be more accurate than old-school arithmetic by hand.

Using a daily business review

Your *daily business review* is a report that you create by recording relevant details (like your sales figures, labor costs, and customer counts) every day. By recording this info in one place, every day, you build a history of your business that allows you to compare figures across previous days, months, and years to establish patterns and determine whether you've gained or lost ground in individual categories.

You can find a sample daily business review in Figure 15-1, but you should develop your own review that tracks data in the categories important to your particular establishment. In our sample, we include a line item (like "Sales") then add a row just below it [Sales (L/Y)] so you can quickly compare your current sales to those from the previous year.

Among other things, a daily business review can help you

  ✔ Determine whether a current promotional event is affecting your sales.

  ✔ Confirm whether your overall volume is increasing over time.

Daily Business Review Week of :								
	Monday	Tuesday	Wednesday	Thursday	Friday	Saturday	Sunday	Totals
Sales								
Sales (L/Y)								
Food Sales								
Food Sales (L/Y)								
Beverage Sales								
Beverage Sales (L/Y)								
Labor Cost								
Labor Cost (L/Y)								
Labor %								
Labor % (L/Y)								
Food Cost % (Est.)								
Food Cost % (L/Y)								
Cover Count								
Cover Count (L/Y)								
Total Credit Card Deposit								
Visa								
Amex								
Mastercard								
Discover								
Cash Deposit								
Food/Bev Mix								
Food/Bev Mix (L/Y)								

Figure 15-1:
A sample daily business review.

✔ Identify whether you have a problem somewhere in your business. For example, if your sales numbers continue to rise, but your profits aren't keeping pace, you have a starting place to begin an investigation.

Because this document, in and of itself, is simply a summary of what happened on a given day, you'll likely need to delve into other documents and operational practices to find the root of any problems.

✔ Clue into trends in your business levels. The trends, in turn, can help you make more-accurate buying decisions and set your *par levels* (or how much stock you should could keep on hand). For more information on setting par levels and keeping your inventory under control, check out Chapter 8.

✔ Keep your cash flow in check. Many people track their cash deposits and credit card receipt totals on this form so they know how much is coming in and when.

Controlling cash flow

Your *cash flow* is simply the movement of money into and out of your bar. Money flows into the bar when patrons buy drinks. Money flows out of the bar when you pay the electric bill. If you think keeping your checkbook balanced is a challenge, consider how tough it is when you don't know what your paycheck (in this case, your sales) is going to be and when it might find its way to you.

Figure 15-2 shows how cash flow fluctuates over the course of a month. We had to make some assumptions about your business to put this example into motion, so here's what we assumed:

❑ You started the month with no money in your account.

❑ You're working on a 30-day month.

❑ Your sales are constant at $2,500 each day.

❑ Your rent is $2,000 each month, paid on the 15th.

❑ Your operating expenses (like food costs, labor, and so on) are 88 percent of your sales.

❑ You pay half of your bills weekly (on the 7th, 14th, 21st, and 28th) and the other half on the last day of the month (the 30th). We include payroll in the bill category here.

❑ Half of your diners pay in cash, while the others pay with credit cards.

❑ Your credit card companies charge you 3 percent of the total transaction for the privilege of taking their cards. They deposit the remaining funds into your bank account with a three-day lag time.

❑ You deposit your cash every day.

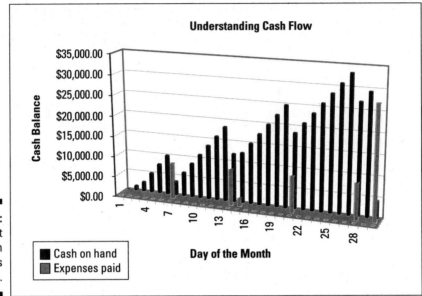

Figure 15-2: Looking at how cash flow works for a month.

After all is said and done, you end the month with a little cash left over *and* you didn't run out along the way. Nicely done! But when you realize how little you had on a few days of the month, you can see that depositing your cash regularly (at least a couple times a week) is essential. And think about how delays in transmitting your credit card charges, and spending extra money when you buy something in bulk, and on and on, can affect your cash flow. Lots to watch out for!

Creating a cost of goods sold (COGS) report

A *cost of goods sold (COGS) report* measures your *actual* food and beverage cost percentages, rather than an estimate. (See Chapter 9 for more on pricing your drinks and meals.) It helps you figure out how much of your food (in dollars) turns into actual sales (in dollars). It shows you how much you're spending on inventory items compared to your sales, which is the ultimate test of how well you manage your inventory.

Write COGS, but say "cost of goods sold." No one really says "COGS."

Take a look at Table 15-1 for a sample COGS report.

Table 15-1	A Sample Cost of Goods Sold (COGS) Report				
	Beginning Inventory (A)	*Purchases (B)*	*Ending Inventory (C)*	*Sales (D)*	*COGS*
Food	957.00	1,200.00	876.00	7,500.00	17.08%
Liquor	2,400.00	2,745.00	1,296.00	18,942.00	20.32%
Beer	895.00	1,200.00	910.00	9,426.00	12.57%
Wine	674.00	350.00	297.00	3,242.00	22.42%
Total	4,926.00	5,495.00	3,379.00	39,110.00	18.01%

To create your own COGS report, follow these steps:

1. **Figure out your beginning inventory (A).**

   If you're just starting and had nothing on the shelf at the beginning of the month, your beginning inventory is $0. If you've been in business, just use your ending inventory number from the previous month's report.

   You can break down your inventory categories in as much detail as you want. The more detailed you are, the better you'll be able to spot trends within larger categories (so you could split beer into multiple categories like Draft and Bottled, or even further like Bottled–Domestic, Bottled–Import, Bottled–Microbrew). Just make sure that you track both your inventory and purchases in a consistent manner so you can get accurate numbers.

2. **Tally your invoices for the products you purchased during the time period you're reporting on (B).**

   Help yourself by keeping an *invoice log* (list of invoices). Assign each invoice to a category that matches with a category on your COGS report. If you make this a habit, you'll save yourself a ton of time when you go to create the report. And you'll make sure you don't miss any invoices.

   If several items from different categories are listed on a single invoice, make sure you put the correct amount in each category, rather than just assigning the total invoice amount to a single category.

3. **Figure out your ending inventory (C).**

   For this report to be truly accurate, you must do a full and accurate physical count of your inventory, and determine the full dollar value it represents. We give you the details for completing a physical count of goods in your bar in Chapter 14.

4. **Figure out your sales for the inventory period (D).**

   Your computer system should track this total for you regularly. If not, add up your daily sales totals from each day during the inventory period to get this total.

5. **Add your beginning inventory and your purchases (A+B). Then subtract your ending inventory (now A+B–C).**

6. **Divide that total by your sales (D), so [(A+B–C) ÷ D] to get your cost of goods sold.**

Your POS system (computerized sales system) may have much of this reporting built in. If it doesn't, you can purchase spreadsheets and forms from several sources, like RestaurantForms.net (www.restaurantforms.net). They sell individual forms and packages of forms in a range of prices. RestaurantOwner.com gives lots of tools free to members; you can find more information at www.restaurantowner.com.

Setting Up Your Payroll System

You will lose good people if you don't keep your word by paying them on time, every time. Setting up a payroll system helps keep you happy — you don't have to hire new employees — and your staff happy — they get paid, which is why they're spending time in your bar in the first place. Heather managed an independent restaurant for an owner who was constantly moving money back and forth between his accounts. Her paycheck bounced two times in a row, and she found another job.

The first rule of payroll (there is no fight club!) is to open two separate bank accounts:

- ✔ **Operating account:** Your operating account is your main account. Money from things like credit card transactions and cash deposits go into this account. You pay all of your bills and invoices from this account.

- ✔ **Payroll account:** This bank account is *only* for payroll purposes. Period. End of story. You move money from your operating account to your payroll account by payday. Never move money from your payroll account to your operating account. As far as you're concerned, the money in your payroll account is no longer your money. If, after payday, an employee chooses to hold his check rather than cash it immediately, so be it. Resist the urge to borrow from this account, even temporarily, no matter how tight money may seem.

Determining your payroll period

There's really no right or wrong way to pay your people, unless you're inconsistent. Remember, this bar is not only your baby; it's your employees' livelihood. It's how they support their families, make car payments, and pay for school. Set up a system and stick to it.

Most bars pay weekly or every other week. (Some choose twice a month, usually the 1st and 15th, but this schedule can make calculating pay for hourly employees really tough.) Here's the rundown on the advantages and disadvantages to you, the bar owner, for both periods.

- ✔ **Weekly:** The upside is that you have a steadier payout of payroll expenses. Each week you transfer roughly the same amount of money to your payroll account. On the downside, you double your management time. Under this system, you have to verify hours, pay rates, and so on, four or five times a month, rather than two or three times.

- ✔ **Every other week:** The upside is that you spend less time managing payroll. You can probably cut your payroll costs in half (assuming you're farming it out) because you need the service less often. The downside is that you have a much larger payroll expense every other week.

Doing payroll yourself or outsourcing it

Depending on the size of your operation, you may opt to do all the payroll duties yourself from start to finish (or assign it to someone in your operation), or you can outsource some of the work to a payroll company.

Here are the basic steps involved in completing the payroll process:

1. **Calculate and verify the hours each of your employees worked.**

   No matter what kind of system you use, you or one of your other managers needs to look at this information and confirm it before paychecks are issued. If you use a computerized system to track hours worked, you can print a report that gives you the recorded hours worked. If not, collect those timecards and start adding.

   By verifying the hours, we don't mean that you need to interrogate every employee ("Did you work 38 hours or 37 hours last week?"). Instead, you just scan over the information looking for discrepancies, especially unexpected overtime.

2. **Confirm employee pay rates.**

   Data entry errors are common, so again someone needs to double-check this important piece of info even if (or especially if) your time clock is computerized.

   After you do this a few times, it becomes second nature. If you notice that your favorite dishwasher worked 32 hours this week at a rate of $132 an hour, you won't have trouble figuring out that something is amiss.

   Starting at this point, a payroll company can take over for you (except for Step 7, probably) or you can continue the process on your own. This process does become a bit more tedious at this point because you have lots of calculations to make.

3. **Crunch the numbers.**

   You have to calculate gross pay and deduct taxes and FICA (better known as Social Security) for each employee to arrive at the *net pay* (the amount owed the employee after all the withholding is withheld).

   Employee checks are issued for the net pay amount, but the check stub should give them details such as their gross pay and itemized deductions.

   As an employer, you send payment for taxes and FICA to the appropriate government agency on a regular basis. Get with your accountant for the details.

4. **Tally the net pay for all of your employees to determine your total deposit for the payroll account.**

5. **Transfer the payroll deposit from the operations account to the payroll account.**

   Keep both accounts at the same bank so you can make a phone call or complete an online transaction to move money from one account to another and post it by the end of the day.

6. **Cut checks for each employee.**

   Print a separate check for each employee. Make sure each check includes details about the number of hours the employee worked, his or her gross pay, and any deductions taken out.

7. **Distribute checks to employees on payday.**

   Establish a scheduled time, usually midafternoon, to distribute checks.

Even if you hire a payroll company, you still need someone in house to double-check the information before checks are handed out. Decide whether a payroll company's service (to basically crunch numbers and issue checks) is worth the amount of money you'll pay for it.

Keeping and Protecting Your Records

All businesses must keep records for all kinds of things . . . just in case of audits, court cases, police investigations, and so on. Right now, it may not seem like such a big deal, but next month, next year, or even five years from now, how do you know what to keep? Does the IRS really need to see how much you spent on keg beer six years ago? Yes, it does, believe it or not. Take a look at Table 15-2. It gives you our recommendations for how long to keep certain documents.

If you get information from a reputable source that differs from the information in this book (like from the IRS, your accountant, or your dentist — no, scratch that last one), follow the most conservative recommendation to cover yourself.

Table 15-2	Recommendations for Keeping Records
Records	*How Long?*
Balance sheets	Permanently
Bank statements	7 years
Cash receipts	Permanently
Cash sales slips	3 years
Contracts: employee, government, and labor union	Permanently
Contracts: vendor (after expiration)	9 years
Credit card receipts	10 years
Employment records (after termination)	10 years
Equipment leases (after expiration)	6 years
Equipment repair records	Life of equipment
Financial statements	Permanently
Franchise documents	Permanently
Garnishments	6 years
General ledger	Permanently

(continued)

Table 15-2 *(continued)*

Records	*How Long?*
Inspection reports	5 to 10 years
Inventory records	3 years
Invoices	7 years
Job applications, nonemployee	1 year
Leases	Permanently
Mortgages	Permanently
Payroll records (after termination)	10 years
Permits and licenses (fire, elevator, liquor, and so on)	Current on file
Profit and loss statements	10 years
Tax records	7 years

Preventing identity theft

Identity theft is regularly in the news today. Basically, crooks steal vital personal information of unsuspecting people and open credit cards in their names, using their Social Security numbers, birth dates, last known address, and so on. They then max out the credit, never pay the bills, and stick the victims with a huge mess to try to unravel. As a business owner, you have a responsibility to protect your customers and your employees from unscrupulous, would-be thieves.

Keep a security camera in your coat-check area. Despite the warnings, people do leave identification in their coats. The IDs can be stolen and used to commit identity theft.

You'll have all sorts of paperwork with sensitive information on it — yours, your employees', and your customers'. Keep your employees' Social Security numbers and other highly personal information locked up in your office, and store bank account numbers for your business and customer credit card numbers out of reach. Locks don't keep criminals and thieves out of your stuff. But they do keep honest people honest. Ultimately, if someone wants to get into your file cabinet, they will.

Hackers be gone! Protecting your computer system

You will probably store just as much sensitive information on your computer as you will in the filing cabinet in your office, so you need to protect your computer from hackers. *Hackers* are computer-savvy criminals who want to gain access to your records to either destroy them or use the information for illegal gain. A *firewall* is a software application that protects the restaurant *and* its clientele from attack from hackers. Talk to the sales rep who sells you your computer system about the best plan for protecting your system. At a minimum, limit access to the system to managers and make sure everyone has their own password so you can track who's doing what in the system.

Hackers can attack your credit card system as well. Make sure that you're using a reputable credit card company. It should have protection, insurance, and *encrypted*, or secure, systems. Talk about what services the company offers, and pick what's best for your business.

Chapter 16

Building and Keeping Your Bar Crowd

- -

In This Chapter

▶ Spreading the word about your bar

▶ Finding new bar customers

▶ Keeping your customers coming back for more

▶ Getting started on the right foot

- -

*Y*ou may pour the best drinks, tell the best jokes, and have the best selection of games on your 35 TVs, but if your potential customers don't know it, you're not going to make any money. Getting people in the door for the first time is half the battle. Keeping them coming back requires you to do an excellent job of entertaining and pleasing them while they're in your place.

In this chapter, we show you how to spread the word about your new bar and keep it spreading. We give you concrete ideas for letting people know about your bar so they can come in to check you out. We have tips for competing with all the other bars and restaurants that are vying for your customers, and we give you ideas for keeping your customers coming back again and again.

Generating Word of Mouth

The best form of marketing and advertising is *word of mouth,* having others speak about your place. People connect and trust other people who've had a good experience. Hearing good comments about your bar from another person makes a potential patron much more likely to stop in than if they had read your ad in the newspaper. In fact, ultimately you want your main advertising to be word of mouth. But you can't have it until you start it. So get going! This section shows you how. For more great information, take a look at *Advertising For Dummies,* 2nd Edition, by Gary Dahl (Wiley). It has a whole chapter on word-of-mouth advertising.

Above all, give your customers excellent service and products. No one complains about them, and no one complains about the price if the food and service are great.

Making sure everyone knows your name (and logo)

Name recognition goes a long way, just ask the politicians. All public relations (PR) is good PR (unless the health department is involved, of course). So get your name out there in front of people.

Ray has a friend who puts his bar's name on everything in his place, from the front door to the line where you sign your credit card. You can have your bar's name printed on just about anything — you make the choice.

Choose a great name and hire a professional to create a great logo. For more on choosing the right name, take a look at Chapter 6.

We recommend putting your name and logo on these items to spread the word:

> ✔ **Local newspaper:** Run a small ad, but run it often. Ask that it be placed in the entertainment section so people see it when they're planning their evenings.
>
> ✔ **T-shirts:** You can sell T-shirts for a small profit and have walking billboards all over town.
>
>   Remember, T-shirts have space on the back. Use it.

> ✔ **Pens and pencils:** Everyone uses them, so give patrons one of yours with your phone number, Web site, or tagline on it.
>
> ✔ **Business cards:** Carry them and hand them out. Put a free drink coupon on the back.
>
>   Consider printing business cards for bartenders and longtime staff members, too. They can pass them out to their mechanic, dental hygienist, or other people they come into contact with.

> ✔ **Bumper stickers:** People put stickers on everything, not just cars. College kids use them to decorate dorms, fraternities, notebooks, beer fridges, and backpacks.

✔ **Frisbees and other toys:** Frisbees are a great choice if your community has large, open parks or campuses where people play ultimate Frisbee or use them as dog toys. Patrons may take other silly toys and set them on their desk at home or work. If a particular gimmick fits your demographic, put your name on it and give it away.

Whipping up a Web site

Web sites are a must-have item for any business these days. A Web site can tell people on the other side of town or on the other side of the world about your place. Its reach is limitless. Your Web site doesn't have to be full of the latest dropdowns, rollovers, superslick graphics, or Flash videos. And it doesn't have to be expensive.

Register your Web site address as soon as you choose a name for the bar. Make sure you make it simple and closely related to the name of your bar. For example, if your bar's name is Muldoon's, www.muldoons.com is a natural choice. Unfortunately, it's already the home of Muldoon's Menswear, so you'll have to pick another one. Keep the address reasonable, like www.muldoonsbar.com or www.muldoonspub.com and so on. (Incidentally, both of these are taken as well, so if you're going to open up a bar called Muldoon's, you're going to have a challenge on your hands when it comes to choosing a Web-site address.) Skip the crazy punctuation or weird spelling (unless the name of your bar is truly unique, Muldoonz, for example).

You can register your address, get design help, and launch a Web site quickly with a company like Network Solutions (www.networksolutions.com), Yahoo! (http://smallbusiness.yahoo.com/services), or NetFirms (www.netfirms.com).

Here are the basics for your bar Web site:

✔ Your address and phone number. Most people look up bars online to order drinks for delivery — no! — to find out the location. If you're really thinking, include a map and directions from different areas of town.

✔ Your hours of operation.

✔ Your menu.

✔ Your calendar of events.

✔ Your drink specials.

✔ An opportunity for patrons to sign up for newsletters, mailings, or Web site updates.

If you have merchandise like sweatshirts, T-shirts, and gift certificates that you sell in the bar, consider making them available for sale. A shopping-cart feature is a little more complicated and expensive, so if you don't want to start out with one, it's okay. You can always add one later.

You only need to update the Web site when you have changes to the menu, entertainment, or specials. It won't be a huge time commitment, but you can reap the benefits.

Getting your employees excited about your place

You want your staff to want to come to work. You want them to encourage other people to come to the bar. You want great synergy between the front of the house (FOH) and the back of the house (BOH). Treat your staff with respect and insist that they treat each other with respect.

Take their ideas to heart. Encourage them to develop new drinks, menu items, or merchandising plans, as the ideas are appropriate in their position. Making employees feel like they have a say gives them a greater sense of ownership and pride in your business. Employees are often the driving force behind community involvement efforts (see the next section, "Making the most of community involvement").

Having daily meetings before opening to explain new menus and hear any suggestions from the employees is very important. Respecting and listening to your employees sets an example that they'll follow with your customers. To show your employees that you appreciate them, have an employee of the week or month, and give them something small to go along with the honor.

Your staff can be your most loyal supporters or your quickest road to ruin. Make sure they're advocating for you, building your bar up in the eyes of your patrons, and representing the bar the way they should.

Making the most of community involvement

Community involvement means being a caring and contributing member of your community. Maybe you give money to charity, host charity events at your bar or, donate gift certificates for silent auctions. Being involved in your community makes people feel like you're a member of their world, like you're all in it together, and they're more likely to make yours a regular stop when they're bar hopping.

Sponsoring amateur sports teams in your town is a no-brainer for a bar. When you're approached by a coed softball team (and you will be, trust us), say yes if you can swing it financially. You'll reap the benefits by getting your name and logo on the uniforms and by, likely, getting the team and their fans in after their games.

Stay away from sponsoring teams with players under 21 years old. You don't want to be seen corrupting tomorrow's leaders. Most kids' leagues have regulations against it anyway, so this likely won't be a problem.

Here are some other ideas that may be less obvious to the bar newbie but can get your bar's name in the public eye:

- ✔ Host charity events. A local bar in Heather's neighborhood sponsors the Red Ribbon Ride to support AIDS research every year. The bar is on the ride's route and hosts the party afterward, too.

- ✔ Sponsor runners or walkers in charity events.

- ✔ Give a check to local hospitals and VA hospitals for charity drives.

- ✔ Help with school or church magazine drives.

- ✔ Search out food-rescue programs that repurpose restaurant food for homeless shelters.

- ✔ Sponsor a team at your local chili cook-off, wing-apalooza, or other food competition.

- ✔ At Christmas, give a bag full of toys and games to Toys for Tots (www. toysfortots.org).

- ✔ Have a fun float for any and all parades (think St. Patrick's Day, Veterans Day, and so on).

You must limit yourself when it comes to community involvement because every nonprofit organization in town will visit you. Prioritize which ones are important to you. Three of the most important for your business are police, fire, and emergency medical technicians (EMTs). You need them.

Keep all records of any donation for a tax write-off. Talk to your accountant to get the complete information on what you can and can't write off.

Also, consider getting involved personally in nonprofit groups that are important to you, whether it's neighborhood revitalization efforts, scholarship programs, Big Brothers/Big Sisters, Habitat for Humanity, or something else. Being a board member or a volunteer exposes you to more people who may be interested in your business and impressed by your largesse. And volunteering definitely makes most of us feel good to genuinely help others.

Getting New Customers in the Door

Before your customers can be regulars, they need to be customers. Getting them in the door is half the battle. And as the line between bars and restaurants becomes more blurry (even before you've had a drink!), you compete with new businesses every day for the almighty drinking dollar. This section helps you help your soon-to-be customers sift through their options and see your bar for what it is: Their soon-to-be favorite place.

Remember, if you start one of these programs and then take it away, it reflects negatively on your business. Do it right the first time. You may not have the opportunity to do it right the second time. Keep an eye on all promos. When they start to get old and don't bring any new customers in, change them! Nothing lasts for ever.

Handling your first customers: The grand-opening crowd

Your grand opening is a great opportunity to get lots of buzz going about your bar. Human curiosity makes people want to try out something new, so opening your place is likely to bring in a crowd looking for what you have to offer. Do it right, and that crowd will continue and build over time. Do it wrong, and that crowd will be the only one you get.

In Chapter 13, we show you everything you need to do to prepare for the grand opening, but here are some basic tips for building on your opening crowd:

- ✔ Make sure your bar, kitchen, and waitstaff are ready to go.

- ✔ Invite business leaders, local celebrities, *beautiful* people, and anyone else whom your demographic relates to or aspires to be.

- ✔ Consider hiring a PR firm to spread the word about your opening. You don't necessarily need to sign a year-long contract with a PR firm, but do seriously consider the benefit a firm provides for getting you off on the right foot.

- ✔ Create a memorable invitation. Don't simply print up your invites on stationery and mail them out. Consider sending them in custom-printed pint glasses, on a coaster, or with logoed items like silicone bracelets, stress balls, or bottled water.

✔ Invite people from the local luxury-car enthusiast club (along with their luxurious cars). Parking sweet rides right outside your door can set a very hip tone for your place.

Make sure you keep those customers coming back by running your bar the right way every day!

Promoting your, uh, promotions

Promotions are special events going on in your bar on a not-so-regular basis. Specials (see the next section) and promotions are the second-best way of getting new customers (word of mouth is number one). Typically, promotions involve some sort of theme or event that goes on for a set period of time — a night, a week, or a maybe a month.

Here are a few examples of promotions that may be successful in your place:

✔ **"Insert-beverage-brand-here" parties:** Your liquor representatives have special liquors or beer they're always promoting. They have all the swag and tchotchkes to go with it: buttons, beads, bumper stickers, and so on. They may also have a staff of attractive young women to walk around your bar and hand out all the stuff. Just ask your salesperson and keep asking.

✔ **Trivia nights:** Teams and individuals compete on electronic trivia games in the bar.

✔ **Karaoke nights:** Everyone can sing or thinks they can.

✔ **Open-mike nights:** You choose the genre — singing, telling jokes, or whatever fits your place.

✔ **Speed dating:** This one is hot. *Speed dating* allows single men and women to meet several potential dates in one evening. Two people talk one on one for a couple of minutes and then move on to the next person. Check out 8minute Dating (www.8minutedating.com), PreDating from Cupid.com (www.pre-dating.com), or HurryDate (www.hurrydate.com) to host an event in your bar. Most parties take place early in the evening and on weeknights when your bar may not be packed already. You also get the benefit of getting mentioned on the dating Web site.

✔ **Bartending contests:** Invite all the bartenders in the area. Choose a theme, like the fastest mixologist, funniest barkeep, or let's-name-a-cocktail-after-the-town.

✔ **Déjà vu celebrations:** Have a grand reopening or birthday party for your bar.

- ✔ **New menu items:** Try adding new ethnic dishes or cocktails. The change, even a temporary one, brings in a different customer.

- ✔ **Customer contests:** Hold a contest to name a new cocktail or dish. Or sponsor a contest to buy a recipe of the best homemade entree in the area.

Don't forget to put your best foot forward during these events because you will have new (and potentially regular) customers in your place. If they get great food and service and have a great time, they're more likely to come back.

Drink and food specials

People like to get a bargain. Sometimes the lure of the bargain helps them decide to visit your place rather than someone else's. Most bars try specials of some sort until they find something that works for them. In the following sections, we explain some of the most common specials.

Cheap food and liquor brings people in the door. Period. But you always have to consider who it's bringing in and how they'll behave after they sit down at your bar and fill up on cheap liquor. If your drinks are too cheap, it can encourage overconsumption and intoxication, both of which can be a headache in terms of liability and the PITA (Pain In The Abdomen) factor. Consider the consequences before you drop your drink prices.

Setting up your happy hour

Happy hours are designed to bring customers into your bar early, let them relax after traditional working hours (9 a.m.–5 p.m.), and, hopefully, get them to stick around. Half-price cocktails, special beer prices, and food are the common fare. Serve appetizer-type foods — items that are small but good quality. Don't have tasteless fried food that just fills up chafing dishes; have items that will make you look *great*, items that people will talk about. Consult with your chef — don't make it just chips and dips.

Early-bird specials

These food specials offer reduced-priced items in the late afternoon to early evening. In most cases, senior citizens take advantage of them and don't stick around. Consider this only if you're ready to split one $5 entree in half and serve it up with two glasses of water.

Have something special food-wise that your patrons can't get anywhere else. Work with your food vendors to find unique, easy-to-prepare appetizers that you can restock easily.

If the food is supposed to be hot, keep it hot. If it's cold, keep it cold. A bad happy hour will hurt, not help, your business. If you're going to do it, do it great. See Chapter 9 for more about setting up a happy hour.

Offering drink nights

Some bar owners choose to discount certain drinks on certain nights. You can focus on a special price or a special category of drinks for a special night.

Thursday night seems to be a popular night for these specials, but remember that you're competing with other bars looking for the same drinking dollars.

Here are a few successful drink-night ideas:

- $2 pints
- $2 domestic bottled beer
- $3 well drinks
- Martini specials
- Margarita specials

Please, never do all-you-can-drink nights. You won't make money, and more importantly you encourage overconsumption and all the legal problems that go along with it.

Catering to certain groups

Depending on your location, you may want to run early-week or early-evening specials for certain groups.

Here are a few ideas for doling out special group privileges:

- **College night:** Discount with a student ID.
- **Greek night:** Discounts for fraternity and sorority members.
- **Ladies night:** Ladies get half-priced drinks (and food). Men and women both come — chicks to get the drinks, dudes to get the chicks. This promo is good for your really slow night, maybe Tuesdays.

  Ladies Nights have been banned in some areas due to gender discrimination. Some bars get around it by offering the discounts to people wearing skirts or lipstick.

> ✔ **Amateur sports teams:** Players in uniform after their game get a discount.
>
> ✔ **Public servants:** Give a nod to police officers, soldiers, firemen, and EMTs.
>
> ✔ **Restaurant employees:** Consider running late-night specials for these night owls.
>
> ✔ **After the game:** Fans can bring in a ticket stub from that day's game for a 10 percent discount.

Cater your specials to your area and clientele. This list is only the beginning.

Promoting specific dishes

You can make every day a banquet. If you serve meals in your bar, offer certain meals only on certain days at a lower-than-average price.

Make Monday *Lobster Night*; Tuesday *All-the-corned-beef-you-can-eat Night*; Wednesday *All-the-pasta-you can-eat Night*; Thursday *Thanksgiving Night* with turkey and all the trimmings; Friday *Fish-fry Night*. You can do just about anything you want (Mexican or Chinese nights, farmers' market nights, potluck nights), but be consistent. Make sure everyone knows what you serve when, and they'll pass the word. As always, make these meals great, or you're wasting your time and money. Most bars don't run specials on the weekends because bars are typically busy during those times.

If you've got a hook, use it: the best burger in town, the biggest burger, the only Buffalo burger, the largest pizza. Big, best, and any words that tell your customers how unique your meals are (in a good way, of course) are the key words.

Making the most of music

Make your current and potential customers aware of your music and entertainment offerings. Check out Chapter 6 to figure out what kind of entertainment works for your bar and how to get it.

After you've decided what entertainment to have, use it as a mechanism to spread your name around town. When you book hot bands, post fliers around the local college campus. Consider running ads on the radio station that plays the same type of music the band plays. Newspapers routinely look for content in the *what's happening* sections and often print entertainment schedules for free.

Don't forget to include professional posters in your own place about upcoming bands and entertainment engagements.

Considering coupons

We don't like the idea of coupons or *buy one, get one free.* It can look like your business isn't doing well, and word travels fast (almost always faster than any positive news coming out of your place). Coupons seem to carry a stigma (think cheap, low quality, cheesy) that you probably don't want associated with your bar, with one exception: Drink coupons for one cocktail to get people into your bar. They work. Offering two-for-one meals won't attract the customers you're looking for. Trust us!

Giving Your Customers a Reason to Come Back

Getting customers in once is good, but creating repeat customers and even regulars is essential to keeping your bar afloat. The surest way to keep them coming back is to give them a quality experience and, to some extent, a value. That's not to say you have to be a bargain, but your customers should feel like they're getting what they pay for at your place.

To make your bar successful, you have to meet your customers' needs, and to meet your customers' needs, you first have to know who they are. After you figure that out, you can figure out what they want and decide how you can give it to them. Try to determine your *demographic profile,* or the set of traits or characteristics the group shares.

For demographic data on the people near your particular location, consider contacting a company like Claritas (www.claritas.com) to do the research for you. They can help you target your customers more effectively than you can on your own.

Here's a list of questions to ask yourself when you're trying to figure out who your customers are:

- ✔ Are they men, women, or both? Are you looking for singles, couples, or a mix?

- ✔ Do you attract a particular segment of the community, like a college crowd, the after-work-people-in-suits crowd, or a hard-hat lunch group? Maybe you get different groups at different times of the day, week, or month.

- ✔ What age are your patrons?

- ✔ What's the economic level of your customer? Does it match the economic level of the area your bar's in?
- ✔ What types of cars fill up your parking lot?
- ✔ Do you draw in tourists, business travelers, locals, or a mix?

You're not trying to exclude anyone from your bar. You're trying to create a picture of the patrons you want to attract so you can gear your products, menus, and entertainment options to them.

Ensuring good customer service

All the marketing, advertising, and promotions don't keep customers. Service brings customers back again and again. Do something right, and a customer will tell *ten* people. Do something wrong, and that customer will tell a *hundred*. In fact, we think good customer service is so critical to your success that we include a whole chapter on the subject, Chapter 11.

Service doesn't begin or end with the person who's handing your patrons their drinks. You as the manager or owner can go a long way toward providing excellent service. Talk to your customers and make sure they're having a great time. Approach a table or patron with open-ended questions like "What can I do for you tonight?" or "How is everything?" rather than "Is everything all right?" (Is "all right" or "okay" your goal? We doubt it.)

Figuring out what your customers want

After you know who your customers are, you have to figure out what they want. (We call this the *psychographic profile.*) You can do this by determining the answers to a set of very simple questions:

- ✔ What do they drink? Do you sell tons of draft beer and hardly any wine? Do your martinis fly off the bar while your sidecar special sits around?
- ✔ What food do they order?
- ✔ Where do they eat and drink when they're not visiting your bar?
- ✔ How often do they visit you?
- ✔ What do they enjoy doing besides sitting in your bar?
- ✔ What do they eat elsewhere that they can't get at your place?

"Great questions, but how do you get the answers?" you ask. Talk to your patrons. Get to know them. And consider creating a comment/suggestion card.

You don't have to change a single thing based on their answers to your questions. It's your bar, for crying out loud! But knowing the answers can help you make better choices when you're ready to make changes. If 50 more people would come in daily for lunch if you only had a nice 8-inch pizza, wouldn't you want to know that?

Start a database of customers and include information such as birthdays, anniversaries, and other special occasions. Place comment cards with table tents and give customers an incentive (like a complimentary appetizer or drink) to join the mailing list.

Turning complaints into repeat customers

Although no one likes to hear what they're doing wrong, many bar owners overlook the immense opportunity that customers provide when they're chewing you out because your place sucks. Granted, it doesn't always *feel* like an opportunity at the time, which is why we're telling you about it now, in a moment of cool, calm collectedness. You do, indeed, want people to complain to you on occasion. The alternative is that a customer is disappointed, doesn't tell you, never comes back again, and tells 15 other people how bad your place is. Yikes!

Okay, so here's how you make sure they not only leave happy but also come back and stay happy.

1. **Listen to the patron.**

   Close your mouth, make solid, continuous eye contact, and just listen. Too many times managers rush to fix the problem without listening to what the customer is telling them. In essence, the manager interrupts them, causing even more problems.

   Remove whatever is disappointing or offending the customer immediately. If it's a drink or food item, remove the glass or plate immediately after you've heard their complaint. If it sits there in front of them, it continues to be a source of negative emotions and can prevent you from turning around the situation.

2. **Apologize or thank them for the feedback, depending on the situation.**

   Believe it or not, many patrons just want to know that you hear their problem and feel their pain. Your sincerity can go a long way in resolving the problem in their mind. Sometimes guests just want to tell you an idea that would make your place better for them, so it's not a complaint, it's just a suggestion. Thank them for their interest in your business and let them know you'll consider their idea.

3. **Fix the current problem.**

 Don't just start comping drinks off their check. If the problem is that
 their glass is chipped, get them a new one. If the Coke in their Jack and
 Coke tastes funny, go check the soda system. Give them a quality experience first, and consider giving something away as a last resort.

4. **Rectify the long-term problem.**

 Let them know that you'll definitely take care of the long-term problem.
 In the chipped-glass example, maybe you institute a more-careful inspection of glassware at some stage in your stocking process. In the Coke
 example, you can set up a system where a barback makes more frequent
 checks of the soda system. Whatever it is, figure out what systematically
 let the offending experience occur and take steps to fix it.

Making patrons feel special

When customers feel like your bar is their home away from home, you know
you're treating them right. One bar owner Heather knows maintains a photo
album of regular guests, including details about them like their favorite
drinks, significant other, kids, alma maters, and profession. He quizzes his
employees during staff meetings about the details of each Very Important
Patron. Almost everyone feels a special connection to the bar because the
staff members can call them by name after just a few times. Talk about creating repeat business.

Who needs a reason to party?

We all do, to some extent. Whether the refrain is
"It's 5 o'clock somewhere!" or "Paycheck
Friday," many people can have a better time
when they celebrate something. Personally, we
celebrate only on days that end in y, but we're
sticklers for that kind of thing.

Here's a list of good reasons to throw a party at
your place:

Back to school

School's out

Graduation

Oktoberfest

Spring Break

Homecoming

Racing events (IndyCar, Formula One, NASCAR)

NBA Finals

Stanley Cup Playoffs

World Curling Championships

World Cup Soccer/Football

Local-team home games

Tour de France

National History Day

National Private Investigators' Day

National Milk Week

Denim Day

National Snack Food Month (February)

Super Bowl Sunday (early February)

Groundhog Day (February 2)

Valentine's Day (February 14)

Anti-Valentine's Day (February 14)

Mardi Gras (the day before Ash Wednesday and the beginning of Lent)

Procrastination Week (March)

St. Patrick's Day (March 17)

Rotten Sneaker Day (March 20)

Benito Juarez's birthday (March 21)

National Goof-Off Day (March 22)

Stress Awareness Month (April)

May Day (May 1)

Cinco de Mayo (May 5)

Doughnut Day (June 6)

National Long Live Lefties Day (June 10)

Clear Off Your Desk Day (June 20)

Bikini Day (July 5)

Video Game Day (July 12)

National Ice Cream Day (July 17)

National Relaxation Day (August 15)

Joke Day (August 16)

Bad Poetry Day (August 18)

Hawaii Statehood Day (Luau theme) (third Friday in August)

Popcorn Day (September 10)

World Peace Day (September 16)

Citizenship Day (September 17)

Talk Like a Pirate Day (September 19)

German/American Day (October 6)

Leif Erikson Day (October 9)

International Newspaper Carrier's Day (October 11)

National Grouch Day (October 15)

National Boss Day (October 16)

Dictionary Day (Daniel Webster's birthday, October 16)

United Nations Day (October 24)

Halloween (October 31)

Dia de los Muertos (Day of the Dead, November 1)

Election Day (dates vary and most bars can't serve liquor until after the polls close)

World Hello Day (November 21)

Boxing Day (Dec. 26)

Create a master schedule with the dates you're interested in. Add to it as you hear of interesting days to celebrate. Make your celebrations and promotions leading up to your championships special, and crowds will follow.

Making changes to your business as necessary

If you're going to run a successful bar, you have to change. Why? Everything changes; some changes are for the better, others . . . well, not for the better. So you need to keep up with the times. Stay in touch with the customers and staff for feedback on what changes to make to better serve your patrons. Maybe they regularly request a brand of vodka that you're not pouring. They may let you know that your restrooms need more attention on weekend nights than they're currently getting. Or if every third chicken sandwich is sent back to the kitchen, you can find the problem. Check out "Maintaining Your Success" later in this chapter for help in analyzing your market and staying on top of the competition.

When you make changes, make them slowly — every other week, for example. For many people, gradual change is better. You can give people a chance to get used to new menu items and drink offerings without too much stress.

Strike a balance between keeping your regulars happy and bringing in fresh meat — we mean, new customers. Your regulars became regulars for a reason. You don't want to unwittingly do away with the reason.

Maintaining Your Success

So you're open. Now what? Maybe you have a feel for what works in your bar, a process to keep it moving and shaking. If you don't, you've come to the right place. Most of the work of keeping your profits pointed in the right direction involves staying on top of what other people are doing and doing it better.

Researching your competition

Know thy enemy is true in any business, and the bar business is no exception. Conduct regular reviews of your competitors, and know what they're doing right and how they're missing the boat.

Here are some questions to help you when you're shopping your competition:

- What's on the menu?
- How much does it cost?
- What's it taste like?
- How's the quality?
- What draft beers are they pouring?

- What's their pricing structure for beer, wine, cocktails, and so on?
- What bottle beers do they stock?
- What's featured on their drink menu?
- What glassware are they using?
- What specials are they plugging?
- What entertainment are they advertising?
- What kinds of customers do they draw?
- How are their bathrooms?
- How's the general atmosphere?
- What's their draw?
- What do they do that's special or intriguing?
- How does their location affect them?
- How was the service?

If you're looking at a specific part of your competitor's business, make sure to include it in your list. Maybe you don't care what their bathroom is like and only want feedback on the chicken wings. Develop your own list of questions that get you answers to *your* concerns.

It may go without saying (too bad, we're saying it anyway), but when you shop (or have someone else shop) your competition, do it very stealthily. Don't sit at the bar asking questions and filling out your little form unless, of course, you approach the bar owner and ask for permission to do so. Instead, you typically get your questions in mind and then experience the bar like any other patron. Yes, like any incredibly observant and curious patron.

Staying marketplace savvy

Knowing what's going on in the bar industry is essential for you to succeed. Stay in the know with trade publications and organizations. Join your local chapter of the National Restaurant Association (www.restaurant.org) or your state affiliate of the American Beverage Licensees (www.ablusa.org). Talk to real estate agents in the area; they know the changing scene. And don't forget the Chamber of Commerce. Folks there may be in the know about long-term plans for different areas in your community.

Subscribe to trade publications such as *BARTENDER* magazine (`www.bartender.com`) to keep up with trends throughout the field. (Yes, a cheap plug — Ray's the founder — but a good magazine.)

The most important advice we can give you is to listen to your customers. Talk to them every chance you get. Get feedback from your servers and bartenders. Ask questions: "What's new in the local places?" "What's hot?" "What's not?"

Part V
The Part of Tens

"Okay, we got one cherry lager with bitters and a pineapple slice, and one honey malt ale with cinnamon and an orange twist. You want these in steins or parfait glasses?"

In this part . . .

For your quick reading pleasure, in this part we include four short and sweet chapters to help you run your bar the right way and keep it *fun!* Here you'll find tips for running a safe bar, myths about the bar business, mistakes to avoid, and Ray's favorite bar jokes to share with your customers (get ready for some groaners!).

Chapter 17

Ten Ways to Run a Safe Bar

. . . .

In This Chapter

▶ Keeping everyone safe in your bar

▶ Following government safety regulations and laws

. . . .

*1*t's all fun and games until someone loses an eye or

- ✔ Loses a purse or wallet.
- ✔ Slips on a spill.
- ✔ Can't find the emergency exit.

Help keep your patrons and employees safe with the pointers in this chapter.

Hiring Safely

Be very cautious when hiring. Make sure applicants provide references and *check* them. Call all previous employers and ask about their experiences with your potential employee. You don't want to find out after you've hired someone that he or she has a criminal record or a history of violent or deviant behavior. Make sure you make the workplace safe for all your employees. Don't hire someone if you have the least bit of doubt.

It's your responsibility to maintain a safe environment for everyone who works for you, and that means protecting your staff from people who may want to harm them, including other employees. Take a look at Chapter 10 for more help on hiring employees.

Practicing Fire Safety

Call the fire department first if a fire starts. Then try and extinguish it with a fire extinguisher. Keep extinguishers near the kitchen, grills, and behind the bar, and make sure all employees know how to use them. You can buy extinguishers from companies that inspect them on a regular basis to make sure they'll work properly when needed. Contact your local fire department to find out what fire codes apply to your bar and for tips on fire safety.

You need to have lighted exit signs at all doors that lead out of your bar. Make sure the signs can remain lighted during a power outage. (The same company that maintains your fire extinguishers can help you with emergency lighting.) Keep all doors unlocked during business hours, and make sure the doors are never blocked. Have fire drills at least every other month, and instruct employees on how to get customers and staff members out quickly and safely.

Using Video Cameras

Video cameras deter criminal behavior, including theft and violent crime from everyone! These days, you don't pay too much to have video cameras installed at your bar. Post signs notifying the public that you have the cameras. Have one camera at the front door and one at the back. They pay off ten times plus in the long run. Check with your insurance company because you may get a discount on your premiums if you install video cameras. And check with the local police — they may want you to have them too. Make sure you change the tapes regularly and keep them up-to-date.

Tell your employees that the cameras are for their own protection and that you're not spying on them. Ultimately, it's your decision where to put the cameras, but never infringe on your employees' privacy!

Using Locks and Alarms

All your supply rooms should be locked, and only managers should have access to the keys. Remember, locks keep honest people honest. Keep these storerooms locked at all times unless someone is actually stocking.

Your liquor and supplies cost you lots of money and have the potential to make you even more money. Keep them locked up!

Make sure employees have lockers with locks. What does this have to do with safety? It stops everyone's temptation to steal. Stealing an employee's keys can lead to much more than stealing their car. It can lead to breaking into their house or worse. Keep everyone safe, not sorry!

All your exit doors need alarms so you know who's leaving and when they're leaving. You don't necessarily need them on interior doors, but they can't hurt.

Most alarm companies install systems for a very low fee and charge you a monthly maintenance.

Consult with both your police and fire departments on alarm systems and which ones they recommend. Sometimes they charge for false alarms; ask them!

Preventing Slips and Falls

Keep floors clean, and use only slip-proof cleaning and waxing supplies. When a spill occurs, make sure someone stays near the spill, or put chairs over it to keep people from walking into the spill. Clean up any spills immediately and place a *Caution Wet Floor* sign in the area until you're sure the floor's dry.

Place rubber mats where possible behind the bar and in the kitchen for better traction. Rubber mats give you the added benefit of cushioning the floor, making it easier on employees' feet. All stairways need rubber treads and handrails. Ask your local fire and building inspectors for guidance. They can work with you.

Taking proactive steps can help you keep insurance premiums down and minimize any legal problems.

Installing Lighting

To ensure safe working conditions, have lighting at all doors and parking areas. Install emergency lighting in all rooms, including the kitchen. Always have backup lighting, which can include flashlights and power lights. If you have the money and space, consider buying an emergency generator, which can also maintain your refrigeration system. If the lights go out, you'll be the only one with COLD BEER! The generator will pay for itself! *Working grids* (lights installed in the floor on the floor) are also very helpful. In case of a blackout, your customers can find their way out.

Checking IDs

Train all front-of-the-house employees how to check IDs. The legal drinking age in every state in the United States is 21 years old. Check carefully. Look for the expiration date, the word *duplicate*, and any smudges. Use a flashlight or magnifying glass to make sure the ID is authentic. If you're not sure, don't serve.

In some communities, no one under 21 is allowed to even enter the premises. Make sure you know which laws and regulations apply to your business.

You can get an ID-checking guide from your beer wholesaler, or contact the Driver License Guide Company, 1492 Oddstad Drive, Redwood City, CA 94063; phone 800-227-8827; Web site www.driverslicenseguide.com.

Serving Hot Food

People want their coffee, tea, and food hot. Train your employees to be very careful when serving hot food. The rule for serving is to serve on the right, pick up on the left. Your servers need to use extreme care when carrying hot food to the table and always tell the guest, "This plate's hot," or "The soup's hot." Keep serving areas free of clutter, and remind your employees to work slowly and safely with hot food. It burns!

Keeping a First-Aid Kit

Make sure employees carry a band-aid in their wallet or purse. Keep first-aid kits behind the bar, in the kitchen and coatroom, and next to the fire extinguisher. Post phone numbers for the ambulance, police, and fire departments. Post instructions for performing the Heimlich maneuver in the locker room and kitchen. Hold first-aid and Heimlich training every two months. It's worth it. You can also find a service company to stock and maintain your first-aid kit.

Following Handicapped and Discrimination Laws

Your bar must be handicapped accessible; that includes the restrooms, entrances, and exits. Make sure you post all state and local ordinances and discrimination bulletins where your employees can read them.

Chapter 18

Ten Myths about Running a Bar

In This Chapter

▶ Looking at some common misconceptions in the bar business

▶ Preparing yourself for the reality of running your own place

You probably came to this business expecting it to be fun. Well, you're right. It can be a ton of fun when you run your business well. But you may have some other ideas that aren't as realistic. This chapter helps you compare your expectations against reality to make sure you know what you're getting into.

The Hours and Days Are Short

The hours and days are long, but time does pass quickly when you're having fun. Busy days go by fast. Slow days last twice as long. Be prepared for long hours.

You're not only the owner; you're also the employee when someone doesn't show up. Hint: Open your tavern six days a week instead of seven when you first start your business. This way you can give everyone, including yourself, a break. It's also a good idea to have two shifts. Overworked people don't perform at their best capabilities. Careful scheduling and good managers make your life easier. Hire well; fire seldom.

Free Drinks All Day, Every Day

Your job is to serve, not drink. Don't make the mistake of sitting around partying with your friends while the business goes on around you. This job is an investment designed to make money. Work hard in your bar. Play hard at other places. Every cocktail is money, so don't drink your profits.

Don't confuse being friendly with your staff and being friends with your staff. If you're hanging out in the bar with your staff, you're in the danger zone. Ultimately, if you're drinking in your place of business, you're taking a risk. At some point you'll embarrass yourself or someone will take advantage of you, most likely by stealing from you in some way.

There's Not Too Much Paperwork

As a bar owner, you take care of lots of details, and many of those details require — you guessed it — paperwork! Your life can be overrun by paperwork: invoices, statements, income-tax forms, state forms, alcohol beverage control forms, and employment forms. And that's just for starters! Have an experienced accountant help you with the bills and taxes to eliminate 50 percent of the paperwork you have to handle. Then you can spend your time with the other paperwork: scheduling forms, monthly promotions calendar, inventory forms, checkbook, order forms, payroll, and other stuff. You're not finished until the paperwork is done.

Your Family Will Want to Work for You

If you're very lucky, your family will help you, and it'll be a pleasant experience for everyone. But always remember that people will disagree (with you or each other), and someone has to be the owner. Have a job description for every position (whether or not family members fill those jobs) so no one's feelings get hurt. Take a look at Chapter 10 for more job-description information.

 If you do decide to work with your family, explicitly go over your expectations with them, especially your rules about handling cash and inventory. When you mix money with family, relatives can become accustomed to unintended perks, including helping themselves to loans, a bottle of scotch, or free draft beers. Make sure they understand what's acceptable and what isn't.

You Can Hire Good Help in a Snap

Help means just that: Help! Good, experienced help is hard to find and harder to keep. As the saying goes, if you pay peanuts, you get monkeys. If your place is busy and everyone makes money, everyone will be happy. But you'll have bumps in the road — slow days, bad weather. Be prepared!

Showing respect to your employees is the most important step in keeping good help. Don't correct anyone in front of customers or other employees. Treat them fairly, always. Good employees are hard to find. And remember, you're only as good as those who work for you!

You Know Everything about Everything

Every owner and bartender at one time or another is asked to settle an argument. Don't be the expert; let the facts speak for themselves. Keep a sports almanac, the latest copy of the *Guinness World Records,* plus a general cinema and movie trivia guide behind the bar. Let these references solve the arguments. If you have a computer, go to your favorite Internet search engine to get the facts. No one can argue with the facts.

Do not get into arguments with customers. Some people are always right, or think they are. Worst-case scenario: Agree to disagree. You don't want to lose customers over a trivial discussion over who was the MVP in the 1977 Major League Baseball All-Star game or who won the 1962 Academy Award for Best Achievement in Sound Editing.

Nobody Would Steal from You

Know your inventories. Watch them daily, monthly, whatever you need to stay on top of your business. Take a look at Part IV for all the details on keeping adequate tabs on your numbers. Check out more strategies for curbing sticky-finger syndrome in Chapter 14.

Here are a few specific rules to help you keep honest people honest:

- ✔ Ensure that all cocktails are rung up immediately.

- ✔ Use a computer-generated ticket that includes the table and check number for all food and cocktails.

- ✔ Keep staff coats, purses, and other personal belongings in a safe place — away from the door.

- ✔ Have your managers and bar staff keep a diary or communication log. Include the opening and closing times, who tended bar, and which wait-staff members were on duty. Immediately write down any problems and the solution. Keep good records; don't rely on your memory.

Everyone Is Trustworthy

Set up effective cash-handling procedures and consistently follow them. Establish your policy for complimentary drinks and stick to it. If you've established a firm policy, it's tougher for employees not to follow it. Take a look at Chapter 11 for establishing procedures.

We strongly recommend that bartenders send the cash drawers to the closing managers rather than count the drawers themselves. At a minimum, the bartender counts the drawer and the closing manager recounts and verifies it. This may seem unnecessary, but double-check all your orders. Check in everything before signing the delivery invoices. Double-check your copies against any mailed statements and pricing agreements to make sure you're charged only for what you receive at the agreed-upon price. Verify everything, *everything*. Keep everyone honest!

Everyone Loves the Boss

No one likes the boss! Respects, admires, fears — yes, it's possible. If you treat people with respect, you'll be respected. But it's nearly impossible to successfully run a bar or tavern *and* be liked by everyone. You're running a business, not running for governor. Write down the rules and regulations and explain them the day you hire someone. Establish a consistent orientation process and go it with employees on their first day. Ask them to read the rules and sign off on them the same day. You'll have fewer mistakes.

Anyone Can Run a Bar or Tavern

The bar business captivates and intrigues people. People think it's glamorous and exciting. Customers see you working where they play and assume that it's always a party. It can be a party, and it can be fun. But to be successful, you must maintain firm control, consistent procedures, and vigilance. Running a bar or tavern is definitely not easy. But hard work, a great attitude, and determination do pay off!

Chapter 19

Ten Bar Owner Sins Not to Make, Ever

In This Chapter

▶ Recognizing errors that can spell disaster for your business

▶ Setting up the ground rules before you begin your venture

Many first-time bar owners can't see the long-term problems that come from seemingly minor or insignificant decisions. By thinking about some ground rules and making decisions before sticky situations arise, you can avoid the consequences of making the wrong decision. Here are our tips for avoiding some of the biggest problems in the business.

Depending on Your Friends and Family

You have to attract and retain customers. Don't depend on your family, friends, or relatives. They probably will patronize your place, but they'll expect to get freebies and deep discounts. Your customers will become like family and friends, only they will pay you for what they eat and drink. For tips on building up your bar business and attracting and keeping customers, check out Chapter 16.

You have to pay your suppliers, not supply your family and friends.

Extending Lines of Credit to Customers

"In God we trust. All others pay." After someone starts a long-term bar tab, it's too easy to say, "Put it on my tab." It will get out of hand. Make it a house policy to not start bar tabs, and put in an ATM so customers have quick access to cash. Do not chase your own money! Credit cards are easy to come by these days if a customer really needs a loan, so let real lenders take the risk.

Starting a nightly tab, with a credit card to secure it, is convenient for both you and the customer. You don't have to do the cash-out dance every time someone orders a drink, but make sure you settle up at the end of every night. With a credit card to secure the tab, you're practically guaranteed that your customer isn't going to "accidentally" leave without settling up.

Some customers (we call them customers, after they walk in the door) will run a tab at your place, and then say they can't pay, but will go down the street and pay cash! Please trust us on this one.

Allowing Gambling or Betting

Without a license that is. . . . In most areas, allowing gambling without the proper paperwork is against the law, and you will lose your liquor license. A patron who loses too much cash will turn you in to the authorities, and you will be out of business. Do not let anyone in your establishment take bets, make bets, or be in any way involved in gambling. Period.

Not Taking the Keys from an Intoxicated Patron

Be safe and you will never be sorry. If a customer who has had too much to drink gets in an accident, he or she will sue you. You will be a part of a lawsuit. Take the customer's keys and call a cab to take the customer home. Always be safe, not sorry.

Train your staff how to recognize when a patron has had enough to drink so they can make these serious decisions. Take a look at Chapter 11 for training tips and for help in dealing with difficult customers.

Believing the Customer Needs "Just One More"

If you are concerned about the rate someone is drinking, slow them down! One more becomes two more becomes three more. Watch your customers; you want them to come back. Bartender training is very important, and so is waitperson training. Monitoring how much customers have had to drink is a team effort. Everyone should watch and help each other. Remember, you want that customer back, so you want them to leave happy and sober.

Lending Money to Anyone

You're not a bank — you're a bar. Like extending credit, the likelihood that you'll see that loaned money again is pretty low. "Neither a lender nor borrower be" is excellent advice. That $10 becomes $20, then $30, and then goodbye friendship, money, and, most importantly, customer!

Becoming Romantically Involved with an Employee

It's not love. It's lust, the liquor, or just being stupid. Don't play where you get paid. It's dangerous. Everyone who works for you will know that you're seeing an employee after hours; there are no secrets in the bar business. Be careful; be smart. Workplace romance causes serious tension for everyone, including the people not in the relationship. The staff's attitudes toward you and your paramour will change because everyone will think you're treating that person better, and that will cause turmoil in your business. Ask any owner!

Drinking and Working

Combine these two and you have the absolute worst cocktail. First of all, you have to be sober when counting and handling money (assuming you want to make sure you get every dime you're due). Second, you are dealing with customers and employees. No one can drink and handle either one. Your job is to supervise, not sip and serve.

You're the innkeeper, not gin sleeper. It's not a good idea to get into the habit of drinking at your bar with customers and employees.

Drinking and Working (Did We Say This Twice?)

Drinking at work: *NO!* Did we repeat ourselves?

Last Call Is Last Call. The End. No More!

Give *last call* (the magic moment when you take final drink orders for the night) at least 20 minutes before closing. When it's 5 minutes before closing, all drinks must be off the tables and the bar. This step must be done as a team. Last call is last call — it's not first call before last call — it's last call. To make enforcing last call easier, allow only one drink per person, not two or three drinks per person. This rule is very important and should never be broken. If you make one single exception, you'll have a losing battle on your hands.

Have the bartenders come out from behind the bar after last call. That way, no one can make another cocktail!

Chapter 20

Ten (Okay, More Than Ten) Bar Jokes You Can Tell Your Customers

*B*ars are havens for jokes and jokesters. Some of those jokes, of course, aren't suitable for printing in this type of book. But we've put together a collection that you can tell to just about any customer, anywhere, anytime.

Bounce This!

A big man approached the bartender and said, "I see by the sign in your window that you're looking for a bouncer. Has the job been filled yet?" "Not yet," the bartender replied. "Do you have experience?" "No," the man admitted, "but watch this!" He walked over to a loudmouthed man at the back of the room, lifted him off his feet, and threw him out into the street. Then he turned to the bartender and said, "How's that?" "Great!" said the bartender. "But you'll have to ask the boss about the job." "Fine," said the man. "Where is he?" "Just coming back in the front door."

Generous to a Fault

A man walks into the tavern, sits at the bar, and says to the bartender, "Give everyone a drink and have one yourself!" The bartender complies. A little later the man says, "Bartender, give everyone a drink and have one yourself!"

Again, the bartender complies. Now the bartender presents the man with a check for $30, and the man says that he has no money. This infuriates the bartender, who immediately comes from behind the bar and bodily throws the man out. About an hour later, the man comes back into the bar and says to the bartender, "Give everyone a drink but leave yourself out. You get nasty when you drink!"

Sign of the Times

Three deaf-mutes walk into a tavern and sit down at a table. The bartender greets them and takes their order using sign language. After returning to the bar, he is complimented by a patron on his knowledge of sign language just to better serve his patrons. After a few rounds of drinks, the bartender notices the three deaf-mutes' hands moving a mile a minute. He quickly grabs a bat from under the bar and chases the deaf-mutes out. When he returns, the same patron who complimented him earlier questions why he ran the three out of the bar. He replies, "If I told them once, I told them a thousand times, *no singing in this joint!*"

If You Haven't Got Your Health . . .

Doctor: "The best thing for you to do is to give up drinking and smoking. Get up early every morning and go to bed early every night."

Patient: "What's the second best thing to do?"

When Do You Open?

The owner of a corner saloon was sleeping peacefully at 3 o'clock in the morning when his phone rang: "What time does your saloon open?" asked a voice. "Eleven o'clock," said the saloonkeeper and slammed down the phone. A minute later the bell rang again. The same voice asked, "What time did you say your saloon opened?" "Eleven o'clock, darn it," roared the proprietor, "and you can't get in a minute before." "Who wants to get in?" said a very hurt voice. "I want to get out!"

Which Are You?

When intoxicated, a Frenchman wants to dance; a German, to sing; a Spaniard, to gamble; an Englishman, to boast; an Italian, to eat; an Irishman, to fight; and an American, to make a speech.

Your Wife's Not Looking for You

A bartender tapped a drinker on the arm and apologized. "Excuse me, mister, but if you're the pale-faced runt who looks like a lop-eared rabbit, I'm to tell you your wife got tired of waiting and drove the car home without you."

Nurse or Bartender?

What's the difference between a nurse and a bartender? A bartender gives you a shot in a glass.

Bartender (bärtndr)

BARTENDER:

1. An irrigation engineer.

2. The only psychiatrist who works in an apron.

3. A good mixer in more ways than one.

4. A person who brings you in contact with the spirit world.

5. A person to whom almost everything is a stirring event.

6. One who knows that the emptiest men in the world are those who are full.

A Horse

A horse walks into a bar, and the bartender says, "Why the long face?"

A Duck

A duck walks into a bar and says, "I'll take a shot of bourbon and put it on my bill."

A Pony

A pony walks into a bar and says, "Bartender, may I have a drink?"

The bartender says, "Speak up, I can't hear you."

The pony says again, "Bartender, may I have a drink?"

The bartender replies, "Look, if you don't speak up, I won't serve you."

The pony replies, "I'm awfully sorry, I'm just a little hoarse."

A Snake

A snake walks into a bar, and the bartender says, "I'm sorry, but I can't serve you."

"Why not?" the snake asks.

"Because you can't hold your liquor."

A Giraffe

A man and giraffe walk into a bar and start drinking. The giraffe passes out, and the man gets up to leave.

The barman says, "You can't leave that lying there."

The man says, "It's not a lion, it's a giraffe."

The Famous Quasimodo Bar Joke

Quasimodo has retired. The priest holds interviews and auditions to fill the vacancy, to which a man with no arms shows up. The priest asks how he intends to ring the bell. The man replies, "With my face." The skeptical priest laughs, the man backs up, runs full tilt at the bell, and smacks it with the bridge of his nose. "That's all well and good," replies the priest, "but my congregation is spread out over 10 miles. I've got to have volume." The man asks for a second chance, backs up farther, runs hell bent for leather, and careens into the bell, which gives a high, resonant bong. Unfortunately, the man ricochets off the left side and falls off the parapet to his death. The priest runs downstairs to the crowd surrounding the body.

People ask him, "Father, do you know who this is?"

"Well, I don't know his name, but his face rings a bell."

Part two:

Three days later, a second man with no arms shows up for the same job. The priest refuses the man admittance, saying he doesn't want to go through that again. "What do you mean, again?" the man asks.

"Three days ago another no-arm guy showed . . ."

"That's my brother! I've been following him for years! How's he doing?" The priest tells him how his brother had unfortunately passed away, whereupon the man urges the priest to hire him so he can spend the rest of his life working where his brother had passed away.

"I've corrected the fault he had on his approach to the bell," he says, "so just let me work here for my brother." The priest hesitates, so the man backs up and hurls himself into the bell, which gives a resplendent bong. But the man falls off the parapet to the courtyard below. The priest rushes downstairs.

Startled onlookers ask, "Do you know this one, Father?"

"No, but he's a dead ringer for his brother."

Part three:

After the second armless man falls off the tower, the priest places another ad in the paper, and a third armless man shows up, the third brother. Once again, the priest explains the rigors of the job and impresses on the man that the "gong" has to be heard all over the city. The man answers that he can do it and is given a tryout. He goes back as far as he can, speeds toward the great bell at an alarming rate, misses the bell completely, goes off the tower, and smashes to the street below.

The priest jumps down the spiral staircase, and when asked by the crowd if he knows the man, states, "No, I don't know his name, and his face doesn't ring a bell with me."

Part VI
Appendixes

The 5th Wave   By Rich Tennant

"I showed Patrick where the pots and pans are. Now he wants to know where to go to sharpen and hone his compensation package."

In this part . . .

The appendixes generally help you find answers to questions. In this case, we present you with a state-by-state listing of alcohol control boards, with all their contact information, and a ton of Web sites to help you answer a variety of questions about running a bar.

Appendix A

State Alcohol Beverage Control Boards

● ●

Alabama
Alabama Alcoholic Beverage
Control Board
2715 Gunter Park Drive W.
Montgomery, AL 36109
Phone 334-271-3840
Fax 334-277-2150
Web site www.abcboard.state.
al.us/home.asp

Alaska
Alcoholic Beverage Control Board
5848 E. Tudor Road
Anchorage, AK 99507
Phone 907-269-0350
Fax 907-272-9412
Web site www.dps.state.ak.
us/abc

Arizona
Arizona Department of Liquor
Licenses and Control
800 W. Washington, fifth floor
Phoenix, AZ 85007
Phone 602-542-5141
Fax 602-542-5707
or
400 W. Congress, #521
Tucson, AZ 85701
Phone 520-628-6595

Fax 520-628-6620
Web site www.azll.com

Arkansas
Alcoholic Beverage Control
Administration Division
1515 W. Seventh St., Suite 503
Little Rock, AR 72201
Phone 501-682-1105
Web site www.arkansas.gov/
dfa/abc_administration

California
California Department of Alcoholic
Beverage Control
3927 Lennane Drive, Suite 100
Sacramento, CA 95834
Phone 916-419-2500
Web site www.abc.ca.gov

Colorado
Colorado Department of Revenue
Liquor Enforcement Division
1881 Pierce St., Suite 108A
Lakewood, CO 80214
Phone 303-205-2300
Fax 303-205-2341
Web site www.revenue.state.
co.us/liquor_dir/home.asp

Connecticut
Connecticut Department of
Consumer Protection
Liquor Division
State Office Building
165 Capitol Ave.
Hartford, CT 06106
Phone 860-713-6210
Fax 860-713-7235
Web site www.ct.gov/dcp

Delaware
Delaware Department of Public
Services
Alcoholic Beverage Control
Commission
Carvel State Office Building,
third floor
820 N. French St.
Wilmington, DE 19801
Phone 302-577-5222
Fax 302-577-3204
Web site http://date.delaware.
gov/dabcpublic/index.jsp

District of Columbia
Alcoholic Beverage Regulation
Administration
941 N. Capitol St. N.E., Suite 7200
Washington, DC 20002
Phone 202-442-4423
Web site www.abra.dc.gov

Florida
Florida Department of Professional
Business Regulations
Division of Alcoholic Beverages
and Tobacco
1940 N. Monroe St.
Tallahassee, FL 32399
Phone 850-488-3227
Fax 850-922-5175
Web site www.state.fl.us/
dbpr/abt

Georgia
Georgia Department of Revenue
Alcohol & Tobacco Division
1800 Century Center Blvd. N.E.,
Room 4235
Atlanta, GA 30345-3205
Phone 404-417-4900
Fax 404-417-4901
Web site www.etax.dor.ga.gov/
alcohol

Hawaii
Honolulu
Liquor Commission
City and County of Honolulu
Pacific Park Plaza
711 Kapiolani Blvd., Suite 600
Honolulu, HI 96813
Phone 808-523-4458
Fax 808-591-2700
Web site www.co.honolulu.hi.
us/liq

Hawaii (Big Island)
Office of Liquor Control
County of Hawaii
East Hi office:
101 Aupuni St., Suite 230
Hilo, HI 96720
Phone 808-961-8218
Fax 808-961-8684
West Hi office:
75-5737 Kuakini Highway, Room 104
Kailua-Kona, HI 96740
Phone 808-327-3549
Fax: 808-327-3550
Web site www.hawaii-county.
com/directory/dir_liquor.htm

Kauai
Department of Liquor Control
County of Kauai
Lihue Civic Center
Mo'ikeha Building
4444 Rice St., Suite 120
Kauai, HI 96766
Phone 808-241-6580
Fax 808-241-6585
Web site www.kauai.gov/liquor

Maui
Department of Liquor Control
County of Maui
Wailuku office:
2145 Kaohu St., Room 105
Wailuku, HI 96793
Phone 808-243-7753
Fax 808-243-7558
Lahaina office:
788 Pauoa St., Room 102
Lahaina, HI 96761
Phone 808-661-9581
Fax 808-661-8375
Web site www.co.maui.hi.us/
departments/Liquor

Idaho
Idaho State Liquor Dispensary
Alcoholic Beverage Control Division
1349 E. Beechcraft Court
Boise, ID 83716
Phone 208-947-9400
Fax 208-947-9401
Web site www.liquor.idaho.gov

Illinois
Illinois Liquor Control Commission
100 W. Randolph St., Suite 7-801
Chicago, IL 60601
Phone 312-814-2206
Fax 312-814-2241
Web site www.state.il.us/lcc

Springfield office
101 W. Jefferson, Suite 3-525
Springfield, IL 62702
Phone 217-782-2136
Fax 217-524-1911

Indiana
Alcohol and Tobacco Commission
Indiana Government Center South
302 W. Washington St., Room E-114
Indianapolis, IN 46204
Phone 317-232-2430
Fax 317-234-1520
Web site www.in.gov/atc

Iowa
Iowa Alcoholic Beverages Division
1918 S.E. Hulsizer Ave.
Ankeny, IA 50021
Phone 866-469-2223 or 515-281-7400
Fax 515-281-7375
Web site www.iowaabd.com

Kansas
Kansas Department of Revenue
Alcohol Beverage Control
Docking State Office Building
915 S.W. Harrison St., Room 214
Topeka, KS 66625-3512
Phone 785-296-7015
Fax 785-296-7185
Web site www.ksrevenue.org/
abc.htm

Kentucky
Kentucky Office of Alcoholic
Beverage Control
1003 Twilight Trail
Frankfort, KY 40601
Phone 502-564-4850
Fax 502-564-1442
Web site http://abc.ky.gov

Louisiana
Louisiana Office of Alcohol and
Tobacco Control
8549 United Plaza Blvd., Suite 220
Baton Rouge, LA 70809
Phone 225-925-4041
Fax 225-925-3975
Web site www.atc.rev.state.
la.us

Maine
Maine Department of Public Safety
Bureau of Alcoholic Beverages and
Lottery Operations
8 State House Station
Augusta, ME 04333
Phone 207-287-3721
Fax 207-287-4049
Web site www.maineliquor.com

Maryland

Comptroller of Maryland
Alcohol and Tobacco Tax Bureau
80 Calvert St., Room 310
Annapolis, MD 21401
Phone 410-260-7314
Fax 410-974-3201
Web site `http:// compnet.comp.`
`state.md.us/Regulatory_and_`
`Enforcement_Division/Alcohol_`
`and_Tobacco_Tax_Bureau`

Montgomery County only

Montgomery County Department of
Liquor Control
16650 Crabbs Branch Way
Rockville, MD 20855
Phone 240-777-1900
Fax 240-777-1962
Web site `www.montgomerycounty`
`md.gov/dlctmpl.asp`

Massachusetts

Alcoholic Beverages Control
Commission
239 Causeway St.
Boston, MA 02114
Phone 617-727-3040
Fax 617-727-1258
Web site `www.mass.gov/abcc`

Michigan

Michigan Liquor Control Commission
7150 Harris Drive
P.O. Box 30005
Lansing, MI 48909
Phone 517-322-1345 or 517-322-1415
Fax 517-322-5188 or 517-322-5046
Web site `www.michigan.gov/cis/`
`0,1607,7-154-10570---,00.html`

Minnesota

Minnesota Department of Public
Safety
Liquor Control Division
Alcohol and Gambling Enforcement
Division

444 Cedar St., Suite 133
St. Paul, MN 55101
Phone 651-296-6979
Fax 651-297-5259
Web site `www.dps.state.mn.us/`
`alcgamb/alcgamb.aspx`

Mississippi

Office of Alcoholic Beverage Control
P.O. Box 540
Madison, MS 39110
Phone 601-856-1301
Fax 601-856-1300
Web site `www.mstc.state.ms.us/`
`abc/main.htm`

Missouri

Division of Alcohol and Tobacco
Control
Truman Building
301 W. High, Room 680
P.O. Box 837
Jefferson City, MO 65102
Phone 573-751-2333
Fax 573-526-4540
Web site `www.atc.dps.mo.gov`

Montana

Montana Liquor License Bureau
125 N. Roberts
Helena, MT 59620
Phone 406-444-0700 or 406-444-6900
Fax 406-444-0750
Web site `http://mt.gov/`
`revenue/forbusinesses/`
`alcohol.asp`

Nebraska

Nebraska Liquor Control
Commission
301 Centennial Mall S.
P.O. Box 95046
Lincoln, NE 68509
Phone 402-471-2571
Fax 402-471-2814
Web site `www.lcc.ne.gov`

Nevada
Nevada Department of Taxation
Web site http://tax.state.
nv.us
(All beverage alcohol permits are
regulated by each individual county.)

Carson City
1550 E. College Parkway, Suite 115
Carson City, NV 89706
Phone 775-684-2000
Fax 775-684-2020

Elko
850 Elm St., #2
P.O. Box 1750
Elko, NV 89803
Phone 775-753-1115
Fax 775-778-6814

Las Vegas
Grant Sawyer Office Building
555 E. Washington Ave., Suite 1300
Las Vegas, NV 89101
Phone 702-486-2300
Fax 702-486-2372

Reno
4600 Kietzke Lane
Building L, Suite 235
Reno, NV 89502
Phone 775-688-1295
Fax 775-688-1303

New Hampshire
New Hampshire State Liquor
Commission
Robert J. Hart Building
30 Storrs St.
P.O. Box 503
Concord, NH 03302
Phone 603-271-3521
Fax 603-271-1107
Web site http://webster.state.
nh.us/liquor

New Jersey
New Jersey Department of Law and
Public Safety
Division of Alcoholic Beverage
Control
140 E. Front St.
P.O. Box 087
Trenton, NJ 08625
Phone 609-984-2830
Fax 609-292-0691
Web site www.state.nj.us/
lps/abc/index.html

New Mexico
New Mexico Regulation & Licensing
Department
Alcohol and Gaming Division
2550 Cerrillos Road, second floor
P.O. Box 25101
Santa Fe, NM 87504
Phone 505-476-4875
Fax 505-476-4595
Web site www.rld.state.
nm.us/agd

New York
New York Division of Alcoholic
Beverage Control
State Liquor Authority
Web site www.abc.state.ny.us

Zone 1
317 Lenox Ave., fourth floor
New York, NY 10027
Phone 212-961-8385
Fax 212-961-8283

Zone 2
80 S. Swan St.
Albany, NY 12210
Phone 518-474-3114
Fax 518-473-2286

Syracuse District
333 E. Washington St., Room 205
Syracuse, NY 13202
Phone 315-428-4198
Fax 315-428-4201

Zone 3
125 Main St., Room 556
Buffalo, NY 14203
Phone 716-847-3035
Fax 716-847-3435

North Carolina
North Carolina Alcoholic Beverage
Control Commission
3322 Garner Road
Raleigh, NC 27611
Phone 919-779-0700
Fax 919-662-3583
Web site www.ncabc.com

North Dakota
North Dakota Office of the State Tax
Commissioner
Alcohol Tax Section
600 E. Boulevard Ave.
Bismarck, ND 58505
Phone 701-328-2329
Web site www.nd.gov/tax/
alcohol

Ohio
Ohio Department of Commerce
Division Of Liquor Control
6606 Tussing Road
Reynoldsburg, OH 43068
Phone 614-644-2360
Fax 614-644-3166
Web site www.liquorcontrol.
ohio.gov

Oklahoma
Alcoholic Beverage Law Enforcement
Commission (ABLE)
4545 N. Lincoln Blvd., Suite 270
Oklahoma City, OK 73105
Phone 405-521-3484
Fax 405-521-6578
Web site www.able.state.ok.us

Oregon
Oregon Liquor Control Commission
9079 S.E. McLoughlin Blvd.
Milwaukie, OR 97222
Phone 800-452-6522 or 503-872-5000
Fax 503-872-5266
Web site www.olcc.state.or.us

Pennsylvania
Pennsylvania Liquor Control Board
Northwest Office Building
Harrisburg, PA 17124
Phone 717-783-7637
Fax 717-787-8820
Web site www.lcb.state.pa.us

Rhode Island
Rhode Island Department of
Business Regulation
Division of Commercial Licensing
and Regulation
Liquor Section
233 Richmond St., Suite 230
Providence, RI 02903
Phone 401-222-2562
Fax 401-222-6654
Web site www.dbr.state.ri.
us/divisions/commlicensing/
liquor.php

South Carolina
South Carolina Department of
Revenue & Taxation
Alcoholic Beverage Licensing Section
301 Gervais St.
P.O. Box 125
Columbia, SC 29214
Phone 803-737-5000
Fax 803-734-1401
Beverage Alcohol Licensing
803-898-5864
Web site www.sctax.org

South Dakota
South Dakota Department of
Revenue
Special Taxes Division
445 E. Capitol Ave.
Pierre, SD 57501
Phone 605-773-3311
Fax 605-773-6729
Web site www.state.sd.us/
drr2/propspectax

Tennessee
Tennessee Alcoholic Beverage
Commission
226 Capitol Blvd., Suite 300
Nashville, TN 37219
Phone 615-741-1602
Fax 615-741-0847
Web site www.state.tn.us/abc

Texas
Texas Alcoholic Beverage
Commission
5806 Mesa Drive
Austin, TX 78731
Phone 512-206-3333
Fax 512-206-3399
Web site www.tabc.state.tx.us

Utah
Utah Department of Alcoholic
Beverage Control
1625 South 900 West
Salt Lake City, UT 84130
Phone 801-977-6800
Fax 801-977-6888
Web site www.alcbev.state.
ut.us

Vermont
Vermont Department of Liquor
Control
13 Green Mountain Drive, Drawer 20
Montpelier, VT 05620
Phone 800-642-3134 or 802-828-2345
Fax 802-828-2803
Web site www.state.vt.us/dlc

Virginia
Virginia Department of Alcoholic
Beverage Control
2901 Hermitage Road
Richmond, VA 23220
Phone 804-213-4400
Web site www.abc.state.va.us

Washington
Washington State Liquor Control
Board
3000 Pacific Ave. S.E.
Olympia, WA 98504
Phone 360-664-1600
Web site www.liq.wa.gov

West Virginia
West Virginia Alcohol Beverage
Control Commission
322 70th St. S.E.
Charleston, WV 25304
Phone 800-642-8208 or 304-558-2481
Fax 304-558-2893
Web site www.wvabca.com

Wisconsin
Wisconsin Department of Revenue
Alcohol & Tobacco Enforcement
2135 Rimrock Road
P.O. Box 8933
Madison, WI 53708
Phone 608-266-2776
Fax 608-261-6240
Web site www.dor.state.wi.us/
faqs/ise/atlicns.html

Wyoming
Wyoming Liquor Commission
1520 E. Fifth St.
Cheyenne, WY 82002
Phone 307-777-7233
Fax 307-777-6255
Web site http://revenue.state.
wy.us

Appendix B

Useful Web Sites for Every Bar Owner

· ·

*W*ith bar ownership, as with all businesses, one of the best ways to stay on top of things is to arm yourself with as much knowledge as possible. Here we give you a few lists of some useful Web sites that contain information indispensable to bar owners. Of course, these lists aren't complete (a complete list of wineries and breweries alone could fill a phone book), but they're a good starting point for arming yourself with everything you need to know about running your bar.

Bar supplies and equipment

A Beautiful Bar, www.abeautifulbar.com. Offers salvaged, restored, and antique bar elements.

AccuBar, www.accubar.com. Offers an inventory system for bars, using cutting-edge technology.

Alcohol Controls Inc., www.AlcoholControls.com. Buy products that will help you increase beverage profitability.

Algerd Crystal Stemware, www.crystalgiftsworld.com. Find a wide range of crystal stemware, decanters, beer mugs, and more.

AutoFry, www.autofry.com. A ventless, hoodless, fully enclosed, automatic deep-frying system.

Bar Rags, www.barrags.com. Order T-shirts for your bar and other alcohol-themed shirts here.

BarProducts.com Inc., www.barproducts.com. This Web site seems to sell everything you need for your bar — except the alcohol!

BarStool Superstore, www.barstoolsuperstore.com. Offers bar stools in wood, metal, and wrought iron and in many styles and sizes.

***BARTENDER* magazine, www.bartender.com.** Coauthor Ray Foley founded this fun and informative magazine for bartenders and anyone who serves alcohol.

Broaster, www.broaster.com. Offers pressure fryers, ventless fryers, frozen foods, and recipes.

The Bumper Tube Company, www.bumpertube.com. Offers coin-operated pool tables and shuffleboards, parts, and supplies.

Candle Services, www.candleservices.com. Sells disposable, refillable candles.

Chef's Emporium, www.chefsemporium.net. Purchase chef uniforms and apparel (including fun hats) at this site.

Clicker Exchange, L.C., www.ClickerExchange.com. Provides liquor inventory control systems.

Cool Bar Stools, www.cool-bar-stools.com. Offers links to companies that sell bar stools, bar tables, pub tables, wine racks, and bar accessories.

CrystALaCarte, www.CrystALaCarte.com. Find beautiful wine glasses, champagne flutes, and cocktail glasses here.

Discount Janitorial Supply, www.discountjanitorialsupply.com. Offers thousands of commercial-quality cleaning supplies.

Drain Scoop, www.icescoop.com. This nifty ice scoop is slotted so the water drains out and the ice stays in, eliminating watery drinks.

Dri-Dek Shelf Liners, www.dri-dek.com. These interlocking tiles keep glassware above wet counter tops.

4Rails.com by Commercial Finished Metals Corp., www.4rails.com. Sells foot rails, glass racks, handrails, waitress stations, and other accessories for bars.

HANDePOS, www.handepos.com. This point of sale system allows your servers to take orders from customers and transfer them wirelessly to the kitchen and bar.

iBarControl, www.ibarcontrol.com. This technology allows you to take inventory and create reports using handheld computers.

Kardwell International, www.kardwell.com. Offers promotional products and other supplies.

Leroy Neiman artwork, www.bartender.com. Prints, serigraphs, and originals by America's foremost artist are available through *BARTENDER* magazine.

Lets Glow 'N Party.Com, www.letsglownparty.com. Offers links to other Web sites that sell bar products that blink, light up, glow, and sell.

MedTech Wristbands, www.medtechgroup.com. Manufactures wristbands, offering a wide selection of colors, patterns, and styles.

Precision Dynamics Corp., www.visaband.com. Offers Visa Band wristbands.

Precision Pours Inc., www.precisionpours.com. Offers a unique system of three ball bearings in precision liquor pours.

Quik n' Crispy Greaseless Fryer, www.q-n-c.com. These greaseless fryers allow you to offer fried foods without the oil and mess.

Rocket Packs, www.rocketpacks.de. This company, located in Frankfurt, Germany, sells portable beverage-dispensing equipment.

S&V Restaurant Equipment, www.customcool.com. Features beverage coolers, reach-ins, under-counter units, and more.

Sharp, www.sharpusa.com/bartender. Sharp offers point of sale systems as simple or as complex as you could ever want, for any size business.

Sunkist Food Service, www.sunkistfs.com. If you expect to make a lot of fruit garnishes, check out the Sunkist commercial sectionizer. It will save your staff time in cutting citrus wedges and slices.

Synrdyne Solutions Inc., www.synrdyne.com. Verify the authenticity of IDs presented for admission with this company's technology.

WedgE, www.wedgeonline.com. The WedgE (yes, it's pronounced wedg-ee), cuts 8 or 16 perfect wedges.

Beer

Anheuser-Busch, www.anheuser-busch.com

Bass Ale (Guinness Imports), www.bassale.com

Beck's Beer, www.becksbeer.com

The Brewery, `http://hbd.org/brewery`. Hundreds of recipes and brewery equipment suppliers.

Budweiser, `www.budweiser.com`

Budweiser Specialty Brewing Group, `www.hopnotes.com`

Coors, `www.coors.com`

Corona, `www.corona.com`

Foster's Lager, `www.fostersbeer.com`

Grolsch, `www.grolsch.com`

Guinness, `www.guinness.com`

Hacker-Pschorr, `www.paulaner.com`

Heineken, `www.heineken.com`

Labatt, `www.labatt.com`

Miller Brewing Company, `www.milleradvantage.com`

Molson, `www.molson.com`

Newcastle Brown Ale, `www.newcastlebrown.com`

Old Milwaukee, `www.oldmilwaukee.com`

Pabst Brewing Company, `www.pabst.com`

Paulaner, `www.paulaner.com`

Sapporo, `www.sapporobeer.com`

Spirits

Absente, `www.absente.com`

Absolut Vodka, `www.absolutvodka.com`

Appleton Rum, `www.appletonrum.com`

Asbach Uralt, www.asbach.de/weiche.htm

Bacardi Rum, www.bacardi.com

Ballantine's, www.ballantines.com

Barton Brands, www.bartonbrands.com

Beefeater, www.beefeatergin.com

Bombay Sapphire Gin, www.AsExpressedByYou.com

Canadian Mist, www.canadianmist.com

Captain Morgan, www.rum.com

Caravella, www.caravellaus.com

Chambord, www.chambordonline.com

Chivas Regal, www.chivas.com

Classic Malts, www.scotch.com

Coco Lopez, www.cocolopez.com

Cointreau, www.cointreau.com

Courvoisier, www.courvoisier.com

Crillon Importers Ltd., www.crillonimporters.com

Crown Royal, www.crownroyal.com

Cutty Sark, www.cutty-sark.com

Dewars, www.dewars.com

Diageo, www.diageo.com

Disaronno, www.Disaronno.com

Fris Vodka, www.frisvodka.com

Grand Marnier, www.grand-marnier.com

Heaven Hill Distilleries, www.heaven-hill.com

Iceberg Vodka, www.icebergvodka.net

Jack Daniels, www.jackdaniels.com

Jägermeister, www.jagermeister.com

J&B Scotch Whisky, www.jbscotch.com

Jim Beam Brands, www.jimbeam.com

Jose Cuervo, www.cuervo.com

Johnnie Walker, www.johnniewalker.com

Kahlúa, www.kahlua.com

Knob Creek, www.knobcreek.com

Laird & Company, www.lairdandcompany.com

Laphroaig, www.laphroaig.com

Magellan Gin, www.magellangin.com

Maker's Mark, www.makersmark.com

Malibu Rum, www.malibu-rum.com

Midori, www.midori-world.com

Niche, www.ourniche.com

Patrón, www.patronspirits.com

Pernod, www.pernod.com

Remy Martin, www.remy.com

Sauza, www.sauzatequila.com

SKYY Vodka, www.skyy.com

Smirnoff Vodka, www.smirnoff.com

Southern Comfort, www.SouthernComfort.com

Stolichnaya Russian Vodka, www.stoli.com

Tanqueray, www.tanqueray.com

Vincent Van Gogh Vodka, www.vangoghvodka.com

Vox Vodka, www.voxvodka.com

Whaler's Original Rum, www.whalersrum.com

Trade associations

Bureau of Alcohol Tobacco and Firearms, www.atf.treas.gov

The Century Council, www.centurycouncil.org. The Century Council is funded by America's leading distillers to fight drunk driving and illegal underage drinking.

Distilled Spirits Council of the United States Inc. (DISCUS), www.discus.org. DISCUS is the trade association representing producers and marketers of distilled spirits sold in the United States.

National Bar & Restaurant Management Association (NBRMA), www.bar restaurant.com

National Beer Wholesalers Association Inc. (NBWA), www.nbwa.org

National Restaurant Association (NRA), www.restaurant.org

NRA Educational Foundation, www.nraef.org. The educational foundation for the National Restaurant Association.

US Bartender, www.usbartender.com

Wines

Banfi Vineyards, www.castellobanfi.com

Bolla Wines, www.bolla.com

Champagne Wines Information Bureau, www.champagnes.com/en_indx

Fetzer Vineyards, www.fetzer.com

Frederick Wildman, www.frederickwildman.com

Geerlings & Wade, `www.geerwade.com`

Italian Wines Direct, `www.italianwinesdirect.com`

Joseph Drouhin, `www.drouhin.com`

Kenwood, `www.kenwoodvineyards.com`

Korbel Champagne, `www.korbel.com`

Matanzas Creek Winery, `http://matanzascreek.com`

Moet & Chandon, `www.moet.com`

Niche, `www.ourniche.com`

Pellegrini Vineyards, `http://pellegrinivineyards.com`

Premium Port Wines Inc., `www.premiumport.com`

Roederer Estate, `www.pacificsites.com/~roederer`

Sonoma, `www.sonoma.com/wineries`

Sterling Vineyards, `www.sterlingvineyards.com`

Winebow, `www.winebow.com`

Wines of France, `www.frenchwinesfood.com`

Index

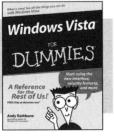
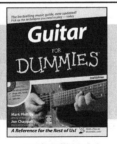

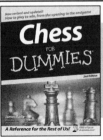

SPORTS, FITNESS, PARENTING, RELIGION & SPIRITUALITY

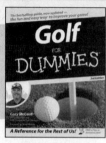

0-471-76871-5

0-7645-7841-3

Also available:

- Catholicism For Dummies
  0-7645-5391-7
- Exercise Balls For Dummies
  0-7645-5623-1
- Fitness For Dummies
  0-7645-7851-0
- Football For Dummies
  0-7645-3936-1
- Judaism For Dummies
  0-7645-5299-6
- Potty Training For Dummies
  0-7645-5417-4
- Buddhism For Dummies
  0-7645-5359-3

- Pregnancy For Dummies
  0-7645-4483-7 †
- Ten Minute Tone-Ups For Dummies
  0-7645-7207-5
- NASCAR For Dummies
  0-7645-7681-X
- Religion For Dummies
  0-7645-5264-3
- Soccer For Dummies
  0-7645-5229-5
- Women in the Bible For Dummies
  0-7645-8475-8

TRAVEL

0-7645-7749-2

0-7645-6945-7

Also available:

- Alaska For Dummies
  0-7645-7746-8
- Cruise Vacations For Dummies
  0-7645-6941-4
- England For Dummies
  0-7645-4276-1
- Europe For Dummies
  0-7645-7529-5
- Germany For Dummies
  0-7645-7823-5
- Hawaii For Dummies
  0-7645-7402-7

- Italy For Dummies
  0-7645-7386-1
- Las Vegas For Dummies
  0-7645-7382-9
- London For Dummies
  0-7645-4277-X
- Paris For Dummies
  0-7645-7630-5
- RV Vacations For Dummies
  0-7645-4442-X
- Walt Disney World & Orlando
  For Dummies
  0-7645-9660-8

GRAPHICS, DESIGN & WEB DEVELOPMENT

0-7645-8815-X

0-7645-9571-7

Also available:

- 3D Game Animation For Dummies
  0-7645-8789-7
- AutoCAD 2006 For Dummies
  0-7645-8925-3
- Building a Web Site For Dummies
  0-7645-7144-3
- Creating Web Pages For Dummies
  0-470-08030-2
- Creating Web Pages All-in-One Desk
  Reference For Dummies
  0-7645-4345-8
- Dreamweaver 8 For Dummies
  0-7645-9649-7

- InDesign CS2 For Dummies
  0-7645-9572-5
- Macromedia Flash 8 For Dummies
  0-7645-9691-8
- Photoshop CS2 and Digital
  Photography For Dummies
  0-7645-9580-6
- Photoshop Elements 4 For Dummies
  0-471-77483-9
- Syndicating Web Sites with RSS Feed
  For Dummies
  0-7645-8848-6
- Yahoo! SiteBuilder For Dummies
  0-7645-9800-X

NETWORKING, SECURITY, PROGRAMMING & DATABASES

0-7645-7728-X

0-471-74940-0

Also available:

- Access 2007 For Dummies
  0-470-04612-0
- ASP.NET 2 For Dummies
  0-7645-7907-X
- C# 2005 For Dummies
  0-7645-9704-3
- Hacking For Dummies
  0-470-05235-X
- Hacking Wireless Networks
  For Dummies
  0-7645-9730-2
- Java For Dummies
  0-470-08716-1

- Microsoft SQL Server 2005 For Dummies
  0-7645-7755-7
- Networking All-in-One Desk Reference
  For Dummies
  0-7645-9939-9
- Preventing Identity Theft For Dummies
  0-7645-7336-5
- Telecom For Dummies
  0-471-77085-X
- Visual Studio 2005 All-in-One Desk
  Reference For Dummies
  0-7645-9775-2
- XML For Dummies
  0-7645-8845-1